# SRI AUROBINDO AND SHAKESPEARE

## Eastern and Western Theories

# SRI AUROBINDO AND SHAKESPEARE

## Eastern and Western Theories

**Dr. Meenu Sodhi Sharma**

*Published by*
**PRABHAT PRAKASHAN PVT. LTD.**
4/19 Asaf Ali Road,
New Delhi-110 002 (INDIA)
e-mail: prabhatbooks@gmail.com

ISBN 978-93-94534-97-1
**SRI AUROBINDO AND SHAKESPEARE**
*by* Dr. Meenu Sodhi Sharma



*Edition*
2025

*Price*
₹ 800.00 (Rupees Eight Hundred only)

*Printed at*
R-Tech Offset Printers, Delhi

# A word of Thanks...

I dedicate my book to all the people who shaped my life in such a loving and affectionate way that I could stand on my feet and accomplish the task of reaching a point or destination in my life where I could return and repay their unconditional love and support by showing my respect and reverence for their positive contribution in forming my personality and character.

The first bow is reserved for my dear departed **parents** Mrs. Surjeet Sodhi and Shri Ranveer Singh Sodhi, who taught me all the good and moral virtues and values which I try to practice till today.

The second place is reserved for the love of my life i.e. my **late husband** Dr. Arvind Sharma. He gifted me with so much trust and liberty to pursue all my dreams. He never pressurized me with any of the orthodox or negative views of the society. He always wanted me to share my work with the world at large so today I am taking my nascent steps towards that purpose.

The third place is reserved for **all those who loved and supported me through my toughest.**

**After marriage I stepped into a new world of nationalism and patriotism because I was married into the family of freedom fighters and social reformers. I am indebted to the Almighty for giving me such productive family and work environment to give way to my thoughts on paper.**

• • •

# Contents

# Foreword

Born in a landlord family on 13th May, 1961, Meenu Sodhi Sharma, Ph.D had spiritual influence of gurudwara and literary inklings since childhood. Spirituality is embedded in her psyche and in her blood as her father Shri Ranveer Singh Sodhi was the Mahant of Dera Baba Dargah Singh which is at Sati ghat, Kankhal, Hardwar and has a historical gurudwara of Guru Amar Das Ji, the third Guru of the sikhs.

Author was married in a family that was totally dedicated to the cause of attaining freedom of the country so much so that they not only gave away much of their money and property to this cause but also pursued a simple and humble life-style befitting the times. The materialism prevailing in the society of our time was far-away from their minds, the only focus being the betterment of the society, mankind and freedom for the nation. Author feels proud to be a part of such a family and such lofty traditions.

Her legacy taught her to serve the humanity and mankind and to pursue charitable endeavors which she passed on to her daughter who currently serves as a dedicated Judge in Uttarakhand Judicial Services. Dr. Meenu Sodhi Sharma left her teaching job and coaching in the year 2012 to be with her daughter. In her quest to protect the environment, she has launched the crusade for making the earth a better and cleaner place to reside in by promoting plantation of trees and organic farming. Also she is a philanthropist involved in various charitable pursuits and works.

She contributed in strengthening the nation by providing career counseling to youth and providing guidance and motivation in preparing for various competitive examinations for the betterment of society and nations as youth is the foundation of a strong nation.

Presently she is occupied in getting her works published for the betterment of society by spreading noble thoughts and making a significant contribution to the literary field which will immensely benefit in widening the horizons of knowledge of the students, research scholars and also help people in their quest for spiritual enlightenment.

Choosing Sri Aurobindo was a natural progression from her background which comprised of freedom fighter family, humanitarians and spiritually evolved souls as Sri Aurobindo was a freedom fighter who was a highly qualified and intellectual person, great writer, poet and seer who was spiritually awakened, evolved and enlightened person. As coincidence would have it, her husband Dr. Arvind Sharma was actually named after him.

Her guide Dr. Ambuj Sharma of Gurukul Kangri University, helped her through the herculean task of comparing Sri Aurobindo, who is so vast in his literary output dedicated to spiritual and philosophical pursuits with William Shakespeare, regarded as the greatest writer in English. It is said that Sri Aurobindo had Shakespearean literature along his bedside when he left his mortal remains.

In her book, the author Dr. Meenu Sodhi Sharma has tried to compare the two legendary writers by comparing the eastern way of thinking with the western way. Deeply immersed in western thought and tradition when Sri Aurobindo returned to India in 1893, the Elizabethan period saw blood shed and gory tales in the writings of Shakespeare while Sri Aurobindo truly follows Indian ethos of one world, one family and the mantra of Ahimsa (non-violence). She underlines the stark similarities and differences in both the writers exploring their sonnets and plays. The structure of plays and sonnets may be same of both the greatest minds but ethos and persona ingrained in their writings is quite different.

**—Radhika Nagrath, Ph.D**

(Writer and Journalist)

# Preface

By the grace of God I was born into such a spiritually rich heritage that left such a huge impact on me which guided my spiritual growth right from the inception of my life; right from my childhood to this day.

Surrounded by all the comforts and luxuries and with the warm presence of loving, caring, humble and down to earth parents Mrs. Surjeet Sodhi and Shri Ranveer Singh Sodhi who lavished all their love and care on me and yet as a child, I didn't have any company of my own age as my elder brother was at boarding school. I was also supposed to follow him as I was also registered at Cambrian Hall, Dehradun; one of the most eminent schools of that time.

As a five year old when my parents took me for joining the school, my mother created a scene and started crying and refused to part with me so Ms. Mannering who was the principal of the school at that point of time being very kind hearted suggested that I could join after one year at the age of six years as I was too young at that time.

That one year never came as my mother won't even hear of sending me to the boarding school as a result of which my father had to use all his influence to get me enrolled in BHE academy, Hardwar which was meant only for the children of officers' of BHEL. So I was an exception, being the only outsider from BHEL community and the condition put by the school was that the commuting of the child will be the responsibility of the parents. Throughout, all my schooling ycars my father would personally drop me and collect me from the school that was at a daunting distance from our house which was at the other end of the town in old Hardwar popularly known as Kankhal area, as he would not trust any driver or servants for this job with his precious daughter.

My parents were highly educated. They graduated from D.A.V. College, Dehradun in the 50's and my father went on to become the topper and the gold- medalist of Gurukul Kangri University, Hardwar in Psychology subject. He was also a lecturer in the Nirmal Sanskrit Mahavidhyalya and never charged a single penny for it.

My parents were not only active participants in the religious and spiritual fields but also totally dedicated to the cause of humanity. They were very active members of the Rotary Club and Inner-Wheel Club. They worked for the betterment of lepers who were supposed to be outcasts and ostracized by the society. They also made significant contribution for the cause of cancer foundation of India.

My parents also founded English medium school, Shri Mahant Sadhu Singh Academy in the memory of their guru and worked in the field of education by imparting free education to scores of students. They helped in their placements in various institutions, factories and banks.

On the social scenario they got many poor girls married by providing all the arrangements and financial help. My parents also initiated the formation of 'Rifle- Club' for the budding aspirants in the field of shooting in Hardwar. My father was the commanding officer of Home-Guards in Hardwar. During the India- Pakistan war he very valiantly performed his duties towards the nation.

I was married to Dr. Arvind Sharma, doctor, astrologer and a social worker par excellence who belonged to the family of freedom fighters. He was actively involved in various charitable pursuits like providing free medical help and advice to those in need and propounded the concept of equality of boys and girls (sons and daughters) and tirelessly worked for eradicating gender discrimination which is deep rooted in the society.

Also he worked for the upliftment of weaker sections of the society and helped many people in securing jobs. In his endeavour to serve the society and humanity he sponsored education of many children who are now occupying eminent places in different kinds of professions and are contributing in nation building.

My husband's grandfather Late Vaidyaraj Sri Ram Chandra Sharma Ji, the founder of 'Vishnu- Pharmacy' in the year 1918 was also the founder of Congress party in Hardwar and in his honor a memorial has been erected on Har-ki-Pauri. He went to jail many times as a freedom fighter.

My husband's grandmother Late Smt. Lal Devi Ji, was a high-spirited and fiery lady who was very active in the fight for freedom. Once she slapped a British official right in front of the public. She was a social reformer and also made a significant contribution in the local administration of the town for almost over a decade. Batukeshwar Dutt Ji who was a Indian socialist revolutionary and independence fighter was hidden in our house by her. Batukeshwar Dutt Ji himself recounted the episode.

My husband's Tauji Late Vaidya Sri Vishnu Dutt Sharma Ji, also was a well known social worker and a freedom fighter, who suffered a lot in the jails in his fight to secure freedom for the nation. Tauji was a totally self- realized person who was a devoted sadhak. A person who was so selfless that if we got more than two dhoti- kurtas for him, he would go out and gift the extra brand new clothes to some needy person. The same was the case with his other personal belongings- be it a new quilt or blanket.

At the time of partition he was devoted day and night to the proper settlement of all the refugees from Pakistan as he was very actively involved in the local administration of Hardwar at that time.

After my marriage, I had the privilege of his august company that I will always cherish. He never let me feel even for a single- day that I had left my own parental home and come into my in-laws home. He made me so comfortable, loved and respected. It is also imperative to mention here that if I required anything even late at night, he being so old (80 plus years) immediately took his walking stick and went out to the market amidst my protestations.

When I was expecting my daughter he took so much tender care of me. After my daughter was born, he took her under his wings and did an amazing job of taking care of her. This care was from a person who never got married and never had a family of his own. I truly hold him in highest esteem and reverence.

My Father-in-law, Late Dr. Surendra Dutt Sharma Ji, was a practicing doctor and lecturer in the Rishikul Medical College, Hardwar. He was a very compassionate person who could do anything to give relief to his patients without charging a single penny. He helped many young aspiring students of medicine in realizing their dreams.

The family was active in the charitable endeavours and gifted away much of their property and assets for the cause of attaining the freedom of the country and for the betterment of society and nation. Free medical help and advice was given to the needy and free education was sponsored for many students, who went on to become eminent personalities in their chosen fields.

So being a part of two such outstanding and illustrious families I feel honored and humbled at the same time. Both the families are remembered and revered by the people because of their immense contribution to the society.

• • •

# Acknowledgements

I owe my gratitude to all those people whose presence was indispensible for the completion of this book.

First and foremost I would like to pay my obeisance to the Almighty for giving me strength and conviction to put my thoughts and views on paper and to successfully complete the book.

I am deeply indebted to my late parents, tauji and my husband, the four most important people in my life. They are physically not present with me, but their spirit always inspires, encourages and guides me.

Words cannot adequately express my indebtedness to my Supervisor, Dr. Ambuj Kumar Sharma, Department of English, Gurukul Kangri Vishwavidyalaya whose able guidance has helped me immensely, in fulfilling my difficult and herculean objective.

My sincerest thanks are due also to Professor M.R. Verma, Department of English, Gurukul Kangri Vishwavidyalya.

I am especially grateful to the Librarian and the staff of S.M.J.N. P.G. College Library, Hardwar, for extending all the possible help. The help provided to me by the librarians and staff of Gurukul University, Khetan-Bhawan's personal library, Hardwar and various other libraries is also gratefully acknowledged.

The one person who deserves to be thanked the most is my dear daughter who stood by me like a pillar of strength and support through thick and thin. I would like to extend my gratitude and blessings to her for her continuous encouragement and feed backs, help and suggestions with regard to the book.

I wish to record my special gratitude to Mr. Sunil Pandey and Dr. Radhika Nagrath for their indispensable support and valuable suggestions regarding the book.

I would like to extend my heartfelt gratitude to the editors, the entire marketing, sales and production teams for their valuable support and hard work.

At last but not the least, I would like to extend my gratitude to my friends and well-wishers who extended their immense support and helped me in the completion of this book. I greatly value their friendship and I deeply appreciate their belief in me.

• • •

# Introduction

Sri Aurobindo is a versatile genius described by critics variously as "a multi-faceted diamond", 'the Himalaya of various extremes of height", "an illumined philospher", "a non Pareil yogi". "The Indian Prometheus", "the modern Vyasa", and so on. Though over shadowed for quite some time by the philosophical and spiritual aspects of his personality, his literary genius has of late attracted great scholarly attention. Considerable light has been shed on Sri Aurobindo the poet by eminent writers and critics both in India and abroad. Quite a few studies of his plays have also appeared in recent years. The critics like P.C. Kotaki can no more complain the "Occasional magazine notices are all that can be had by a way of critical appreciation of his {Sri Aurobindo's drama}". However no serious attempt seems to have been made to study influences on Sri Aurobindo's Poetry and Plays. Though he himself admits such influences when he says that "his aesthetic temperament and being were impregnated with an early cult for the work of the great builders in Sanskrit and Greek, Italian & English poetry."

Shakespeare is amongst the writers Sri Aurobindo holds in highest esteem. His comments on Shakespeare show his deep love and sincere admiration for this poetic celebrity, who according to him, has always been for the poetic and aesthetic mind "the object of its sincere admiration and a powerful presence and influence." Sri Aurobindo's admiration for the great dramatist resulted in obvious Shakespearean influences on him. He adopts for his plays the Elizabethan model of drama perfected by Shakespeare's genius. He writes poetic plays like him and like him again he prefers an existing story to an invented one for his plays. Critics like M.K. Naik hear "persistent and loud Shakespearean echoes in character, incident and even dialogue" in Sri Aurobindo's plays.

Shakespeare's influence is traceable also in Sri Aurobindo's sonnets. They do not only adopt the Shakespearean form of sonnet but also seem to have in them echoes of his language and style.

Even more marked proof of Shakespeare's influence Sri Aurobindo is the parallelism between the two writers. Sri Aurobindo had a special love for Shakespeare. Apart from his own poems which were unavoidiably there, he had in his room no books of poetry, wrote Sri Aurobindo to one of his disciples, except the works of Shakespeare. K.D. Sethna accounts for this special consideration by saying that in his creative ideal, Sri Aurobindo has "certain general affinities with his favourite Shakespeare." Both of them do not merely "hold as it were, the mirror upto nature," but recreate human life. They have in them a "greater and deeper life power." This is not satisfied "with mirroring or just beautifully responding, but begins to throw up at once around them its own rich matter of being . And so creates something new, more personal, intimate, full of an inner vision, emotion, passion of self – expression."

Thus, there is an obvious need to study Shakespeare and Sri Aurobindo together to bring our affinities that may be there between their creative ideal and vision and their poetic and dramatic art, along with the former's influence on the later.

In the proposed study, an attempt will be made to fulfil this need and to contribute, in some measure to the appreciation of Sri Aurobindo's poetry and plays. It will also briefly touch upon the Indian response to Shakespeare. It will focus mainly on Sri Aurobindo's numerous insights and critical observations on him, for they may well be regarded as India's most significant contribution to the understanding and upraisal of Shakespeare's genius, and as such will help understanding the great dramatic poet.

• • •

CHAPTER-I

# Early Indian Response to Shakespeare

V. Rai in his book *Willam Shakespeare,* writes about Shakespeare's dramatic art that– For more than two and half centuries after his death critical approach to Shakespeare was based upon the assumption that he was an untutored genius. For Milton he was 'sweetest Shakespeare Fancy's child' singing 'his wood notes wild'; for Dryden he was naturally educated and did not look at nature through the spectacles of books; he looked into his own heart and found her there. Gray, in the *Progress of Poesy* pictures this 'Darling of Nature' as receiving undismayed, two valuable keys from her, one capable of opening the gates of laughter and the other the founts of tears. The Romantic critics of the early nineteenth century in Germany and Coleridge in England emphasized the element of conscious art in his play, but even they failed to relate his plays to the conditions of the stage, and Lamb confidently assured that *King Lear* cannot be acted. It was left to the theatre critics of the present century headed by Granville-Barker to explore the age-old myth and remind us that Shakespeare was a man of the theatre and wrote his plays for the performance on the Elizabethan stage, the peculiar conditions of which determined the shape structure of those plays, whose stage- success bears witness to his keen theatrical knowledge and consummate artistry. The present position has been neatly summed up by W.H.Clemen:

> At every turn in Shakespeare's early and middle plays we encounter conventional usage, forms of style, literary artifices and dramatic features which have their origins and many parallels, in the pre-Shakespearan drama. But already in his early plays, from *Richards III* onward, we constantly feel ourselves in the presence of something entirely new

and unexpected: Something that belongs to him alone, even though he may have borrowed so much of his material, the themes and situations from pre Shakespearean drama. For what is so often used there as a single detail, a mere matter of technique, a superficial trick of style, turns up again in Shakespeareorganically related to the play as whole...

For a long time indeed, right upto the Romantic period, critics were unwilling to credit Shakespeare with this highly finished and conscious artistry, and his finest strokes were put down tonature and not to art; but this supreme artistry will be clear and obvious if his work is approached along the lines we have just indicated.[1]

The purpose here is to study the nature of Shakespeare's art and the line of his development in this respect, which will involve the breaking up of the play, a living organism, into its various constituents for the sake of convenience. It should never be imagined that Shakespeare's development was continous and every second play was better and maturer than what had gone before. The fact is that even in his maturest period he produced plays which bear the stamp of hurry and imperfect grasp over theme, style and character and the plays of the last period betray a slackening in plot-architecture and relaxation in style and art of characterization, either due to tiredness or a fresh experiment in a new direction.[2]

We begin with the plot which, in Shakespeare, is at all stages made up of borrowed materials drawn from all available sources. But, from the very beginning he shows his originality in altering the stories in such a way as to disimprison the soul of drama latent in them and sharpen the balance and contrast of characters.

As he advances in his career he frequently combines several stories in such a way that help one another as the limbs of a living body. The apt illustrations are provided by comedies like *A Midsummer Night's Dream and The Merchant of Venice.* In history plays, like *'King Henry IV'* two distinct words are combined together for balance and contrast, which unite to form a complex whole. Then there are plays where underplots are added to the main plots and their interweaving and integration shows a cunning hand. The study of *Twelfth Night, Hamlet, King Lear* will prove rewarding in this respect. But the plot must have rhythm and movement and the story must pass through well-marked stages, through suspense and expectation raised, sustained and gratified along the clear curve with its climax, denouement and resolution. Aristotle has called the plot the soul of tragedy and defined it as a structure of  episodes and incidents which are bound together by the law of probability and necessity in such a way that the removal of any one of them may cause injury or distortion to the whole. In W.Shakespeare, however, the unity is not classical but Gothic, a unity which underlies superficial diversity and richness of details in comedies and romances, moreover, we find the elements of improbability, coincidence and sudden changes and unexpected turns which are not properly motivated. In the tragedies, it is true the plot movement is determined by the clash and interplay of circumstances and characters, but chance is quite in evidence here also. In *Hamlet* and *Macbeth,* and other great tragedies chance plays an important part and the plots have no inevitability about them, as till the last moment, we are not sure about the result to the fencing match in Hamlet and are taken aback when Leartes is wounded and confesses his own crime with a frank exposure of the machination of Claudius, which stings the dying Hamlet into a violent fit of activity of his delayed revenge.[3]

When we examine the plotting in relation to the stagability of the plays we are struck with the dexterity and subtlety of Shakespeare's craftmanship. The point has been elaborately discussed by Granville-Barker in his series of P*reface to Shakespeare* which must be consulted for the complete information. The initial difficulty comes in the opening scenes which must be effective, dramatic and capable of engaging the attention of the audience at once. In this respect Shakespeare's opening scenes are dramatically quite effective, though his method varies from play to play. Thus *Twelfth-Night* opens with a lyrical demand for 'music, as the food of love' which at once strikes the key-note of the play and fixes the peculiar nature of Orsino, the lover, in our mind. Sudden and effective is the brief opening science in *Macbeth,* with the appearance of the three weird sisters on the heath amid thunder and lightening and their departure with the significant motto, symptomatic of the nature of the play, 'Fair is foul and foul is fair'. *Hamlet* opens in a cold and bitter atmosphere in the dead silence of midnight with whispered colloquies of suspense ridden guards, which gradually opens out, like a folded fan. In *King – Lear* the opening scene is on a low pitch of prose conversation, but *Othello* opens in an atmosphere charged with alarm and excitement; *Julius Ceasar* with a holiday crowd in the street and *Romeo- Juliet* with a quarrel, all of which are theatrically effective and dramatically important.[4]

In the comedies the pace of the plot is accelerated by the demand of happy ending. Events crowed and changes are quick and unexpected, even logic and probability may be sacrificed so that Jack may have his Jill and the final curtain may ring down to the accompaniment of the marriage-bells. Critics have taken an exception to this tendency and have subscribed to Dr. Johnson's indictment. "In many of Shakespeare's plays," said Dr. Johnson, "the latter part is evidently neglected. When he found himself near the end of his work and in view of his reward, he shortened the labour to snatch the profit." More severe still is the criticism of the forced happy ending in the 'dark' comedies, especially in *Measure for Measure* which Colridge described as painful, hateful, disgusting, horrible and degrading.[5]

'In the tragedies Shakespeare, like other great artists, shaped many a well-rounded story into a consciously wrought beginning, middle and end; and in them his characters live and move and have their being in artistic and psychological accord with the end as well as the means of the action'[6]. But here also the lack of front curtain necessitated the advance of action a little beyond the climactic point, with a touch of the anti-climax, the calm setting upon the scene of tragic heat and fever. The death of Hamlet is followed by the speeches of Horatio and Fortinbras leading to the final march of soldiers with the dead body of the prince amid the sound of muffled drums.

In the final romances, however, the last scenes are solemn and ritualistic, dealing with recognition, reconciliation and resolution of discord and tension. Music and moving poetry are the instruments to achieve this purpose, 'These plays are romances with the readily recognizable characteristics of the type : an idealized background, crowded action, an occasional melodramatic emphasis upon situation, or a striving for surprise at the expense of characterization- especially of the secondary characters. It is to be expected that these conditions should have their effect upon the endings of these plays.[7]

The final forgiveness in Shakespeare's dramatic romances is to some considerable extent, earned by suffering. Not mere surprise for the audience but agony suffered by the chief offenders motivates the end. And, to turn to the side of the forgivers, Imogen, Hermione, and Prospero have been mellowed and humanized by time and suffering. In short, the 'unbelievable forgiveness' of these dramatic romances is not unbelievable. It is the serene mercy which grows out of suffering, ripening into wisdom and charitable judgement, "The rarer action", says Prospero, is "in virtue than in vengeance". Prospero may not be Shakespeare but this style is Shakespeare's very own, one of the noblest and most definite of the moral conviction of the maturity.[8]

In between the two extremes, the beginning and the end, the plot passes through a series of brilliant or striking situations, which create a flexible rhythm out of which single scenes sometimes, stand out as the peaks of a mountainous range. The 'trial scene' in *The Merchant of Venice,* the "storm – scene" *in King Lear,* the 'play within –the play' and the exciting 'fencing scene' in 'Hamlet', the scene in *Troilus and Cressida* where the fickle heroine is watched by three observers differently, interested in her and the 'Banquet' and 'sleep-walking' scenes in *Macbeth* are only a few of the numerous cases in point. The pattern of the scenes is a curious contrivance of checks and balances, relief and contrast with alternations in pitch and tempo. Thus the lyrical last scene in *The Merchant of Venice* serves to dissipate the gloom of the trial scene and bring the play to the plane of comedy and the continuous rise and fall in the tempo of the action in *Hamlet* is in perfect keeping with the deliberate inaction and impulsive spurts of violent but spasmodic activity which characterize the nature of the hero, placed in the heart and centre of the play.[9]

K.R. Srinivasa Iyengar comments about Shakespearen Tragedy :

The tragedies are a vast continent, jungle like in their complexity and range. The tragedies resist easy generalisation and refuse to fit into our neatly contrived systems. The surge and roar of evil is obvious enough, but in the long run the forest fires exhaust themeselves and are somehow put out. Evil is beaten back, the Truth, Goodness, Beauty and Love have a chance to prevail again. Apart from the violence of the first explosion, there are the chain reactions, wave upon wave of widening destrucion that go on till the whole earth itself and the atmospheric envelope seem to be involved in the catastophe. Claudius poisoning his brother in the orchard, Macbeth murdering his kinsman and king, his guest and his benefactor : Goneril and Regan driving their old father out to face the naked fury of the elements. They let loose forces of evil that can be brought under control only after incommensurable damage has already been accomplished. So, once evil has been unleased, it sweeps avalanche like over all, the guilty and the innocent suffer alike, and the calm that concludes the tragedy is rather like the calm that follows a cyclone. The two avengers, Hamlet and Laertes, are reconciled in the end. Lear is reconciled to Cordelia, Othello recaptures the faith he had lost, Antony dies reconciled to his Cleopartra-but all this happens just a little too late."In the tragedies, then, the potency of evil and its seeming irresistibility are in terrible contrast to the apparent powerlessness of innocence and goodness. Not poetic justice, only rough justice is possible in the end."[10]

Shakespeare has offered no formal definition of Tragedy. Rossiter points out that, although the word tragedy, tragic and tragical appear 24 times in all in Shakespeare's plays, these are either in the earlier plays or are of a very casual nature. Shakespeare indeed seems to have avoided the world in the mature-tragedies which may perhaps, be taken as an indication that what he was trying to write was something different from what was usually taken for 'tragedy' let's take a glimpse into the world of Shakespearian tragedy. Let us take of chance and open *Macbeth,* These are hero's first words:

So fair and foul a day I have not seen.[11]

Our first view of the tragic world cannot be better or more forcefully described. Already, in the very first scene, the witches have declared in chorus:

Fair is foul, and foul is fair.[12]

And here Macbeth, by a purposeful coincidence, echoes the idea.

The day is foul, the day is fair, contradictions confound us in this world, and we are a prey to a perpetual siege of contraries. From *Titus Andronicus* to *Coriolanus* we have a dozen or more tragedies, including *Richard II* and *Richard III;* and what a world! The Elsinore of *Hamlet,* the cyprus of *Othello,* the Inverness of *Macbeth,* the Alexandria of *Antony* and *Cleoptra* and Heath and the Hovel in *King Lear*-what a world! Thus lady Macbeth advises her husband to "look like the innocent flower, but be the serpent unde't."[13]

It is a day of victory for Duncan, but the victory is to be a prelude to his death. It is a day of rejoicing, but the "obscure bird" clamours the livelong night, Banquo thinks that . (I , iii, 124)

The instruments of darkness tell us truths.

Win us with honest trifles to betray's.

In deepest consequence.

Macbeth is tantalised by the pattern of evil and good and thinks that intervention by the witches "cannot be ill; cannot be good." In *King Lear;* Cordelia is aghast at her sisters' perfidious hypocrisy, and achieves this unspoken thought. (I, i, 75)

Then poor cordelia!

And yet not so.

Poor and not poor![14]

When Lear is in a towering rage, kent. taunts him with a paradox.

(I, i, 163)

Kill thy physician, and the fee bestow

Upon the foul disease.[15]

To the King of France, Cordelia-although disowned and disgraced by the father is "most rich, being poor; /Most choice, forsaken; most lov'd despis'd (I, i, 250) Edmund gloats over his cunning strategy hoping that he, the base, shall nevertheless top the legitimate, (I, ii, 20). "The prince of darkness," says Edgar the bedlambbeggar, "is a gentlemen" (III, iv, 140). In *Othello,* Cassio is "a great arithmetician -----a fellow almost damn'd in a fair wife" (I, i, 19) Iago swears by the "Divinity of hell" and plans to turn Desdemona's virtue into pitch and "out of her own goodness make the net that shall enmesh them all ". (II, ii, 339) In *Antony* and *Cleopatra* the hero's "Captain's heart.... is become the bellows and the fan to cool a gipsy's lust .... the triple pillar of the world transform'd into a strumpet's fool"(I, i, 6). Kingdoms are clay and very falsehood is decked in excellence. Chameleonic Cleopatra is herself a whole world of splendid witchery and ceaseless fascination. The defection of Enobarbus only brings out Antony's magnanimity, which in turn shames the former into committing suicide[16]. Let us open *Antony* and *Cleopatra* and read on:

Cleo : If it be love indeed, tell me how much .

Ant : There's beggary in the love that can be
reckon'd.

Cleo : I'll set a bourn how far to be belov'd .

Ant : Then must thou needs find out new heaven new earth.[17]

In *Antony* and *cleopatra* amorous love is lifted out of all imaginable limits, and it is this that rules the tragic world of the play. Love here is primordial Eros, illimitable, untameable all consuming, all preserving; it sways the destinies of nations empires, it swings the lovers between the extremes of pain and ecstasy. Love completely destroys them, love also finally rehabilitates them. There is more than mere "brag" in Antony's dying declaration. (IV, xv.14):

Not Caesar's valour hath o'erthrown Antony.
But Antony's hath Triumph'd on itself.[18]

Likewise Cleopatra too is transfigured by the power of love, and losing everything she also redeems everything . (v, ii. 278):

Give me my robe, put on my crown : I have
Immortal longing in me.... Husband, I come
Now to that name my courage prove my title!
I am fire and air, my other elements.
I give to baser life.[19]

No bourn could be set to such love as Antony's or Cleopatra's; therein lay the glory of their life together, and there in also lay the spring of their tragedy.

There is no use advising Romeo and Juliet to love in Moderation, or Macbeth to nurse ambition only within reason, or Othello to keep the green-eyed monster in restraint, or Timon to put curbs on his misanthropy; they are helpess, they are carried along by the heady current of the ruling passion that sweeps them to its estuary by its own irresistible momentum. As easily control this force as contain a Niagara or a Padma in all her native fury! This all inclusive, all consuming, all preserving force may be called, after Masefield, the " 'tragic obsession; or we may characterise this phenomenon of excess as the "tragic flow" or "tragic - error" or simply, the "tragic-trait". Othello loved Desdemona, not moderately nor wordly – wisely, but too well, almost to the pitch of frenzy. (III, iii. 91):

Excellent wretch ! Perdition . catch my soul

But I do love thee; and when I love thee not

chaos is come again.[20]

If only he could feel less and think more- but no! That were asking Othello to be somebody else. These tragic powers are what they are, and we must take them even as they are. Lear's obstinacy and Cordelia's righteousness, Regan's perfidy and Edmud's villainy, all are aboslute forces that meet and clash at the infinite range of the tragic world.

"Tragedy", says C. Narayan Menon, "is a complicated arrangement of lenses having a simple focus, the hero"[21] Not only is the hero progressively isolated from his companions, divorced from his material supports, but the isolation is carried out also in the realm of the spirit ; his soul too is thus isolated and exposed , and it draws us towards it with an irresistible force. The lesser novelist or dramatist is content with describing the trivialities of small talk, tame action or formal social behaviour. But the great tragedian focusses attention on just those dynamic and purposive traits that determine the zig-zag movements of a Hamlet's mind and the incommunicable disturbance in his soul. So isolated so pinned down, so exposed to our gaze, Hamlet cannot escape us- Othello and Lear and Macbeth cannot escape us- and we too cannot escape them. Hamlet, Macbeth, Othello, and Lear loom immense against the sky, each a colossus in his own right and each in some strangely inexplicable way a projection of ourselves, of what nature is Shakespear's alchemy that he is able to make pain itself a pleasure, to transform a story of defeat into almost a hymn of transcendental triumph. A tregedy ought to rebel us, on the other hand, tragedy is no running away from life but rather a bold collision with life at its intensest and profundest and fearfullest-a collision that is also a close embrace. The aesthetic experience of tragedy is of the order titiksha, the confrontation, the mastering, and the beyonding of all the shocks of existence and is very different from the familiar everyday feeling of jugupsa, the shrinking and slinking away. Great tragedy, it has been said is never depressing, for great tragedy, it has been said is never depressing, for great tragedy is someshow an affirmation of the everlasting Yea. In Shakespearian tragedy, there is in the catastrophe itself something of a direct affirmation of imperishable value – a sense of the illimitable and the eternal– a sense of absolute goodness, truth, valour, beauty, innocence, love-that we refuse to accept the defeat and the death at their face-value. On the contrary, it is the point of no return for these our tragic heroes and heroines and upon such scarifices as we have witnessed "the gods themselves throw incense."[22]

Tragedy is a confrontation of life not a turning away from it; tragedy is not the experience of evil alone but rather is the experience of good beyond the evil. One summary way of reading Shakespeare's great tragedies would be to see in *Hamlet* the implied passage from death to immoratality, from the fear of what may happen after death to the certainty of 'felicity', in *Othello*, the passage from falsehood to truth, from Iago's cunning fabrication to the truth that is Desdemona as at last revealed by Emilia's self –sacrificing devotion to her dead mistress; in *King Lear* from the darkness of the world of Goneril and Regan to the light that is Cordelia's love; in *Macbeth*, from the play of evil and the resultant chaos of values to the grace of Grace and the return of order; in *Antony* and *Cleopatra* from insatiable sensuality to fulfilment in death and the deathless marriage on the other side and Shoal of Time; and in *Coriolanus* "from the assertion of self to the defeat of self and its transcendence in death, It is wading through poison and reaching at nectar: amritam Vishasamrishtam in Valmiki's resplendent phrase."[23]

K. R. Srinivasa Iyengar comments that ever since Heminge and condell grouped Shakespeare's 36 plays under comedies, Histories and Tragedies in the Folios edition of 1623, superficial readers have been apt to assume that these terms are clear-cut, and were so understood in Elizabethan and Jacobean times. But it was not so because Shakespeare and his contemporaries had less rigid ideas about history, tragedy, and comedy than a look at the 'catalogue' prefixed to the First Folio would seem to warrant. It is certainly convenient to seperate the 10 history plays, *King John* to *Henry VIII*, from rest and read the two tetrologies as the 'tragedy' of England and of the English people, conveying a cumulative sense of horror, and suffering and futility but also of nobility and humanity, and reawakening strength. If an epic could be defined as a significant evocation of events and characters that are of paramount interest to a particular nation but also of general interest to all mankind, then Shakespeare's history plays have certainly an epic intention and sweep. England's trails, her search for unity and stability through monarchic legitimacy and strength, her trying to learn, under the strees of experience, to reconcile in practical action the contradictory pulls of order and impulse, are the basic theme of the history plays. "But since England's history is also human history, these plays make a profound human appeal as well."[24]

In Comedies and the Tragedies as distinct from the Histories- the theme is seized from the human end. *Macbeth* belongs to the history of Scotland (Tillyard has a chapter on *Macbeth* in his *Shakespeare's history plays) Lear* and *cymbelins* to early British History; Caesar, Brutus, Antony, Octavius, Coriolanus and Titus Andronicus are Roman historical characters. While Timon has some sort of niche in Athenian history. Perhaps, there was a prince of Denmark corresponding to Hamlet and a Moorish General of the Athenian army named Othello. But from the beginning these characters are seized inwardly and presented imaginatively; they are not studies in national type of heroism but sparks of primordial humanity and creatures of infinity who have survived all changes in a fast changing world. No doubt characters in fiction and drama - no matter how the writer may have seized them inwardly, need to be clothed and given a set of habits before they are let loose among us. In the English history plays, Shakespeare sought to present certain political situations and characters, and incidently he also brought out what was of primary or universal human interest in them. In the comedies and the Tragedies, on the contrary, Shakespeare started with certain archetypal human situations, worked his way to the human core, and touched both character and plot with universality and imposed on them his individual vision of the human predicament on earth and what man may hope for. Inspiration comes to him from diverse sources: books, observation, personal involvement, intellectual excitement. But not all this is processed by the solvent of the imagination can they crystallise into great art. In the final evaluation the play is really the child of his imagination. The 'subject' has exhasted and is dead : the dramatic artist too has exhausted himself in the act of creation and is 'dead' for the time being. From the funeral pyre of the poetic consort and the poet, there has emerged the work of Art. The 'child' of the poet's imagination. Each of the plays has thus been a creation, a birth; each of the play is unique in its own right. "Yet it is not all together illegitimate for the Critic to play the census enumerator and number the plays, group them and catalogue their common characterstics."[25]

In *The Comedy of Errors* and *The Taming of the Shrew,* Shakespeare wrote farces in *The two gentlmen of Verona* a play about romatic lovers with a certain admixture of comedy, in *Love's Labour's Lost* a witty comedy trembling on the borderland of, romance and in *A Midsummer Night's Dream* a fantasy that seemed to laugh at love and lovers – both the married lovers in the play and tragic lovers in the play within the play. Even in *A Midsummer Night 's Dream,* although the love juice makes Titania dote upon an ass, and makes asses of both Lysander and Demetrius, and cats of Helena and Hermina, it leaves the emotional attachment of these young ladies undisturbed, it is the men who are made to play quick change artists in love. Nevertheless, romantic love's as an absolute – the ideal forcefully presented in sonnet 116 ("Love is not love / which alters when it alteration finds") and in 'The Phoneix and the Turtle'-

Single nature's double name

neither two nor one was called.[26]

Has figured nowhere except in *Romeo an Juliet.* So, how was Shakespeare to project in comedy this vision of 'romantic love'? This can be done only if the reality of a power higher than Death- a power that is also function of the spirit of man, of the human personality can be successfully, convincingly, projected before our consciousness. Love – love that is the trinity of Beauty, truth and rarity - could be the power. It is the sun that dispels the darkness of Death. But this sun has to be veiled, it has to be seen through the circumambient air, the fog and the mist and the smog and even through the massed floating clouds-and even beyond a sudden total eclipse. Hence Shakespeare felt the need to present 'romantic love', not in splendid isolation, but along with much else that seemed to obscure its lucent splendour. Thus 'romantic love', which is an Absolute, is made to co-exist with other kinds of love the relativities, ambiguities, perversions and even the negations of love; and with varieties of 'hate' as well.

In the Tragedy like *Romeo-Juliet,* the projection of the transcendent power of love is viewed as a 'mere wonder'. The light has been too soon put out, and the love has to be inferred from the death, the light from the darkness. The wonder is conceded but not quite credited, it is extolled but not accepted as a living faith.

In the mature Tragedies the darkness is all that there seems to be; the light, when it trickles through, comes as a plot reflected light, or something very remote like the stars, mere pins of light. The Tragedies are about apparent death; and yet it is the tragedians role to convince us that death - even when it tauntingly confronts us-is not the end. Death is somehow defeated by some other power. This power is not Love – that union of 'Beauty', 'truth and 'rarity' – except perhaps in *Othello* and perhaps also *Antony* and *Cleopatra*: but it is not this trinitarian splendour, what helps to defeat death is at least a speck, an emanation, of this power. It is some 'value' or spiritual measure that out-bids death's dread measure any positive value would do courage, integrity, innocence, endurance- even if it were mixed up with much that is dross or worse. Thus Tragedy too affirms through apparent negation; it posits 'life' through the presentation of 'death'; and it is the tragedians vision and the power of his poetry to communicate it that makes the 'lie' of this paradox the higher 'truth' of Tragedy.

What is the 'world' of Romantic Comedy? The Elizabethan audience was taken to Venice (and Belmont), to Messina, to the Forest of Arden , to Illyria. It is a far country, rendered strange, alluring and unpredictable by the fact of distance in space and time.

"The advantage of the Romantic preference for remoteness in time and space", says Mark-Hunter, "is obvious", and adds: "remoteness weakens or completely removes the impression of improbability; for of course Romance, though depending for its effects on the improbable, does not aim at conveying an impression of improbability, but rather seeks to invest the strange and wonderful with an air of likelihood".[27]

We are prepared for anything that might happen , and many strange things do happen, some hundreds of years ago perhaps– therein far – off Messina or unheard – off Illyria, in the inaccessible Forest of Arden or an enchanting Belmont under the moon there, perhaps, such things did take place, and such persons did live. But on closer scrutiny, this Messina – this Venice was not much odder than "London –A street – Enter two citizens". Launcelot, Dogberry and Malvolio were no different from their English Counterparts, Silvius and Phoebe were no strangers to the English country side, nor was Arden itself. Even 'Illyria', was by no means an impossible address in Elizabethan England. The spell of strangeness was thus followed by the pleasant shock of recognition, and it was the privilege of the dramatist to cast the one as well as administer the other. As Gorden finely puts it "it is in his power over these two worlds, in his ostensible alternation between Nowhere and England, that Shakespeare's romantic comedies excel all others."[28]

A Romantic comedy may indeed, perilously edge towards Tragedy (as in *Merchant of Venice* and *Much Ado about Nothing*) yet not actually touch it. History with its excessive addiction to fact wouldn't mix either with the seeming incredibilities of Romance. The lash of satire or open didactic exhortation too might destroy the illusion of Romance. On the other hand when they are in a minor key and mingle purposefully with the many notes in the symphony, they too can co-exist with Romantic comedy. In such a place, in such an atmosphere, "Love is the central light, the infallible intelligence, the chief source of life and happiness. And this Love is identified primarily with a young woman She is the Shakti of this universe, she is beauty, truth and rarity, and inspires similar virtues (or values) in her lover."[29] In a Romantic comedy the main stress is on the story of these lovers – a story, says Mark Hunter," treated seriously, moving through a number of checks and trying complications to a prosperous ending". It is, besides, " a story not only of high life but of the highest in each particular case possible". But allied to the main story, there are invariably other stories also, but silken threads of diverse colours- all are cunnigly woven into a single texture:

"Through complexity of plot is secured a compensating variety, both variety of character – interest, and variety of delight afforded by the alternation of two or more Romantic themes, together with a greater or lesser admixture, of pure comedy not Romantic".[30]

In this world ! love sometimes rages like an epidemic; in *The Merchant of Venice* there are three marriages at the end of the play, in *Much Ado* there are two, in *As you like it* there are four and in *Twelfth Night* three." "In this climate of romance," says Gorden, "It is off – course, the rule that all the lovers shall love at once, and love absolutely, Nothing else in this world is permitted", But this is no homogeneous or monistic world; while the lovers are sighing or singing , just round the corner in a tavern or even down –stairs in the buttery there are carefree creatures swearing by cakes and ale. Shakespeare would make these two antagonistic worlds co-exist somehow; and dualism of the worlds of Romance and comedy is exceeded by Visishtadvaita of dramatic artistry. In Gordon's words again:

"Shakespeare proceeded, as he always does by compromise. If comedy laughs, Romance is not to be offended; if love sighs, comedy promises to put up with it to a point! to a point !...... The low therefore, is one of decency and measure. The solemnity of Love is relieved by the generosity of laughter, and the irresponsibility of laughter by the seriousness of Love."[31]

The comic scenes provide contrast and relief to the Romantic Scenes and this in itself is an advantage. But they have another role too, namely to create a climate of realism in which the Romantic Imprubility also may be accepted without question. To quote Mark Hunter once more:

"The men and women in Shakespeare's comedies are of varying degrees of moral worthlessness, and from none, it may be truly said, is more measure of sympathy withheld; but the character for whom most sympathy is demanded are, on the moral ground, essentially noble, even balanced and proportioned types."[32]

The world of the Shakespearian Romantic comedy is thus a gay and happy world and also essentially a 'moral' world. And the synoptic centre of this world, its savitar, is the Romantic heroine, who incarnates the power and glory of Love, She has "Beauty, truth and rarity, / Grace in all simplicity". The Shakespearian Romantic heroine is that rare creature, her mind, heart and soul in splendorous harmony. In these heroine, as H.B. Charlton says in his Shakespearian comedy, "hand and heart and brain are fused in a vital and practicable union, each contributing to the other, neither of them permanently pressing demands to the detriment of the other. Yet each asserting itself periodically to exercise its vitality, even if the immediate effect be a temporary disturbance of equilibrium, for not otherwise will they be potent to exercise their proper function when the whole of their owner's spiritual nature-struck into activity."[33]

A heroine like Rosalind has graduated from the school of Adversity and the lesson she has learnt is that, even in life's darkest extremities, she should not forget the claims of love and sacrifice, nor lose the innate joy of living. In the hands of woman like Portia, Beatrice, Viola and of course Rosalind, the frivolous comedy of the ancients recedes and its place taken by a transmuted 'divine comedy 'which effectively links "the kindred points of heaven and home." The heroine "She only, she alone, is the whole incarnation of the idea of the Shakespearian Romantic comedy. Ruskin probably had this in mind when he said that Shakespeare had no heroes but only heroines. A love story plotted with ethical seriousness and ending happily; a heroine who is the mind, heart, and soul of the play, its laughter, its love, and its infalliable wisdom-these are the 'elements' that mix and make the 'substance' of Shakespearian Romantic comedy.

Shakespeare's tragedies belong to Renaissance England. They are essentially different from Greek drama. At the same time they differ in certain respects from the rest of the Renaissance tragedies. It may be next to impossible to define this Shakespeare stamp completely and scientifically but there is no doubt that its presence is felt by all. Among Shakespeare's own tragedies the four major plays stand out as a group apart. They have been linked together for centuries. Bradley made the quarter popular with his classic on Shakespearean Tragedy. It is primarily these four plays people have in mind when they speak of Shakespearean tragedy. Renaissance tragedies are of two kinds. These are romantic tragedies of Marlowe and Shakespeare and these are tragedies written in accordance with classical model as those of Ben Johnson. The great Greek tragdies portray a situation instead of a series of situations as in Engilsh tragedies. These are exceptions but in most of the important tragedies we see great concentration on a single situation which leads to a unified tragic effect ." In *Othello,* the best constructed tragedy of Shakespeare, we see a single dramatic situation developing after the second act".[34]

Every tragedy of Shakespeare has a meaning. But this meaning cannot be read on the metaphysical or theological plane. Read tragedy as the fall of man or of his damnation, *Othello* and *Macbeth* would appear to be meaningless. But seen in a more realistic and secular context they are full of meaning for all human beings. The meaning of a tragedy depends on our understanding of the characters involved, their social situation and our response to their suffering. The meaning of a tragedy is not an idea that can be grasped in an intellectual way. The meaning can be understood only through sympathy. Macbeth is a murderer; Othello is a semibarbarian; Hamlet is a sick and doubting intellectual; Lear is an old man gone mad because of uncontrollable passion. If we understand the heroes in this way, failing to sympathise with them, then all tragedies would be meaningless." A criticism that sees only sickness in Hamlet, only crime and damnation in Othello and Macbeth and only the lunacy of a helpless old man in Lear would indeed become meaningless."[35] A Shakespearean tragedy moves on two planes simultaneously; one is the social-moral plane of the external world and the other is the subjective plane of human consciousness. The conflict spreads to both the planes. Hamlet finds himself in contradiction with the world of social relations based on greed, lust and selfishness. To this world he is not reconciled. He gets sick of this world not because he is essentially morbid; we see enough of the other Hamlet to convince us how his genius would have flowered in a different situation. He gets sick of the world because of its ugliness which he perceives more sharply than others because of his innate sense of what is good and beautiful in life. The Conflict spreads to his own consciousness. Hamlet gets the better of his melancholy and dies triumphantly avenged on his enemies." The meaning lies in our increased awareness of the sordidness of the world which Hamlet hated, in our increased sympathy for that is represented by Hamlet and others in the play. And the meaning of the tragedy also lies in our experience of human suffering revealed in all its magnitude unknown to us before."[36]

In *King Lear* the conflict between the two worlds becomes still sharper. Instead of a duel we have an armed conflict between Lear's party and his opponents. Machiavellian ethics in its extreme form confronts the moral values holds dear by the people. Our emotional responses to the two sets of moral values are strengthened. And the meaning of the tragedy lies in our experiencing the sorrows of Lear which have no equal in world drama.

In *Othello* Machiavellian egoism faces a hero, partly corrupted by it. The conflict between the two sets of moral values has becomes more complex but it is there. Iago and Othello in their normal awareness stand for two different worlds. Our sympathy and disgust in the given social situation are strengthened. But Othello has a bit of Iago in himself and Iago has a few admirable qualities of Othello in himself. Both when we admire Iago and Othello and also when we hate them, the difference between the two sets of values remains. The meaning of the tragedy also lies in our experience of the appalling magnitude of Othello's suffering.

In *Macbeth* there is an external conflict between Macbeth and his opponents. This conflict differs qualitatively from a similar external conflict in *King Lear* there is no sense of triumph in the destruction of Macbeth as there is in the destruction of Goneril and Regan. This is because Macbeth is not a Goneril or Regan. He is more like Othello, a mixture of good and evil. He follows the Machiavellian path of destroying everything that hinders the realization of his ambitions. But to destroy good outside is easier than destroying the good within him. That is why he suffers. On the moral plane we do not lose sight of good and evil, our proper responses are strengthened. And once again we experience the ecstasy of a sensitive soul on the rack.

Between loyalty and treachery, between charity and social injustice, between love and callousness, between refined aesthetic responses as those of Hamlet and formalist dullness as that of

Polonius, between sensuality and moral purity, between gratitude and ingratitude, Shakespeare always makes us take sides, He does not simply ask questions. He was a modern decadent intellectual, one of the beaten angry young men of this generation. He was a great Renaissance humanist who leaves us in no doubt of his moral sympathies. On the subjective plane he reveals to us the intricacy of human motives. We have glimpse of the unfathomed world of powerful and often contradictory human impulses. He brings to the surface the under-currents of human consciousness, designated today as the unconscious."This knowledge of the human mind coupled with deep sympathy for all who suffer should give a meaning to the tragedies of Shakespeare."[37]

Shakespearean tragedy is both romantic and realistic. Romanticism provides a kind of enveloping atmosphere of the inner realistic kernel. Shakespeare used the rich material of native folklore for the purpose. The witches and the ghosts have a good deal of specific, English colouring. In *Othello* he provides the romantic background familiar to an *Elizabethan*, audience, through travel books. In *king Lear* the romantic element is hardly separable from the realistic. The storm, the belly pinched wolf, the cub-drawn bear and similar images belong not to the world of imagination but to the world of reality. They are romantic only in the sense that they do not come within the sphere of the experience of the average spectator. A good deal of the life of Edger has also the exotic colouring of a tramp's life. *King Lear* thus shows a skilful blending of the romantic and realistic elements and is the most realistic of his tragedies since the romantic elements themselves are not unreal.

In *Macbeth* the romantic covering penetrates the kernel; it is also present through a major part of the play. The bizarre, the grotesque, the ugly images rousing our disgust, all help strengthen the feelings which harmonise with our responses to the main action of the play. In *Othello* the romantic atmosphere rids itself of the purely fantastic and imaginative. It is more of this world though in its exoticism it does not cease to be fantastic. This romanticism is skilfully used for accentuating the variation in human character and styles of speech. In *King Lear* the storm harmonizes with the raging storm within Lear's own mind'. "Shakespeare further uses storm image, occurring so frequently in his plays, to emphasize the enduring contradiction between man and nature, to show the affinity of all living creatures in their struggle against nature for survival".[38]

There is an element of poetic-justice in the tragedies of Shakespeare. Virtue may or may not triumph but vice is never seen victorious. Evil never triumphs in the tragic world of Shakespeare. "The romanticism underlying his concept of poetic justice is an essential component of Shakespeare's humanism. He believes in the ultimate destruction of evil. Good will survive even though reduced in a very large measure. The concept of poetic justice is also a subtle artistic device for saving a tragedy from a totally pessimistic conclusion and for making it bearable to the spectators."[39]

The device of buttressing the emotional impact of the main plot through a sub-plot is also a characteristic feature of romantic style. It stands in sharp contrast with the economy of material and the unity emotional impression in classical plays. The sense of the massiveness of suffering and its universality is created by the inter linking of the two plots in *King Lear* The two stories support each other, make Goneril and Regan convincing, show a variation in the world of evil and bring out the immensity of Lear's suffering in contrast to Gloucester's. In *Hamlet* the play within the play and all that accompanies it retells the stories of Claudius and Gertrude and also reveals the happy aesthetic aspects of Hamlet's personality. Polonius and Leartes, in the story of their domestic relationship, bring out the sharp contradiction between the two world of Hamlet and Claudius. The grave – yard musings of Hamlet have something of the typical melancholy of the nineteenth century French romantic poets. In a general way all the four tragedies are symbolic. *Lear* stands as a symbol of man against nature and social injustice. *Hamlet* is a symbol of the sensitive Renaissance intellectual unable to reconcile himself to the new civilzation with its mercenary ethic *Macbeth* is a symbol of the criminal who is impelled to crime by powers beyond the control of his reason and who realize in the end the futility of his crime. *Othello* and 'Iago' stand as symbols of the romantic hero deceived by the realistic Machiavellian. Shakespearean tragedy is deeply poetic. There is no reason to mock at those critics who sometimes talk of Shakespeare as a poet. The poetic and the dramatic are interwoven and constitute one integral art. Shakespearean tragedy is made of both prose and verse. That itself is symbolic of its dual romantic – realistic nature. "The most distinctive feature of Shakespearean tragedy is the volume and depth of human suffering that the dramatist exhibits..... The intensity of suffering is such that it transports the sufferer beyond himself; it makes him forget himself for the time being and have a taste of infinity. The ecstasy is for a moment or a few moments but the agony is stretched out."[40]

There is a similarity of pattern in the emotional disturbance and the unfolding of the suffering of the hero in Shakespearean tragedy. The heroes feel guilty for one reason or another. 'Hamlet' feels guilty because he is unable to carry out the wish of his dead father at once. He deep gloom can be explained on the basis of a secret sense of guilty love for his mother or Ophelia in preference to love for his father. 'Lear' feels guilty for being unjust to Cordelia and perhaps also to Kent. 'Macbeth' feels guilty for his crime; possibly Lady Macbeth also feels guilty for having incited her husband to crime and thereby caused his and her own suffering. 'Othello' feels guilty for having murdered Desdemona. In *Macbeth* and *King Lear* the deed which causes awareness of guilt is done In the earlier part of the play. In *Othello* the deed and the full realization of guilt come only at the end. In Hamlet it is the absence of the deed that creates the sense of guilt "Suffering is a great teacher to Shakespeare's heroes. It helps them to cleanse their soul of egoism and other impurities."[41]

In all the four great tragedies woman also die. The deaths of Cordelia, Ophelia and Desdemona, provide what is more pathetic than tragic in the play. There is immense pathos because of their helplessness. In the case of Lady Macbeth the pathetic borders on the tragic. Around this pathos there arises tragic pain which becomes sublime because of the struggle waged by the hero and his partial responsibility for some of his suffering. At the end of a tragedy there is no complete relief, no calm of mind all passion spent. The awareness of pain remains at the end of a tragedy in varying digress.

Shakespearean tragedy moves on several planes all at once. It reflects the contradictions of social life during the Renaissance. It reflect the contradictions of Renaissance culture. It anticipates the development of realism and romanticism in the nineteenth century. It reveals the hidden depths of the human unknown to literature before. "Above all it is the finest evidence of Shakespeare's humanism which shows such a profound understanding of the human soul in pain."[42]

U.N. Jha, in his essay on 'Honour' in Shakespeare's plays writes that-

In Shakespeare's plays 'Honour' has been accorded a very important place. In many of his plays honour is inseparable from chivalry. "...Most of the protagonist of the History plays, the Roman plays and the Tragedies has a high sense of honour and they express it in their words and deeds. In the comedies, where women play more important roles, there is an emphasis on their honour......"[43]

In Shakespearean plays, 'honour' is a word of very high frequency. In the 37 plays that are usually ascribed to him, this word occurs in as many as many as 657 lines which gives us an average of 18 for a play. The distribution, however, is not even. In the comedies of both the period-with the single exception of *All's well That Ends well*- the word is not used frequently, the figure varying from one in '*A Midsummer – Night's Dream*' to nine in 'As you like it'. As against this we find fifty-one occurrence in Henry VIII, thirty-six in Measure for Measure, thirty-five in *Coriolanus,* thirty-two in *Cymbeline,* twenty-eight in *The winter's Tale,* twenty-five each in *Henry VI,* and *Timon of Athens* and so on. These figures, it is true, include addresses to persons of rank, quality and oaths, but percentage of such occurrences is rather small. "In all other example we find some character speaking about honour and the important that the speaker or some other character or the world attaches to it. The quality of the statement is always in keeping with the character of the speaker. Kings and Princes are naturally always conscious of their honour even if the king is like John or Henry IV, not particularly possessed of heroic virtues. Hero's do not attach much importance to life. For Hector:

Mine honour keeps the weather of my fate:
Life every man holds dear; the dear man
Holds 'honour' for more precious-dear than life.[45]

(*Troilus & Cressida,* V. iii,27)

And Julius Caesar:

If it aught towards the general good,

set honour in one eye death i' 'the other,

And I will look on both indifferently. [46]

(*Julius Ceaser,* I, ii. 86)

Blinded by Cleopatra's beauty Antony forgets honour and he has to be reminded by her that

'your honour calls you hence'[47]

(*Antony and cleopatra.,* I, iii. 97')

but once roused, it is the familiar hero who exclaims :

Tomorrow!, soldier,

By sea and land I'll fight : or I will live,

Or bathe my dying honour in the blood

Shall make it live again. [48]

(*Antony and Cleopatra,* IV. ii.114)

But it takes all sorts to make the world. If there are people who in the mocking words of the cynical Jaques are –

Jealous in honour, sudden and quick in quarrel,

Seeking the bubble reputation

Even in the canon's mouth,[49] (As you like It, II. vii.151-53')

Othello asks to be reported as an 'honourable murderer'

For naught did I in hate

but all in honour. [50] (V. ii. 292)

In *Hamlet* there are not frequent references to honour, though the Prince appears to be obsessed with the thought that the Queen, his mother, has dishonoured the royal bed of his father by marrying his uncle. Yet in one of soliloquies we find him saying:

Rightly to be great

Is not be stir without great argument,

But greatly to find quarrel in a straw

When honour's at the stake.[51] (*Hamlet*, IV, iv.53-56)

Brutus whom Antony with cheap irony describes as 'an honourable man', is indeed a true Roman, that is, an honourable Roman and, had rather be a dog, bay the moon, than such a Roman, as would

Sell the mighty space of all our honours

For so much trash as may be grasped thus'[52]

(*Julius Ceasar*, IV, iii. 21)

The chivalrous idea of defending one's honour at the point of the sword is quite common in Shakespeare. And honour raises man to the level of gods. In *Cymbeline*, Iachimo, describes Leonatus in these words:

He sits 'mongst man like a descended god;

He has a kind of honour sets him off,

More than a mortal seeming.[53]

(*Cymbeline*, I.vi. 169-71)

In Shakespeare's comedies and Romances, he refers frequently to the honour of women. While in the case of men honour is the product of valour, in the case it is always linked with chastity and conjugal fidelity, but it is an equally prized possession for both. Shakespearean heroines, too, prefer death to dishonour. Most representative of this attitude are Hermione's speeches when she is charged with infidelity to her loyal consort:

For life, I prize it

As I weight grief, which I would spare: for honour

'Tis a derivation from me to mine,

And only that I stand for.[54]

(*Winter Tale*. III, ii. 43-46)

On hearing reports against his wife, Eleanor, Gloucester says to Queen Margaret:

Noble she is, but if she have forgot

Honour and virtue ,and convers's with such

As, like to pitch, defile nobility.

I banish her, as a prey, to law and shame,

That has dishonour'd Gloucester's honest name.[55]

(*2 Henry* VI. II.i.192)

In the play after play, the theme of feminine honesty or honour has been worked out to a happy conclusion but in Othello the moor's eyes are opened when it is too late. The allegedly dishonest Desdemona who has now been transformed into honesty itself lies dead, a victim to the machinations of 'honest' Iago and Othello's world has come with a mighty crash. So,

Why should honour outlive honesty?[56]

In the Renaissance, men had a high sense of honour and though they had sense enough not to tilt at the wind mill, were not so reasonable as to regard discretion as the better part of valour.

In N.M Roa's essay on Hawk and Handsaw- A study of Hamlet' he remark that-

Hamlet had the habit of telling the truth, but this truth was often expressed in a cryptic manner. One reason for this was the puns, quibbles, proverbs and other clever way of saying things were, no doubt, part of Elizabethan, refined conversation In fact 'wordplay was a game the Elizabethans played seriously.'[57]

It was not only a means of making conversation lively, but a reflection of the intelligence, skill and learning of the speaker. Such word play, however, fell into disuse after Shakespeare's days; only in our time has interest in it been received. As professor Mahood observes, Where the Augustans disapproved of Shakespeare's wordplay and the Victorians ignored it was now acclaim it ... Shakespearean criticism today recognizes world play as a major poetic device'

The Elizabethan may have regarded wordplay more as a show of wit than as a poetic device. But to Hamlet, in Shakespeare play, wordplay is more than a way of showing wit, it is a devise to discover and express reality. Wordplay gets involved in Hamlet's struggle with the problem of reality.

Hamlet makes use of the proverb 'I am but mad north-north–west; when the mind is southerly I know a hawk from handsaw' (2.2.382-83) when he welcome his friends Rosencrantz and Guilderstern, Hamlet's class-mates, who had been sent by Claudius to find out if he was actually mad. Commenting as Hamlet's play upon 'hawk' and 'handsaw' Dover Wilson point out that it is ...

'One of Hamlet's pregnant quibbles... Any how, we need not hesitate to take Hamlet's words as meaning... I am only mad on one point; in other respect I have wit enough to tell chalk from cheese. But as usual he has a second purport, which Rosencrantz and Guilderstern are not intended to catch... The whole passage... can be readily understood in terms of falconry. Hawking at herons were a favourite sport. Thus Hamlet also implies that he has 'an eye of ' his seeming friends and know that to be birds of prey'.[58]

Hamlet seems to assert that he is capable of workman - like approach to his problem and can clearly distinguish contraries like 'hawk' and 'handsaw'. It also means, since a hawk is some kind of a tool and handsaw a quibble on heronshaw, that Hamlet recognizes his school fellows as the kings tools, sent after him as birds of prey are loosened in the royal sport of falcoury'.[59] Such an awareness shows that Hamlet is not mad. Hamlet's awareness of his position as a heron among hawks suggest that he should be cautious in expressing his thoughts. At the same time, he is relieved to find that he still retains in spite of the disturbance recent event have caused him, the faculty of reason which helps him to distinguish 'hawk' and 'handsaw' or appearance and reality. Hamlet's use of proverb suggests his involvement in a larger problem than revenge; he is deeply concerned with 'the problematic nature of reality, and the relation of reality to appearance.[60] One reason for this is that he is perhaps the most well educated of Shakespeare's characers. Wittenberg's university, where he studied, was associated both with Luther and liberal thinking. In his efforts to distinguish 'hawk' and 'handsaw', or reality and appearance, he uses, chiefly, three devices:

1- the 'antic disposition which he had informed his friends in Act I that he might put on;'

2- Careful observation of Polonius,Claudius, Rosencrantz and Guilderstren; and.

3- the play within the play, variously called 'The Mouse – Trap' and 'The Murder of Gonzago' Though he makes fun of his antic disposition or madness, saying he is mad only when the wind blows north – north west, and asking his mothers to tell Claudius that he is mad 'in' name.[61] He uses it to advantage. (That I essentially am not in madness/But mad in craft'). (3. 4. 187-88)

Hamlet observes the people around him in order to know the the reality about them. He quickly finds out that Polonius is fishing for his secrets in order to please the King. When Polonius asks him, 'Do you know me, my lord?' he tells the truth, ' Excellent well, you are fishmonger'.(2.2.173-74). as this example shows Hamlet expresses most of his observations in the form of quibbles, proverbs and images; these as Wolfgang Clemen points out.

Seems... designed to unmask men... And to show them up in their true nature. (They) reflect his ability to penetrate to the real nature of men and things and his relentless breaking down of the barriers raised by hypocrisy.[62]

It is interesting that though Shakespeare has used theatrical imagery in all his plays, it is only in 'Hamlet' that it is so wide ranging and deep. In this way acting to Hamlet, to Shakespeare and to us, becomes a metaphor for revealing reality, for expressing and objectifying deep emotions. The mirror metaphor runs through the whole play. The play within the play not only mirrors but releases a number of realities. In the closet scene when Hamlet meets his mother, he says ' You go not till I set you up a glass where in you may see the inner most part of you.' (3.4.19-20) The play – within the play not only mirrors Claudius villainy and guilt, but reveals to Claudius Hamlets hostility towards him. That makes Claudius act firmly: he sends Hamlet to his death in England 'In fact, the play series is one of a series of ironies, the crowning one being that Hamlet never does avenge his father's death, except in the most off-hand and accidental way : he kills Claudius in direct retaliation for the wound he has himself been given'[63]

To this may added another irony, and that is the inevitability of killing Claudius. Hamlet kills Claudius when he himself is dying, and delay is no longer possible. The killing comes when hamlet knows that his quest for reality has been brought to an end. Even in his last moment Hamlet wants to ensure that reality lives on: he tells Horatio, 'report me and my cause aright' (5.2.337) The play 'Hamlet' has a special appeal for creative writers and audiences alike because the theme of appearance and reality 'appears to reflect our own growing awareness of the discrepancy in our modern world.'[64] That means, we are still trying to tell 'hawk' from handsaw;

Prof. M.M. Mahood comments in his essay- 'A Mid Summer Night's Dream' – As Exorcism, that-

Each of the play's three components, lovers, fairies and those that Shakespeare in an authorial direction unblushingly calls the rabble, enacts the exorcism of one of these basic fears, by purging it away in a comic catharsis. Or rather, since modern psychoanalysis provides a fitter image than does Aristotle's physiology, we may say that. *A midsummer- Nights Dream* Works towards the liberation of its most important spectators not by the Freudian method of bringing their hidden anxieties into the light but by Jungian concentration of the dramatic experience upon those antique fable and fairy toys that Theseus so blandly dismisses in the last act. It is not to suggest that Shakespeare deliberately planned his wedding play as an assault upon the 'bad–spirits; of deep rooted anxiety. Yet the repeated allusions to mimesis and to the power of the imagination suggest that here as in The Tempest the process of writing the play brings vivid awareness of the dramatists art as magic – if it is possible to restore to the word some of its original force. This self-awareness may have been helped by the fact that in. A Midsummer Night's Dream Shakespeare was inventing his own plot or combination of plots, so that it was natural for him to ask himself what he was up to in shaping the play in this particular fashion. In critical writings on the play this self- awareness has perhaps received more than its fair share of attention. Here the play's action shall be traced as the exorcism of anxiety.[65]

The first act of is *A Midsummer Night's Dream* allows the spectators to contemplate the hazardous courses of true love from a very safe distance. The catalogue of ills recited in lines 134 to 140 by Hermia and Lysander can only have aroused the response 'how different from us!' in the newly married pair of Elizabeth Carey, grand-daughter to the lord chamberlain, and Thomas, son to Lord

Berkeley, in February 1956. For this marriage was between young social equals, and it was a love match, the couples affection for each other had begun some months previously. Nor were they safe from having to 'choose love by another's eyes', but they were safe for ever from the dreadful alternative placed before Hermia, that of 'withering on the virgin thorn'.

Shakespeare in part neutralize it by the idea that virginity is theologically the better part – 'thrice blessed they that master so their blood', but real appeasement to the Queen Elizabeth comes from the mirror of princely behaviour held up in the person of Theseus. Like the Duke of Athens, The Sixteenth Century monarch could be called upon to arbitrate between parent and child in matrimonial matters.[66] "In wider judicial context, his or her duty was to arrive at equitable settlements without flouting common law. Romantic and juvenile notions of love have to be put to the test in the wood near Athens, not a place of intellectual enlightenment such as is the Forest of Arden, but a bewildering tangle wood in which the fool has to persist in his folly in order to become wise. Some such paradox may underlie Shakespeare's odd inconsistency about moonlight. At the beginning of the first act the old moon is waning, so the event that follow should happen at the dark of the moon, and before the honeymoon of Theseus and Hippolyta.

Anxieties that were beginning to stir in the play's first act are brought to the surface in the second. Apart from the diminutive choirboy fairies the 'trains' of Oberon and Titania were probably such adult figures as are envisaged by the illustrator of Rowe's edition, and the quarrel that ensures between the first married couple we have met in the play is painfully human and life-sized. As is in the way of such scenes, the couple hurl accusations of affairs at each other, and fight over a child. And because they are the rulers of the fairly land, their quarrel has repercussions far beyond their personal unhappiness. While Oberon is planning is bewitchment of Titania, the Athenian lovers have arrived in paris, preparatory to Shakespeare's employment of them in the transformation of a second fear, the dread of being forsaken. This is closely associated with the dread of having made a wrong choice, just as the two interests in the play are linked through Oberon's little purple flower. In the scenes with the Athenian lovers, Shakespeare frequently calls upon the resources of the couplet, many of which he learned from Chaucer, to stylise and to distance the emotions portrayed. The effect can be explosively funny when he exploits the couplet symmetry:'

Lysander, If you live, good sir awake!

And run through fire I will for thy sweetsake![67] (2.2.101-2)

Blank verse too, when the alternating syllables are given a strongly marked beat, throws into relief the personal voice rhythms of four speakers, creating the effect of operatic duos, trios and quartets. The doleful Helena speaks with a falling rhythm, her words in counterpoint to the metrical feet: an effect helped by occasional displacements of stress and by famine line ending:

I am your spaniel: and Demetrius,  
The more you beat me I will fawn on you,  
Use me but as your spaniel, spurn me, strike me,  
Neglect me, lose me; only give me leave,  
Unworthy as I am, to follow you.[68] (2.1.203-7)

Finally, through Puck's intervention, they all come together once more in an exhausted sleep from which they awake sorted out at last into a right and natural pairing. After this the Athenian workman are faced with the problem that while drama gives pleasure as an imitation of life, such on imitation of it is to be faithful must include much that in life is not pleasurable. To leave the killing out, as Starveling suggests, they do, is to kill off the play. Bottom's proposal is much better. The audience is to be reminded that what it is watching is only a simulation, and this is to be done in two ways. Bottom and snug will step out of their parts to reassure the audience and moon and wall will be impersonated in a highly stylished fashion. All this gives the lie to Puck's description of Bottom as 'The shallowest thick skin of that barren sort'.[69] (3.2.13). The concern he has shown over the ladies fear is anything but thick skinned, and his buoyant inventiveness at the rehearsal distinguishes him from 'the barren sort'. Shallow he is certainly not; his grasp of dramatic illusion shows an understanding of the principle of aesthetic distance which is to stand the test, though through hilarity rather than through pity and fear, in the play acted before the Duke. Oberon's plan to humiliate Titania by making her fall in love with a grotesque, fool thus completely misfires, and this is the Shakespeare's further strategy for dispelling the fear of having made a wrong choice in love. Though Bottom may, as are result of finding himself with an ass' jaws show an occasional craving for oats and dried peas, it is not really possible to make an ass of bottom. His name implies level-headedness the stability of a well built ship. The quality makes it easy for him to keep his aplomb when wooed by the queen of the fairies. It is admittedly, possible to play the Bottom-Titania scenes of the third and fourth acts as if the Athenian workman is too slow-witted to respond to the seductiveness of a beautiful woman. But it is equally possible and a good deal more effective to play them in such a way that Bottom is shown exercising at once his sense of reality and his power of imagination, the very combination that endows him with an understanding of the nature of drama. He is Bottom the weaver who knows his place and his worth and how to humour this very eccentric great lady. Titania may experience a momentary revulsion when Oberon shows her that she has embraced a human with, hobnailed boots and an ass' head; but when puck removes the 'transformed scalp', Shakespeare has completed his exorcism of the fear of wrong choice. The answer to the dread. 'shall I find I have married an ass?'[70] Is that no man is an ass. Our fairy prince or princess is certain to prove in the end an ordinary man or woman, but as such being capable of bottomless dreams.

Just as the spectators were led by the allurements of lyric verse, song and dance, to enter into Titania's experiences so they have become painlessly familiar with the lover's tribulations through amusement at their stylised speech and movement. In the big scene (3.2) between the four, there are verse change which subtly affect the mood of our receptivity. At the point where Helena turns on Hermia, Couplets give way to a blank verse which admits strong overtones of emotion than any spoken so far:

O, is all forgot?

All school days' friendship,

Childhood innocence?....[71] (201 following)

The whole speech is compounded of passionate words, as Hermia says. The four young people in the acting space are however still being hounded by Puck, a situation suggestive of anxiety-ridden nightmares, until that all collapse in an exhausted sleep. Puck can now apply the antidote to Lyander's eyes while Oberon seeks out Titania who, lost in her infatuation, readily yields up the Indian boy to him: a scene which had to be reported, perhaps in spite of Shakespeare's original intention, in order to keep the play to a reasonable length for a private entertainment. The different doubts and fears of love's continuance vanish with the approaching dawn, like 'the fierce vexation of a dream'. Titania's reconciliation with Oberon is celebrated in their dance. As is the way with a marriage between great personages, the couple's rediscovered happiness flows out to those around them, as they 'rock the ground where on these sleepers be' (4.1.85). The four lovers in their turn wake to the noise Theseus' hounds which other forces of nature, echoes from rock and tree, are transforming into 'one mutual cry', and with their own mutual cry discover that each is safe with the right partner at last. Theseus has only to gives his approval to the way their affections have sorted themselves out(with some supernatural help, though he will never believes it), and they are left to reflect on their adventures in words of peculiar power. Liberation from the fear of having a mistake has been brought out by the direction of king Oberon, and liberation from the fear of desertion has been stage-managed by Duke Theseus.[72]

S. Viswanathan in his essay on 'Shakespeare's Metamorphoses of Acteaon' states that-

One of the most Fascinating of the classical legends to cast its spell on the Renaissance, the myth of Actaeon the hunter's transformation into a stag hunted and killed by his own hounds as condign punishment for seeing Diana engaged the attention of the Renaissance mythographers. It is hardly surprising that the apokatastasis of Actaeon seized the imagination of the poets and playwrights of the period like Spenser, Sidney, Marlowe, Chapman, the love sonneteers and above all Shakespeare.

Before considering striking dramatic variations which Shakespeare makes on the motif of Actaeon's 'translation', a mention would be briefly made to indicate the plethora constructions put on it by the interpreters of the times and some of the suggestive force of the legend with the dominant metaphor of 'Venery' and hunting in the vast body of the late medieval and Renaissance love literature, together with the ubiquitous 'heart-hart' pun in English love convention led the poets to invoke Actaeon's plight, directly or indirectly, often enough and perhaps made it convenient for them also to highlight the paradoxical nature of love and the reversals and inversions(not always comic) it could bring about by way of the transformation of the hunter into the hunted. Leaving aside the extreme instance of mythographic typological ingenuity which made one interpreter see a prefiguration of Christ's martyrdom in Actaeon's fate.[73]

The availability to Shakespeare and his contemporary audience, in varying degrees, of the other learned as well as popular significances seen in the myth lends the Shakespearian uses of the myth, sometimes a telling ironical force and sometimes a rich ambiguity or ambivalence, both in terms of the total communication of words and stage picture together. If the legend promoted and was in turn promoted by the 'heart-hart' pun an approximation, by the same argument , was between Actaeon's horns and those proverbial ones of the cuckold in the popular imagination. Renaissance of mythology explicated Actaeon's punishment as the wages of the sin of excessive physical passion, Actaeons own libido eating him up, as it were, in the likeness of his hounds . The beastly degeneration is the result of animal passion .This interpretation is the one adopted of the legend by chapman in the 'Hymmes in Cynthiam', 'The Shadow of Night'[74]. As the two modern English explicators of Bruno's treatise, Yates and J.C.Nelson.[75] Point out, in Bruno's almost visionary interpretation, what the myth connotes is the mytique of the love quest, the ultimate pursuit of the ideal Divine through its reflection in earthly love, the love of woman, the hunt for the vestiges of reflected Divine Glory on earth and the viewing in a glimpse of it by Actaeon in his act of seeing Diana bathing and finally, the pursuer of love becoming in the process the quarry pursued, an identification or atonement achieved at the cost of death and destruction after which, and in fact in and through which, alone, according to the Neo-Platonist assumption the fulfilment and unification in love are to be had. This mystical Interpretation unfolded in Bruno's treatise, and also one very central to the main thesis of the work, which was published in England and dedicated to Sir Philip Sidney, just as the other moral interpretations of the Actaeon legend and its popular associations as well, cannot not have altogether escaped Shakespeare's notice or knowledge. Given Shakespeare's through mastery of the ins and outs of the love conventions in general, evident in his subtle handling of it, and given the 'half – ironical' dallying with Petrarchan and Neoplatonist assumptions and theories about love he makes in his Sonnets, Venus and Adonis and the comedies in general, and especially in Love's Labour Lost, A Midsummer Night's Dream and also in Romeo and Juliet Shakespeare's acquaintance with Bruno's interpretation of the Actaeon story can hardly be considered unlikely, though, as will be seen, his probable use of the interpretation is 'more than half' ironical. Besides making direct reference to the Actaeon idea in two of his plays, Shakespeare employs the idea allusively in terms of words, and stage – image alike in some other plays and exploits the associations of the Actaeon myth in similar fashion in yet other plays.

Although Actaeon is not directly invoked in the hilarious concluding scenes of *The Mives of Windsor* it is a forceful dramatisation of the Emblematic and perhaps to no less degree the popular associations of the Actaeon story. Sleadman's article already cited is the definitive exposition of the Emblematic aspects of the scene; but while the motifs of beastly degeneration and the closing in of the attackers (the fairies in place of the hounds in the Actaeon story ) are fully brought out in Steadman's explication, we should not miss the fairly obvious irony of the use in reverse of the popular identification of Actaeons horns with the proverbial horns of the cuckold with Falstaff's attempt to cuckold the citizen in the horned state bringing about his discomfiture:

The scene in *As you like It* (VI. ii) in which the First Lord is made to wear the head of the stag killed by him on his head as a trophy and to join in a dance and song is reminiscent of the horn dance such as that of Abbots Brombley; but the whole company after crowing the First lord with the deer's (and the cuckold ) horns at Jacques ' instance would appear to close in on the figure with the deer's head and to 'bring him home'. (11.10-15) The visual impression presented at this point is that of an Actaeon like horned figure, and the closing in on him by the company of ' forester-lords is reminiscent of the 'Actaeon – deer' being closed in on in the illustrations of Ovid or the Emblem book.[76]

The most familiar instance of Shakespearian allusion to the Actaeon myth also seems to be the one in which Shakespeare touches upon the ambivalence of interpretative meaning attaching to the myth.

Curio : Will you go hunt, my lord?

Duke : What, Curio?

Curio : The hart.

Duke : why, so I do, the noblest

That I have .

O ! When mine eyes did see

Olivia first'

Methought she purg'd the air of pistilence.

That instant was I turn'd into a hart ,

And my desires, like fell and cruel hounds.

E'er since pursue me.

(Twelfth Night I. i 16-24)

Douglas Bush wondered whether Shakespeare was making a conscious allusion to the Actaeon legend or merely indulging in a casual conceit.[77] The delicate and intricate play with the love convention both Petrachan and Neplatonist which Shakespeare makes in *Twelfth Night* and the way the play as a whole subsumes and surpasses the sophistications, the unrealities and also in a sense the indispensability of the 'game' of love and the mystique of love and virginity should alert us to the need for multiple response to Orsino, his utterances and his predicament in the opening scene is an exploration of the relation of the play to the 'game'. No caricature, this figure, nor is he a satirical portrait of one who is merely in love with being in love. It is he who uses nearly the whole gamut of the range of the fairly transparent conceits of love in this scene and later. The wagging 'characters mongering' critic who wonder if Orsino has ever step out of his palaces to fall in love at first sight let also pay court to Olivia may have been right. Among the marks to know a lover exhibited by the Duke is a certain familiarity with the refinement as well as the common place elements of the tracition of love. The ambivalence or doubleness of respnose towards the character which Shakespeare evokes, perhaps also invites us, his spectators and readers to consider whether Orsino-so to speak, the process of perfecting himself as a paradigm of the love melancholic, 'had not also read his'

Bruno on 'The Heroic Enthusiasts 'of love or at Least got wind of his and other interpretation of Actaeon.

There are indeed reminisces of the Emblematic interpretation of the Actaeon story in the Nemesis which overtakes Stephano, Trinculo and Caliban in *The Tempest* (IV, i.) as they are marching to execute their conspiracy against Prospero and are, in an anti-masque like situation in the play, hunted down and out by a pack of hounds, disguised spirits, set on by Ariel with prospero watching the whole show remaining invisible, Ariel, so has driven the trio hand enough so that they are all but drowned in a cesspool. The trio yield to the temptation of the glistering apparel hung out by Ariel, and the two, though not Caliban are guilty of theft. It is then that they are hunted down and driven out by the spirit hounds a punishment for their lustful designs on Miranda and their theft including the usurpation they plan as the mythographer Natalie Come and the Emblem writers interpreted Actaeons fate. The range of the situations in which Shakespeare in the course of his plays, either directly or indirectly, invokes the image of Actaeon is considerably wide. More remarkable is the range of variations Shakespeare makes on the myth and on the interpretative ideas and contexts which had come to surround the legend in his day. It may not be and exaggeration to say that Shakespeare in his use of myth 'Out-Ovids Ovid' by way of his metamorphises of Actaeon. It was, after all, not for nothing that a contemporary of Shakespeare[78] as early as 1598, thought that the soul of Ovid was reincarnated in Shakespeare.

# REFERENCES


1. V. Rai, *William Shakespeare* (Varanasi : Bhartiya Vidhya Prakashan, 1966), P. 240
2. Ibid., P. 241.
3. Ibid., P. 242-43.
4. Ibid., P. 243.
5. Ibid., P. 243-44.
6. Ibid., P. 244.
7. Ibid., P. 244-45.
8. Ibid., P. 245-46.
9. Ibid., P. 246.
10. K.R. Srinivasa Iyengar, *Shakespeare : His world and His Art* (New – Delhi : Sterling Publishers Private limited ,1964),P.442
11. Ibid., P. 444.
12. Ibid .
13. Ibid., P. 445
14. Ibid., P.445-46.
15. Ibid., P.446.
16. Ibid.
17. Ibid., P. 447.
18. Ibid.
19. Ibid.
20. Ibid., P. 448.
21. Ibid., P. 451.
22. Ibid., P.454.
23. Ibid., P. 469.
24. Ibid.,P. 329.
25. Ibid., P. 330.

26. Ibid ., P. 331.
27. Ibid ., P. 334.
28. Ibid.
29. Ibid., P. 335.
30. Ibid .
31. Ibid ., P. 336.
32. Ibid ., P. 337.
33. Ibid.
34. Ram Bila Sharma, *Essays on Shakespearean Tradegy* (Agra : Shiva Lal Agarwala & Company , 1970), P. 175
35. Ibid., P. 189.
36. Ibid., P. 189-190.
37. Ibid., P. 191.
38. Ibid., P. 192.
39. Ibid ., P. 193.
40. Ibid., P.200.
41. Ibid., P. 206-207.
42. Ibid., P. 208.
43. U.N. Jha, "Honour in Shakespeare's plays "Papers on Shak speare, ed. By , R.S Varma, P. 38
44. Ibid.
45. Ibid., P. 39.
46. Ibid.
47. Ibid.
48. Ibid.
49. Ibid.
50. Ibid., P. 41.
51. Ibid.
53. Ibid., P. 44.
54. Ibid., P. 45.
55. Ibid., P. 46.
56. Ibid.
57. N.M. Rao, "Hawk And Handsaw : A study of Hamlet", *Essays*

*on Shakespeare,* ed . by ,T.R. Sharma, P. 231.

58. Ibid., P. 232.
59. Ibid.
60. Ibid., P. 233-34.
61. Ibid., P. 235.
62. Ibid., P. 236.
63. Ibid., P. 240-41.
64. Ibid., P. 241.
65. M.M.Mahood , "A Mid Summer Night's Dream- As Exorcism" *Essays on Shakespeare,* ed. By, T.R. Sharma , P. 138.
66. Ibid., P. 138-39.
67. Ibid., P. 143.
68. Ibid., P. 144.
69. Ibid.
70. Ibid., P. 145.
71. Ibid.
72. Ibid., P. 147.
73. S. Viswanathan, "Shakespeare's Metamorphoses of Actaeon", *Essays on Shakespeare,* ed. by, T.R. Sharma, P.P. 47-48.
74. Ibid., P. 47.
75. Ibid., P. 48.
76. Ibid., P. 52.
77. Ibid., P. 53.
78. Ibid., P. 56.

□

# CHAPTER-II

## Sri Aurobindo's Views on Shakespeare

Sri Aurobindo's whole life has been one of intensely packed activities. These activities since his stay at Pondicherry in 1910, were internal than external. They have been divied into three distinct division :

(i) A life of wide and sound scholarship and of academic profession and pursuits.

(ii) A life of ardent political thinking, writing and action determine to wrest independence for his country.

(iii) A life of exclusive spiritual sadhana or discipline aimed at a still higher goal which was nothing less than the completest possible liberation of all mankind.[1]

It sounds rather incredible that one single human being could compass, during the seventy- eight years of his life, all these varied big dreams and aspirations and the naturally outsemming actions and disciplines, involving an immense amount of suffering and sacrifice, vigilance and perseverance, work and meditation. One's scepticism, if any, gets, however dissolved when one stands before the tremendous mass of his writings. Another thing which cannot fail to strike one is the rich variety of subjects and interests which the Aurobindonian literature covers. His works are as large as the life itself. One cannot help saying : here is God's plenty, indeed but there is no feeling of sheer multiplicity, and certainly not of chaos, in the Aurobindonian universe.

The Shakespearean world which is mostly the product of a God like vital creative inspiration and imagination is rather bewildering in its variety and multiplicity. But its critics are not all agreed on the principles or even motives which provides the underlying unity to that 'multitudinous' creation. The Aurobindonian unity of visions, idea and purpose, on the other hands, is visible everywhere. The variety and multiplicity, which Sri Aurobindo presses into service to fill out this big universe of life and thought are on a magnitude which leave Shakespeare, and even in certain respects, Dante, for behind.

Sri Aurobindo as a critic glances at the over all picture of English poetry thus-

> "Thus high energy of English poetry has done great and interesting things; it has potrayed life with charm and poetic interest in Chaucer, made thought and character and action and passion wonderful to the life soul in us. In Shakespeare, seen and spoken with nobility and grandeur of vision and voice in Milton, intellectualised vigorous or pointed commonplace in Pope and Dryden, played with elegance and beauty on the lesser things with the Victorians or cast out here and there a profounder strain thought or more passionate and aspiring voice, and if the most spiritual strains have been few, yet it has dreamed in light in Shelley or drawn close in Wordsworth to the soul in Nature...."[2]

> "The best poetry does not usually come by streams except in the poets of a supreme greatness though there may be in other than the greatest long continued wingings at a considerable wingings at a considerable height. The very best comes by intermittent drops, though sometimes three or four gleming drops at a time. Even in the greatest poets, even in those with the most opulent flow of riches like Shakespeare, the very best is comparatively rare."[3]

According to Sri Aurobindo, "That highest intensity of the revelatory poetic word from which the mantra starts."[4] Such a supreme intensity can when "all is powerfully carried on the surge of a spiritual vision which has found its inspired and inevitable speech."[5] It does not belong to any particular style and is not dependent upon any conceivable mould, pattern of formula of language. It may reveal its beauty and power in such varied linguistic structures or patterns as "the decorative imaged style" bare and direct expression where language seems to the used as a scarcely felt vaulting board for a leap into the infinite"[6] Such as we often find in the Upanishadic poetry, or a style "which uses either the bare or the imaged form at will, but fills every word with the utmost possible rhythmic and thought suggestion".[7] Such as Sri Aurobindo himself or Shakespeare can easily command. And it is here that the sublime mantric poetry of the Veda and the Upanishads and the Gita for example, easily gains ascendency over nearly the whole gamut of English poetic achievement.

Sri Aurobindo tells us about one particular and distinctive quality of the greatest poets of the world which is quite true. It is that such poets have been always "those who have had a large and powerful interpretative and intutive vision of Nature and life and man and whose poetry has arisen out of that - in a supreme revelatory utterance of it. Homer, Shakespeare, Dante, Valmiki, Kalidasa, however much they may differ in everything else, are at one in having this as the fundamental character of their greatness"[8] Why is it that Shakespeare, for example, is so much superior in expression to Bacon whose one short essay is packed with more thought than a whole play of Shakespeare? It is simply because "It was the constant outstreaming of from thought and image from an abundant vision of life which made Shakespeare, whatever his other deficiencies, the sovereign dramatic poet"[9], and it was "the very nature of his thought, power and the characteristic way of expression of the born Philosophical thinker"[10] which hampered Bacon in his poetic expression when he tried to write poetry.

Against this achievement of the continental language and literature we find, says Sri Aurobindo, that "to the present day Shakespeare and Byron are the only two great names in English poetry which are generally on the continent and have had a real vogue"[11]. Sri Aurobindo thinks that Elizabethan poetry cannot be said to come up to the standard of excellence attained by the greatest ages of the Greek and Roman poetry. It "falls too short in aesthetic ..... has an inferior burden of meaning, and ... no settled fullness of spirit and a less adequate body of forms. No doubt, the great magician, Shakespeare, by his marvellous poetic renderings of life and the spell his poetry casts upon us, conceals this general inadequacy"[12] also, "the whole age which he embodies is magnified by his presence."[13] Even the lesser figures of the period "catch something of the light... of his glory and appear in it more splendid than they are."[14] Yet, by whatever standards we judge him, Shakespeare will appear to be "a miracle of poetic force"[15] and survie "untouched all adverse criticism, not because there are not plenty of fairly large spots in this sun, but because in any complete view of him they disapper in the greatness of his light."[16]

Sri Aurobindo, defining 'Dramatic poetry' asserts that it "cannot live by the mere presentation of life and action and the passions, however truely they may be potrayed or however vigorously and abundantly..... It may have, to begin with, as the in that vision an explicit or implicit idea of life and the human being; and the vital presentation which is its outward instrument, must arise out of that harmoniously, whether by a spontaneous creation, as in Shakespeare, or by the compulsion of an intuitive artistic will as with the Greeks." It is doubtful whether the large majority of the Elizabethan dramatists understood these subtle and complex conditions of dramatic poetry. As the proper understanding was lacking, so it is not suprising if their actual successful performance came off "only rarely, imperfectly and by a sort of accident."[17] Even Shakespeare, who carried off the thing so well "seems to have divined these conditions or contained them in the shaping flame of his genius rather than perceived them by the artistic intelligence"[18] No wonder if "their tragedy and comdey are both oppressively external." What is more, their tragedy is "irrational"[19] and their comedy has "neither largeness nor subtlety of idea"[20] and both are "mixed together too without any artistic connection such as Shakespeare manages to give to them so as to justify thoroughly their co-existence."[21] It was in the Elizabethan period, says Sri Aurobindo, that the English poetic speech for the first time "got into it a ring and turn of direct, intuitive power, a spontaneous fullness of vision and divine fashion in the utterance."[22] Even the lesser poets of the period are touched by this intuitive power "but in Shakespeare it runs in a stream and condenses to a richly – loaded and crowing mass of the work and word of the intuition almost unexampled in any poetry."[23]

> "Poetry too take this turn, rises and deepens to a new kind of greatness and at the summit in this kind we have Shakespeare."[24]

Shakespeare and Goethe are aptly compared by Sri

Aurobindo in the following lines :

> ...Shakespeare was a supreme poet and one might almost say, nothing else, Goethe was by far the greater man and the greater brain, but he was poet by choice, his minds choice among its many high and effulgent possibilities, rather than by the very necessity of his being."[25] "Both Dante and Shakespeare" says he, "Stand at the summit of poetie fame, but each with so different a way of genius that comparison is unprofitable. Shakespeare has power that Dante cannot rival; Dante has heights which Shakespeare could not reach; but in essence they stand as mighty equals.[26]

Sri Aurobindo classified the words greatest poets in three rows :

Ist row - Homer, Shakespeare, Valmiki.[27]

2nd row – Dante, Kalidasa, Aeschylus, Virgil, Milton.[28]

3rd row – Goethe.[29]

Sri Aurobindo compared Goethe and Shakespeare and after a deep analyses he came to the conclusion that Goethe goes much deeper than Shakespeare ; he had an incomparable greater intellect than the English poet and sounded problem of life and thought Shakespeare had no means of approaching even. But he was certainly not a greater poet; he did not find himself ready to admit either that he was Shakespeare's equal. He wrote out of a high poetic intelligence, but his style and movement nowhere came near the poetic power, the magic and sovereign expression and profound or subtle rhythm of Shakespeare. Shakespeare was a supreme poet and one might almost. Say, nothing else; Goethe was by far the greater man and the greater brain, but he was a poet by choice, his mind's choice, among its many high and effulgent possibilities, rather than by the very necessity of his being. He wrote his poetry as he did everything else with a great skill and an inspired subtlety of language, and effective genius but it was only part of his genius and not the whole. There too a touch is mostly wanting- the touch of an absolute, an intensely inspired or revealing inevitability; quite a few supreme poets have that in abundance, in others it comes by occasional jets and flashes.

According to Sri Aurobindo's comments on Drama- poetry, drama and fictions also are not bound to be historically accurate;

they cannot indeed develop themselves successfully unless they deal freely with any historical material they may choose to include or take for their subject. One can be faithful to history if one likes but even then one has to expand and deal creatively with character and events. In many of his dramas Shakespeare takes names from history or local tradition, but uses them as he chooses; he place his characters in know countries and surrounding but their stories are either his own inventions or the idea only is borrowed from facts and the rest is his own making: or else he indulges in pure fantasy and cares nothing even for geographical accuracy or historical possibility . It is true that sometimes he follows closely the authorities he had at his disposal , such as Holinshed. In plays like *Julius Caesar* he sticks to the main events and keeps many of the details, but not so as to fetter the play of his imagination.[30] Sri Aurobindo in his essay on The course of *English poetry-2* comments about Shakespeare-

"The great magician, Shakespeare, by his marvellous poetic rendering of life and the spell his poetry casts upon us, conceals this general inadequacy. The whole age which he embodies is magnified by his presence and the adjacent paler figures catch something of the light and kinship of his glory and appear in it more splendid than they are. Shakespeare is an exception, a miracle of poetic force; he survives untouched all adverse criticism, not because there are not plenty of fairly large spots in the this sun, but because in any Complete view of him they disappear in the greatness of his light."[31]

Commenting on Elizabethan drama he wrote – The Elizabethan playwrights were men of a confident robust talent, some of them of real genius; they had the use of the language of an age in which the power of literary speech was a common possession and men were using language as a quite new and rich instrument, lavishly, curiously, exulting in its novel capacities of expression; the first elements of the dramatic from, the temper and some of the primary faculties which go to make dramatic creation possible were there in the literary spirit of the age, and all of them in more or less degree possessed these things and could use them. But these things are enough only to produce plays which will live their time on the stage and in the library; they are not, by themselves sufficient for great dramatic creation. Something else is needed for that, which we get in Shakespeare, in Racine, Corneille and Moliere, in Calderon, in the great Greeks, in the Sanskrit dramatists.

According to Sri Aurobindo drama must have, to begin with, as "the fount of its creation or its heart an interpretative vision and in that vision an explicit or implicit idea of life and the human being; and the vital presentation which is its outward instrument, must arise out of that harmoniously, whether by a spontaneous creation, as in Shakespeare, or by the compulsion of an intuitive artistic will, as with, as with the Greeks."[32] This interpretative vision and idea have in the presentation to seem to arise out of the inner life of vital types of the human soul or individual representatives of it through an evolution of speech leading to an evolution of action. Drama is the poets vision of some part of the world- act in the life of the human soul, it is in a way his vision of karma, in an extended and very flexible sense of the word. To satisfy these conditions is extremely difficult and for that reason the great dramatist are so few in their number. Shakespeare himself seems to have divined these conditions or contained them in the shaping flame of his genius rather than perceived them by the artistic intelligence. The rest have ordinarily no light of interpretative vision, no dramatic idea. Their tragedy and comedy are both oppressively external; this drama presents, but does not all interpret; it is an outward presentation of manners and passions and lives by vigour of action and a quite outward going speech; it means absolutely nothing. The tragedy is irrational, the comedy has neither largeness nor subtlety of idea; they are mixed together too without any artistic connection such as Shakespeare manages to give to them so as to justify thoroughly their co-existence.

Shakespeare stands out alone, both in his own age when so many were drawn to the form and circumstance were favourable to this kind of genius, and in all English literature, as the one great and genuine dramatic poet, but this one is indeed equal to a host. He stands out too as quite in this spirit, method and quality. He does not need to lay violent hands on life and turn it into romantic pyrotechnics; for life itself has taken hold of him in order to recreate itself in his image, and he sits within himself at its heart and pours out from its impulse a thought of being, as real in the world he creates as men are in this other world from which he takes his hints, a riot of living images carried on a many coloured sea of revealing speech and a never failing surge of movement. This dramatic method seems indeed to have usually no other intellectual purpose, aesthetic motive or spiritual secret : ordinarily it labours simply for the joy of a multiple poetic vision of life and vital creation with no centre except the life-power itself. "It is this sheer creative Ananda of the life-spirit which is Shakespeare; abroad everywhere in that age it incarnates itself in him for the pleasure of poetic self-vision."[33]

All Shakespeare's powers and limitations-for it is now permissible to speak of his limitations arise from this character of the force that moved him to poetic utterance. He is not primarily an artist, a poetical thinker or anything else of the kind, but a great vital creator and intensely within marked limits a seer of life. His art itself is life arranging its forms in its own surge and excitement, not in any kind of symmetry – for symmetry here there is none. While he has give a wonderful language to poetic thought, "he yet does not think for the sake of thought, but for the sake of life; his way indeed is not so much the poet himself thinking about life, as life thinking itself out in him through many mouths."[34] in many moods and moment, with a rich throng of fine thought effects, but for any clear sum of intellectual vision or to any high power of either ideal or spiritual results. "His is not a drama of mere externalised action, for it lives from within and more deeply than our external life. This is not Virat, the seer and creator of grose forms, but Hiranyagarbha, the luminous mind of dreams, looking through those forms to see his own images behind them. More than any other poet Shakespeare has accomplished mentally and legendary feat of the impetuous sage Viswamitra; his power of vision has created a Shakespearean world of his own and it is inspite of its realistic elements, a romantic world in a very true sense of the world."[35] It is needful in any view of the evolution of poetry to note the limits within which Shakespeare did his work, so that we may fix the point reached; but still within the work itself his limitation do not matter. And even his positive defects and lapses cannot lower him, because there is an unfailing divinity of power in his touch which makes them negligible. He has however much toned down, his share of the Elizabethan crudities, violence's extravagances, but they are up bore on a stream of power and end by falling into the general greatness of his scheme. The claim made for him that he is the greatest of poets may well be challenged- he is not quite that, but that he is first among dramatic poets cannot well be questionded. So, he keeps his soveregin station. Sri Aurobindo thinks that Elizabethan age was "The greatest age of utterance – though not of highest spirit and aim, -of the genius of English poetry"[36] is the age of vital and sensous poetry. As Sri Aurobindo says "Elizabethan poetry is an expression of this energy, passion and wonder of life."[37] Shakespeare alone seemed to have divined intuitively or contained in the shaping flame of his genius what Sri Aurobindo demands as the essence of Drama, "the poets vision of some part of the world- act in the life of the human soul; it is in a way his vision of Karma in an extended and very flexible sense of the world."[38] Sri Aurobindo has a special fascination for Shakespeare and one of the happiest things, in his writings is his superlative admiration for Shakespeare. *The Future Poetry* records his great ecstasy over Shakespeare. He calls shakespeare 'the great magician', 'a miracle of poetic force[39] who by his marvellous poetic renderings of life and the spell of his poetry conceals the general inadequacy of his age. "Shakespeare stands out alone, both in his own age when so many were drawn to the form and circumstances were favourable to this kind of genius, and in all English literature, as the on great and genuine dramatic poet but this one is indeed equal to a host. He stands out too as quite unique in his spirit, method and quality."[40] This supremacy of the dramatic poet he attributes to his complete hold on life, "for life itself has taken hold of him in order to recreate itself in his image, and he sits within himself at its heart and pours out from impulse a throng of beings, as real in the world he creates as men are in this other world from which he takes his hints, a multitude, a riot of living images carried on a many-coloured sea of revealing speech and a never failing surge of movement."[41] Behind the dramatic method of Shakespeare, there is no intellectual purpose, aesthetic motive or spiritual secret but "the joy of a multiple poetic vision of life and vital creation with no centre except the life – power itself .....It is the sheer creative except the life-spirit which is Shakespeare; abroad everywhere in that age it incarnates itself in him for the pleasure of poetic self-vision."[42]

Voicing his great admiration for the supreme genius and finding its roots in life and not in Art, Sri Aurobindo deviates from the established literary criticism on Shakespeare. While the modern criticism emphasises Shakespeare as a conscious artist, he expressed the view that Shakespeare is not an artist: "He is not primarily an artist, a poetical thinker or anything else of the kind, but a great vital creator and intensely, though within marked limits, a seer of life."[43] But, Shakespeare's "is not a drama of mere enternalised action, for it lives from within and more deeply than our external life."[44] Sri Aurobindo compares him with Vedic sage Viswamitra who in his sacred wrath created a new heaven and earth: More than any other poet Shakespeare has accomplished mentally the legendary feat of the impetuous sage Viswamitra, his power of vision has created a Shakespearean world of his own, and it is, inspite of its realistic elements, a romantic world in a very true sense of the word."[45]

In Sri Aurobindo's view Shakespeare is a great poet and dramatist but to try to make him out a great philosopher would not increase but rather imperil his repute. Sri Aurobindo points out that "Shakespeare is neither an intellectual or philosophic thinker nor a mystic one."[46] He further says, "He yet does not think for the sake of though, but for the sake of life; his way indeed is not so much the poet himself thinking about life, as life thinking itself out in him through many mouths, in many moods and moments, with a rich throng of fine thought effects ... in his vision and therefore in his people motives Shakespeare never really either rises up above life or gets behind it."[47] T.S. Ellist has raised the same sort of problem- "Did Shakespeare think at all?"[48]

Sri Aurobindo has compared Shakespeare with Dante, Goethe and Milton and with Kalidas with valiant competence. He sees all the subtle forces at work within or behind Shakespeare. Thus the numerous insights and observations of Sri Aurobindo on Shakespeare may be regarded as "India's most significant contribution to the understanding and appraisal of Shakespeare's genius."[49] To quote K.D. Sethna: "Through his comments on Shakespeare we can have an inkling of the whole general insight and outlook of Sri Aurobindo- the literary critic."[50]

As a master of rhythm and language, as an artist of words, Sri Aurobindo comes close to Shakespeare, while Shakespeare's is the easy outflow of luminous words. Sri Aurobindo's is the search for the right transcription of the overhead inspiration. Shakespeare's world is essentially the world of the vital. Sri Aurobindo's poetic world is that of the higher mind, of a greater conciousness that penetrates deep into the heart of matter and beyond, a world of matter, life and spirit. While Sri Aurobindo does not have Shakespeare's infinite mastery of human character and situation. Shakespeare can never plunge the depths or scale the heights of which Sri Aurobindo is the master.

From the point of view of the medium of expression, particularly blank verse, characterization and plot structure, Sri Auronbindo's plays seem to have been greatly influenced by the Elizabethans. Shakespeare's influence is visible almost everywhere, particularly in the dramatic romance of Sri Aurobindo.[51]

Oriental influences is, of course, the prevailing influence in Sri Aurobindo's plays. According to Sri Aurobindo, the Hindu dramatists put stress on the depiction of 'gentleness, patience, self-sacrifice, purity the civilised virtues, in the place of 'martial fire, brute-strength, revenge, anger, hate and ungovernable selfwill' which are greatly stressed upon in the display of the former qualities ie... gentleness, patience etc. Show the mark of oriental influence over them. But all these diverse influences are fused into in his plays. In one of his letters Sri Aurobindo refers to 'the high secret of mental alchemy that all the poets of the first order possess. Sri Aurobindo, like Shakespeare, undoubtedly possesses this mental Alchemy. He gather his material from the heap of myths, folklores and historical facts and with the help of this 'mental alchemy' fuses them all into new organic wholes. The white heat of Sri Aurobindo's imagination transforms the mental gathered in the crucible of his mind into rich and strange work of art. His pen moves like Prospero's wand and the Ariel of imagination springs into action to create his plays out of the basic materials of Indian, Arabic, Hellenic and Scandinavian history and legends. Furthemore, though Sri Aurobindo's wide sympathies prompt him to choose theme of various countries and climes-Arabic, Scandinavia, Greece and India-yet art gives a universal colouring to each of these themes. Thus, it may be said that Sri Aurobindo was only a great visionary but an accomplished craftsman. His verse dramas are the creations of a supreme artist who was also 'pregnant with celestial fire.'[52]

Ancient legends and myths form the sources of the plots of Sri Aurobindo's plays. But once he choose a legend or a myth as his source-material, his technique is to have full-possession of it and to rearrange it in such a way as to give it altogether a new look. Fresh scenes are created, life –like and vigorous characters are introduced, cosmic visions and dimensions are stringed so much so that nothing but merely the outline of the old story remain while everything else becomes completely Aurobindonian.

The plots of Sri Aurobindo's comedies, as is the case with Shakespearean comedies, deal with a love story. *Thus The Viziers of Bassora, Eric, Vasavadutta and Prince of Edur* deal with the love stories of Nureddene and Anice-aljalice, Eric and Aslaug, Vutha Udayan and Vasavadutta and Bappa and comol Cumary respectviely. Their love faces external obstruction temporarily and appears to be frustarated and disrupted but is ultimately brought to a happy ending. These plays include a subplot or subplots. The action in these subplots necessarily creates a lot of confusion and strife mainly in order to obstruct the smooth sailing of the protagonists. But in the end confusion, conflict and strife are happily resolved. The singleness and the unity of the theme are never disturbed by any effective variation or digression upon the main body. The subplots or diversions on the main plots are limited in number and are introduced so skilfully as not to overburden and completed the main plot.

The act-division of Sri Aurobindo's plays run parallel to the five-act structure of Elizabethan plays. In fact the five act structure of a play was originally started by Seneca, a Roman playwright. Except *Prince of Edur,* which is incomplete all the five plays of Sri Aurobindo are divided into five acts and have typical pyramindal pattern. The German critic Gustav Freytag in *Techniquce of the Drama* described the structure of plays in terms of exposition, rising action climax or crisis, denouement and catastrophe.

If we study the structure of Rodogune the only tragic play of Sri Aurobindo we will again find the pyramidal shape of a play in five acts. It clearly displays Exposition, Rising action, Crisis, Denouement and Catastrophe and as such is very near to an Elizabethan tragedy in point of plot construction. A comparative study of the plot–construction of Macbeth and Rodogune will make the point clear.

### Macbeth[53]

1– Exposition – Appreciation of Macbeth as a great warrior and conferring of honour upon him.

2– Rising action – The forecast of the witches and the birth of ambition to rise in Macbeth .

3– Crisis – conflict between the desire to rise and the sense of loyality.

4- Denouement – Experience of the utter insignificance of life and mental tortures.

5– Catastrophe – Duel with Macduff, fall of Macbeth.

### Rodogune[54]

1– Exposition – Arrival of the twin sons of Cleopatra in the city of Antioch.

2– Rising action – Cleopatra's selection of Timocles for the kingship of Syria.

3– Crisis – Antiochus' revoult, Antiochus and Rodogune's escape from Antioch, civil war.

4– Denouement – Eremites forecast, Thoas information, Antiochus' return to Antioch.

5– Catastrophe- Antiochus' murder, Rodogune's death.

In *Perseus the Deliverer,* Sri Aurobindo follow the principle of the three unities almost to Jonosonian perfection and in this regard it may be placed beside *The Alchemist, The Viziers of Bassora, Eric, Vasavadutta* and *Prince of Edur* are dramatic romance in the fashion of Shakespeare's romantic comedies and his romances attach little importance to the three unities.

The play of Sri Aurobindo are written in blank verse with frequent use of prose. The use of prose and verse in these plays is based generally on the same principle as was followed by the Elizabethans, ie , the primary characters usually speak verse while the characters of humble position speak prose. The black verse of Sri Aurobindo, as that of Shakespeare and Milton is not linear.

The sense does not end with every line but moves on from line to line. So that rhythmic unit is the paragraph rather than the line. As an example of the black verse speech or paragraph of Sri Aurobindo the following lines may be quoted :

Antiochus is dead , is dead , and I
Shall see at last the faces of my sons.
I could cry upon the palace- tops
My – exultation ! Gaze not on me so,
Eunice. I have lived for eighteen years
With silence and my anguished soul within
while all the while mother's heart in me
cried for her children's eyelids, wept to touch.
The little bodies that with pain I bore.
The long chill dawnings came without that joy.
Only me hateful husband and his crown,
His crown![55]

In this unit the verse is not linear. The meaning moves on from line to line. Furthermore, we note that there are variations in place of the pause: it does not necessarily occur after one particular place. That is why this blank verse of Sri Aurobindo is characterized by freedom and simplicity. If we scan the blank verse of Sri Aurobindo we will also find that the movement is not entirely iambic. Other feet for iambic are at times substituted. Lastly, we will find that Sri Aurobindo, like Marlowe or Milton gives his verse weight and sonority by repetition of high sounding words and by bringing together a number of proper names. Example

From *Rodogune.*

Ecbatana, Susa and Sogdiana,
The Aryan country which the Indus bounds.
Euphrates stream and Tigris' golden sands,
That oxus and jaxartes and these moutains

vague and enormous shouldering the moon

with all their dim beyond of nations huge:

This were an empire ! what were Syria, Greece.

And the blue litoral to Gader? They are

Too narrow to contain my soul, too petty

To satisfy its hunger and its vastness.[56]

Sri Aurobindo's blank-verse is born out of his inspired conciousness that keeps itself gazing, even amid the concerns, tumults and myriad complication and contortions of this earthly life, upon the Divine. It is as K.R.S Iyengar says throught Elizabethan in cast though with modern nuances of idiom,"[57] and is perhaps even more responsive to the reflection of human emotion and behaviour than its Elizabethan counterpart. Sri Aurobindo has unique graps over words. He uses them in new ways and often their musical and emotional qualities are beautifully utilised to present a situation in it's entirety. Let us for example, consider these lines spoken by Vasavadutta:

There is fire within me and a cry.

My longings have all broken in a flood.

And I am the tossed spray! O my desire

that criest for the beauty of his limbs

And to feel all his body with thyself

And lose thy soul in his sweet answering soul,

Will thou not all this night be silent?[58]

Exquisite in musical quality these lines beautifully delineate the peculiar situation in which Vasavadutta finds herself as she oscillates between the two ends of duty and love. In Sri Aurobindo's plays, as in Shakespeare's prose has two main uses. It is used in comic scenes and it is assigned to the characters of humble position, out of his six plays only two, *The Viziers of Bassora* and *Prince of Edur* include comic scenes. In *the Viziers of Bassora,* Shaikh Ibrahim, the old Suprintendent of the Caliph's garden of all pleasures and in *Prince of Edur* Canaca, the jester of the court of prince of Cashmere, provide comic relief. These comic characters come on the stage. Particularly, at such moments when the story is passing through some of the most tense moments. Wit and humour, which have received their due share in Sri Aurobindo's plays come mainly through these minor characters. The wit and humour created by Preissus *(Perseus the Deliverer)* Prose is never coarse:

He cannot be satisfied, his nose is too long, it will not Listen to reason for in thinks all the reason and policy in the world are shut up in the small brain to which it is a long hood outlet.[59]

He reminds us of Shakespeare's Falstaff while Shaikh Ibrahim is a prototype of Molvolio of *Twelfth Night.* Shaikh's tomfooleries make us roar with laughter:

Indeed thou art a sweet fish, but somewhat overdone.
Thou hast four lovely eyes and two noses
Wonderfully fine with just the little
curve at the end; 'tis a hook to hang
my heart upon. But verily there are
Two of them and I know not what to
do with the other. I have only one
heart beauty.[60]

The prose used by these characters is remarkable for an abundance of metaphors and images. These metaphor and images are no doubt mostly common place, nevertheless they are apt and striking. We may surmise that in Sri Aurobindo's plays action is almost completely limited to verse and that prose is used largely for the sake of fun, wit and humour. The element of suspense is well maintained in all these plays.

These plays are remarkable for their wide range of characterization. If through his characters 'Kalidasa excels in depicting the emotions of love, from the first suggestion in an innocent mind to the perfection of passion;'[61] Sri Aurobindo succeeds in catching, the whole of love's inner heart -the freshness, the surrender, the assuagement of a dream-thirst, the transforming and creative penetration of the consciousness, the humble and happy gratitude as for a gift of the gods.'[62]

The technique of bringing music in a play through songs brought to perfection by Shakespeare, has also been utilised by Sri Aurobindo. Song occurs in four of his plays. *Rodogune* and *Perseus* the Deliverer contain two songs each and *The Viziers of Bassora* contain eight songs. Shakespeare and Sri Aurobindo both bring in song in their tragedies to provide relief in the moments of intense tragic passion. Desdemona's willow song in *Othello* and Ophelia's song when she appears in deranged mental state in *Hamlet* are some such examples in Shakespeare and the two songs, 'will you bring cold gems to crown me/child of light?'[63] and 'wilt thou share Love with rosy brightness/ To make him stay with thee?'[64] are example in Sri Aurobindo. The two songs in *Rodogune* not only provide relief in intensely tragic moments but also reflect the mood to Timocles at whose behest the songs are sung. In comedies both the play wrights use songs as the 'the food of love'[65] form an integral part of Shakespeare's and Sri Aurobindo's comedies which are pre-eminently the comedies of love. In comedy both use songs in order to create an atmosphere of romance and gaiety. In Act IV of *The Viziers of Bassora* the songs sung by Nureddene, Saw you Shaikh Ibrahim the grave old man?' Anice-aljalice 'white as winter is my beard' and Shaikh Ibrahim, 'chink a chunk a chink'/we will kiss and drink', and 'when I was a young man',[66] respectively form part of the general comic structure of this act. Their wording and texture are such as to add an extra ounce of fun and frivolity to the general comic atmosphere of the play. Often songs of this play are remarkable not only for their functional significance but also for their poetic value. They throw upon the theme through their auditory imagery. For instance this song sung by Anice-aljalice.

The Emperor of Roum is great;

The Caliph hasa mighty state;

But one is greater, to whom all prayers take wing;

And I, a poor and weeping slave,

When the world rises from its grave,

shall stand up the accuser on my king.[67]

Here the image of prayers taking wings and a poor weeping slave standing up as the kings accuser on the Day of judgement create a dramatic atmosphere of suspense with anxiety. All these songs like 'love keep terms with tears and sorrow.' Have evocative power and are lyrical. The two songs of *Perseus the Deliverer* sung by cydone lend beauty and grace to the play which is otherwise sombre and grave. These songs are:

O the Sun in the reeds and willows !

O the Sun with the leaves at play !

Who would waste the warm sunlight?

And for weeping there's the night.

But now 'tis day.

.......................................................

Look ! morn opens : Look how bright

The world appears ![68]

and-

"Marble body, heart of bliss

Or a stony heart and this,

Which of these two wilt thou crave ?

One or other thou shalt have."

"By my kisses shall be known

which is flesh and which is stone

Love, thy heart of stone ! it quakes

sweet, thy fair cold limbs ! love takes

.......................................................

"And will not marble even grow soft,

Kissed so warmly and so oft?"[69]

These songs have romantic nostalgia and sadness about them. The images are remarkable for their richness and suggestivity. They produce the desired effect of with drawing us from the world of harsh reality to one of romance, The song sung by Aslaug, 'Love is the hoop of the Gods' in *Eric*, is as much functional as poetically significant. Songs, thus play an important part in the plays of Sri Aurobindo.

All these features of plotsructure and style of Sri Aurobindo's plays prove, beyond doubt, that he was not only a visionary but a mature craftsman as well.

*The Viziers of Bassora-*

The reason why Sri Aurobindo gave this play the sub-title 'a dramatic romance' can be easily surmised. First, the play deals with love. Love is here depicted as the force that purifies and perfects. It supplants conflict and turmoil with harmony and peace. In its heat the forces of evil destruction while the force of good shine bright.

As in Shakespeare's romances, *Tempest, Winter's Tale, Cymbeline* and P*ericles,* we find towards the end the older people delighting in the happiness of children, in this play as we find Ibn sawy and

Haroun al Rasheed sayings:

End, end embraces ; they will last our life,

Thou dearest cause at once of our woes

And their sweet ender! Cherish her, Nureddene,

Who saved thy soul and body.

Fair children worthy of each other's love

And beauty ! till the sunderer comes who parts

All wedded hands, take your delights on earth

And afterwards in heaven.[70]

Song and music lend a perfect romantic atmosphere to the play. The Duke in *Twelfth- Night* says 'music is the food of love' and it is often played in this dramatic romance. It is significant that most of the songs are sung by Anice. They are short songs but two of them merit reproduction.

Love keep terms with tears and sorrow?

He's too bright.

Born today, he may tomorrow

Say goodnight.

Love is gone ere grief can find him;
But his way
Tears that falling lag behind him
still betray.[71]

King of my heart, wilt thou adore me,
call me goddess, call me thine?
I too will bow myself before thee
As in a shrine.
Till we with mutual adoration
And holy earth defeating passion
Do really grow divine.[72]

These songs remind us of the songs in Shakespeare's comedies and romances. Furthermore we find that imagery in the play is often drawn from music. Here are few examples-

I have a touch upon the lute will charm
The winds to hear me, and my voice is sweeter.
Than any you have heard in Bassora.
And I shall take my lute.
And buy you honey-crusts with my sweet voice.
For is not my voice sweet, my master?[73]

There's a rhytm
Will Shatter hardest stone; each thing in nature
Has its own point where it has done with patience.
And starts in pieces; below that point play on it
Nor overpitch the music.[74]

These images enhance the romantic effect of the play. Third as we have seen the play abounds in bright and colourful images drawn from Nature. We are transported to a fairyland where brooks flow, flowers smile and sweet birds chirp. The world of this dramatic romance reminds one of Shakespeare's Illyria *(Twelfth Night)* and the forest of Arden *(As you like it)*. It is all enchanting here.

Life is lived here lightly and lovingly. The religion which this play preaches is not the religion of the moralists and puritans but that of the lovers are each other saints.

*Prince of Edur:* In this play the pair of Comol Cumary and Coomood Cumary reminds us of the pair of Rosalind and Celia in Shakespeare's As you like it. Take for example these dialogues by Coomood Cumary and Celia respectively-

For when the nuptial fire is lit and when

The nuptial bond is tied, I'll slip my raiments hem.

Into the kept that weds your marriage robes
And take the seven paces with you both.

Weaving my life into one piece with your for ever.[75]

While teachech thee that and I am one.

Shall we be sund'red? Shall we part, sweet girl?

No let my father seek another heir

Therefore devise with me how we may fly,

Whither to go and what to bear with us.

And do not seek to take your charge upon you.

To bear your griefs yourself and leave me out;

For, by this heaven, now at your sorrow pale,

Say what thou canst, I'll go along with thee.[76]

These statements reflect almost similar sentiments and express the desire of their respective speakers to give company to their friends in all weather. In Sri Aurobindo's play, as in Shakespeare's life has been lavished upon the minor characters as well. Rana Curran is an opportunist. He can go to any limits to get his personal causes well served. Coomood Cumary aptly remarks about him:

..... the brain's too politic.

A merchant's mind into his princely skull

Slipped in by some mischance.[77]

Torman is the prince of Cashmere. He though the prince of a big state, is a coward and a hypocrite. He very much boasts of his bravery but at the very first confrontation with the Bheels in the forest of Dongurh becomes 'a mass of terror – stricken flesh.' Canaca the jester of the court of Torman provides most of the fun and frolic of the play. Sungram is a Rajput warrior and the captain of Bappa's army while Kodal is a Bheel soldier.

*Perseus the Deliverer-*

Sri Aurobindo also remarks that in *perseus the Deliverer* one will find the story of life –impulses on the Elizabethan model. The Elizabethans thought in terms of a 'chain of being extending from God, the highest being, to the inert matter, the hierarchy had its apex God in Trinity followed by angels in their hierarchy, men, animals, vegetation and inanimate matter. Man placed in the middle of the chain was therefore a link between spirit and matter. The idea was that man by ascending the 'chain' could become an angel and by descending degrade himself to the level of beasts. This idea is extensively used by Shakespeare who compare the good characters to angles and bad ones to beasts ; For instance in King Lear, Cordilia is called an angel and Edmund, Regan, Goneril are called adders, wolves, tigers and so on. In *Perseus the Deliverer* Athene symoblises the heavenly forces which raise man to divinity and poseidon symbolises that animal passion which degrade man.

*Eric-*

In this play Aslaug like Hamlet who sees the hand of providence even in the fall of a sparrow : "there's a special providence even in the fall of a sparrow" sees 'Fate even is a sparrow's flight; At times this power is called by the general name of the god's who make some innocent human beings their medium :

From light lips and casual thoughts.

The gods speak best, as if by chance, nor knows.

The speaker that is an instrument

But thinks his mind the mover of his words.

At times that power is called necessary 'the gods that rules all me.' Aslaug says that it was the necessity that spoke through her lips; she herself did not use the song 'love is the golden hoop' only her lips were used. It is again called world's mystic will....'

Fate orders all and Fate I now

Have recognised all the world's mystic will

That loves and labours.[78]

*Rodogune-*

A great tragedy does not leave us in a depressed state of mind because we are made to feel that the victories of the mind or soul are superior to those of the body or matter. *King Lear* at the end the play stands purified or purged of his baser self. The wilful egotistical monarch ceases to exist and a new Lear is born. As Kenneth Muir puts it 'he is resurrected as a fully human being?[79] But where as we need the concept of catharsis to interpret the process of purification in *King Lear* or *Oedipus,* in Rodogune we must interpret it in terms of Sri Aurobindo's own theory of evolution. He is of the opinion that man is still passing through the 'Mind' stage and as he will remain in this stage he shall have to bear the agonies of internal strife and clashes. But the moment he will come in contact with the 'supramental consciousness' he will be above these earthly limitations. He will then come to live in the realm of eternal blissfulness. The character of Antiochus is an approximation to this ideal. So long as he is passing through the 'mind ' stage he challenges and fights and takes pride in his victories. In the heat of this new light his self melts down and in its place rises a new self. This new Antiochus is above the feeling of earthly pains and pleasures. His Sacrifice is thus ' the celebration of human greatness'[80] his tragedy is essentially an expression, not of despair, but of triumph over despair , and of the confidence in the value of human mind.'[81]

In *Rodogune* Sri Aurobindo has largely followed Aristotelean and Elizabethan standards in both the structure and conception of tragedy. The catharsis is achieved in *Rodogune* as in any great tragedy, in yet another way. Antiochus, though defeated wins a kind of spiritual victory at the. J.W. Krutch says in *Tragic fallacy* 'we accept gladly the outward defeats which it. (tragedy) describe for the sake of the inward victory which it reveals?[82] The tragic heroes of sophocles and Shakespeare die but not before they have revealed that greatness of soul which makes their death seem unimporatnt. This is true of Antiochus who says :

What were Death then but wider life than earth

Can give us in her clayey limits bound?

Darkness perhaps! There must be light behind.[83]

and-

Yes, sleep

I have done with; now for an immotal waking.[84]

His dramas are but dramas, and not commentaries on his philosophical poetry, A mixed vintage containing the best in Greek, English and Indian drama, Sri Aurobindo's plays project a life – vision of great intensity and not surprisingly echo occasionally the classical dramatist or Shakespeare. On the other hand, although modelled on Shakespeare, the plays are no pale imatations but carry the distinct Aurobindoian stamp.

Sri Aurobindo's translations of Kalidasa's 'Kumar-Sambhava' and 'Meghaduta', which reads almost like an original creation, for he manages to avoid the heaviness of literal rendering. when accused of "a false imitation of Elizabethan drama" in this translation, Sri Aurobindo justified his style on the ground that the plays of kalidasa did indeed resemble the Elizabethan romantic comedy.

Sri Aurobindo's comments on Shakespeare, which show his deep love and sincere admiration for this poetic celebrity, are good enough hints regarding the latter's formative influence on the former. According to Sri Aurobindo this "great and genuine dramatic poet,"[85] has always been for the poetic and aesthetic mind "the object of its sincere admiration and a powerful presence and influence"[86]. In a letter to a disciple he wrote that apart from his own poems which were unavoidably there, he had with him in his room no books of poetry except the works of Shakespeare. The special consideration to Shakespeare is not without significance. His admiration for Shakespeare results into obvious influences of the great dramatist on him"[87]

Prema Nandkumar says : Conciously he chose the Elizabethan model, for the five-act structure affords the greatest scope for the imaginative recreation of an age that is now past. Shakespearean drama is a plastic instrument for a creative writer who wishes to project colour, movement of thought, dramatic contrast and distinctive characterization as an integrated whole.[88]

Like Shakespeare Sri Aurobindo write poetic plays and like him again he preferred an existing story to an invented one for his plays. There are echoes of Shakespeare in the language of his plays. Shakespeare influence is evident on The witch of Ilni in which reverberations of his plays like *A Midsummer Night's Dream, As you like it, Romeo* and *Juliet, Macbeth* and the tempest can be heard particularly where the dramatist unfolds the story of Alaciel, the witch of Ilni, and the effect of her sorcery on Melander, a sylvan poet. A good number of Aurobindonian characters seem to be modelled on characters from Shakespearean world. For example, Basil and Brigida in *The Maid in the Mill* are reminiscent of Benedick and Beatrice; King Phillip has similarities with the exiled Duke in *As you like It.* A good portion of *The Viziers of Bassora* which alludes to Timons of Athens seems to be similar to the play and also to *Romeo and Juliet.* Similarly, Caliph in *The Viziers of Bassora* reminds us of the Duke in Measure for Measure who plays the role of a masked providence. Perissus in *Perseus the Deliverer* resembles Shakespeare's Falstaff.

# REFERENCES


1. S.K. Prasad, *The Literary Criticism of Sri Aurobindo* (Patna : Bharati Bhawan, 1974), P. 42.
2. Ibid., P. 233.
3. Ibid., P. 303.
4. Ibid., P. 336.
5. Ibid., P. 337.
6. Ibid.
7. Ibid.
8. Ibid., P. P. 339-40
9. Ibid., P. 340.
10. Ibid.
11. Ibid., P. 350.
12. Ibid . P. 373.
13. Ibid.
14. Ibid.
15. Ibid.
16. Ibid. P.P. 373-74.
17. Ibid., P. 376.
18. Ibid.
19. Ibid.
20. Ibid.
21. Ibid. P.P. 376-77
22. Ibid., P. 406.
23. Ibid.
24. Ibid., P. 412.

25. Ibid., P. 452.
26. Ibid ., P.P. 452-53.
27. Ibid ., P. 453.
28. Ibid.
29. Ibid.
30. Sri Aurobindo, *The Future Poetry And Letters* (Pondicherry : Sri Aurobindo Ashram, 1972), P.P. 425-426.
31. Ibid ., P. 65.
32. Ibid ., P. 67.
33. Ibid., P. 71.
34. Ibid.
35. Ibid., P. 72.
36. Prem Tyagi, *Sri Aurobindo, His Poetry and Poetic Theory* (Saharanpur : Ashir Prakashan, 1988), P. 186.
37. Ibid.
38. Ibid.
39. Ibid.
40. Ibid.
41. Ibid., P.P. 186-87.
42. Ibid., P. 187.
43. Ibid.
44. Ibid.
45. Ibid.
46. Ibid.
47. Ibid.
48. Ibid., P.P. 187-88.
49. Ibid. P. 188.
50. Ibid.
51. A.K. Sinha: *The Dramatic Art of Sri Aurobindo* (New Delhi : S. Chand & Company Ltd., 1979), P 207

52. Ibid., P. 208.
53. Ibid., P. 148.
54. Ibid., P. 149.
55. Ibid., P. 151.
56. Ibid., P.P. 151-52.
57. Ibid. P. 152.
58. Ibid.
59. Ibid. P. 153.
60. Ibid.
61. Ibid., P. 155.
62. Ibid.
63. Ibid., P. 159
64. Ibid., P.P. 159-60.
65. Ibid., P. 160
66. Ibid.
67. Ibid.
68. Ibid., P.P. 160-61.
69. Ibid. 161.
70. Ibid., P. 47.
71. Ibid.
72. Ibid.
73. Ibid., P. 48.
74. Ibid.
75. Ibid., P.P. 53-54.
76. Ibid.
77. Ibid., P. 59.
78. Ibid., P. 102.
79. Ibid., P. 124.
80. Ibid., P. 125.
81. Ibid.

82. Ibid., P. 140.

83. Ibid.

84. Ibid., P. 141.

85. S.S. Jaiswal, *Sri Aurobindo's Plays- A thematic study* (New Delhi : Classical Publishing Company, 1993), P. 14.

86. Ibid.

87. Ibid.

88. Ibid. P.P. 14-15.

□

Sri Aurobindo

# CHAPTER-III

## Plays of Shakespeare and Sri Aurobindo: A Comparative Study of the Themes, Characters, incidents and dialogues.

It was observed by Mr Pope that– "If ever any author deserved the name of an original, it was Shakespeare, The poetry of Shakespeare was inspiration indeed! He is not so much an imitator, as an instrument of nature; and it is not so just to say that he speaks through him. His characters are so much nature herself, that it is a sort of injury to call them by so distant a name as copies of her."[1] Each picture like a mock-rainbow, is but the reflection of a reflection. But every single character in Shakespeare, is as much an individual as those in life itself. It is impossible to find any two alike. To this life and variety of character we must add the wonderful preservation of it. Never, perhaps, was there so comprehensive a talent for the delineation of character as Shakespeare's. It not only grasps the diversities of rank, sex and age, down to the dawnings of infancy, not only do the kings and the beggars, the hero and the pick-pocket, the sage and the idiot speak and act with equal truth; not only does he transport himself to distant ages and foreign nations, with a few apparent violations of costume. He opens the gate of the magical world of spirits calls up the midnight ghost, exhibits before us his witches amidst their unhallowed mysteries, people the air with sportive fairies and sylphs and these beings, existing only in imagination, possess such truth and consistency, that even when deformed monsters like Caliban, he extorts the conviction, that if there should be such beings, they would so conduct themselves. "In other words he carries nature into the regions of fancy, lying beyond the confines of reality."[2]

If Shakespeare deserves our admiration for his characters, he is equally deserving of it for his exhibition of passion, taking this world in its widest signification, as including every mental condition, every tone from indifference or familiar mirth to the wildest rage and despair. "Of all the poets, perhaps, he alone has portrayed that's the mental diseases – melancholy, delirium, lunacy–with such inexpressible, and, in every respect, definite truth, that the physician may enrich his observation from them in the same manner as from real cases."[3] The objection that Shakespeare wounds are feelings by the open display of the most disgusting moral odiousness, harrows up the minds unmercifully and tortures our senses by the exhibition of the most insupportable and hateful spectacles, is one of much greater importance. "He has never, in fact, varnished over wild and blood-thirsty passions with a pleasing exterior, never clothed crime and want of principle with a false show of greatness of soul, and in that respect he is every way deserving of praise. Twice he had portrayed downright villians-Iogo and Richard the third."[4]

Shakespeare's comic talent is equally wonderful. It stands on an equal elevation and posssesses equal extent and profundity. He is highly inventive in comic situation and motives. His comic characters are equally true, various and profound. Not only has delineated many kinds of folly, he has also contrived to exhibit mere stupidity in a most diverting and entertaining manner. In his tragic scenes, there is always something wanting, but his comedy often surpasses expectation or desire. His comedy pleases by the thoughts and the language, and his tragedy, for the greater part, by incident and action. "His tragedy seems to be skills, his comedy to be instinct."[5] Cymbeline is one of the most delightful of Shakespeare's historical plays. It may be considered as a dramatic Romance, in which the most striking parts of the story are thrown into the form of a dialogue, and the intermediate circumstances are explained by the different speakers, as occasion renders it necessary. The principal characters are brought together and placed in very critical situation and the fate of almost every person in the drama is made to depend on the solution of a single circumstance - the answer of Iachimo to the question of Imogen respecting the obtaining of the ring from Posthumus. Dr. Johnson is of opinion that "Shakespeare was generally inattentive to the winding up of his plots, we think the contrary is true and might cite in proof of this present play, but the conclusion of *Lear, Romeo* and *Juliet, Macbeth, Othello,* even of *Hamlet* and other plays of less moment, in which is the last act is crowded with decisive events brought about by natural and streaking means. The pathos in Cymbeline is not violent or tragical but of the most pleasing and amiable kind. A certain tender gloom overspreads the whole,"[6] Posthumus is the ostensible hero of the piece, but its greatest charm is the character of Imogen. Posthumus is only interesting herself from her tenderness and constancy to her husband. It is the peculiar excellence of Shakespeare's heroines that they seem to exist only in their attachment to others. They are pure abstractions of the affection. We think as little of their persons as they hearts, which are more important. No one ever hit the true perfection of the female character, the sense of weakness leaning on the strength of its affection for support, so well as Shakespeare - no one ever so well painted, natural tenderness free from afffection and disguise - no one else ever so well showed how delicacy and timidity, when driven to extremity, grow romantic and extravagant. "His women characters were exquisite logicians; for there is nothing so logical as passion. They knew their own minds exactly, and logical as passion. They knew their own minds exactly, and only followed up a favourite purpose which they had sworn to with their tongues, and which was engraven on their hearts. They were the prettiest little set of martyrs and confessors on record."[7] Speaking of the early English stage, the women in those days were not allowed to play the parts of women, which made it necessary to keep them a good deal in the background, that is why there was a want of prominence and theatrical display in Shakespeare's female characters. Of all Shakespeare's women, Imogen in perhaps the most tender and the most artless. Her incredulity in the opening scene with Iachimo, as to here husband's infidelity is much the same as Desdemona's backwardness to believe Othello's jeolousy, when Pisano, who had been charged to kill his mistress, puts her in a way to live, she says:

Why, good fellow,
What shall I do the while? where
bide? How live?
or in my life what comfort, when I am
Dead to my husband?"[8]

Yet when he advises her to disguise herself in boy's clothes and suggest, 'a course pretty and full in view,'[9] by which she may 'happily be near the residence of Posthumus',[10] she exclaims -

Oh, for such means,
Though peril to my modesty, not death on't,
I would adventure.[11]

She all along relies little on her personal charms, which she fears may have been eclipsed. She relies on her merit, and her merit is in depth of her love, her truth and constancy. There are two descriptions given of her, one when she is asleep and one when she is supposed dead. Arviragus thus addresses her :

- With fairest flowers,
while summer lasts, and I live here, Fidele,
I'll sweeten thy like thy sad grave;thou salt not lack
The flowers that's like thy face,pale primrose, nor
The azur'd hare-bell like thy veins, no, nor
The leaf of egalantine, which not nor to slander,
out-sweeten'd not thy breath."[12]

Iachimo admires her beauty, when he steals into her bed-chamber:

'Cytherea,
How bravely thou becom'st thy bed !Fresh lity,
And whiter than the sheets ! That I might touch -
But kiss, one kiss - 'Tis her breathing that
Perfumes the chamber thus : the flame o'the' taper
Bows toward her, the would under-peep her lids
To see th' enclosed lights now canopied;
Under the windows, white and azure, laced
with blue of Heav'n's own tinct-on her left breast.
A male cinque-spotted, like the crimson drops
I'th' bottom of a cowslip."[13]

There is a moral sense in the proud beauty of this last image, a rich surfeit of the fancy, an inimitable picture of modesty and self-denial. The character of Cloten, the conceited, booby lord, and rejected lover of Imogen, though not very agreeable in itself is drawn with much humour and quaint extravagance. The other characters in this play are represented with great truth and accuracy. There is affinity and harmony in different characters. Shakespeare's scenic description finds no parallel, for example the forest Arden in As you like it can alone compare with the mountain scene in Cymbeline. Yet how different the contemplative quiet of the one from the enterprising boldness and precarious mode of subsistence in the other. "Shakespeare not only lets us into the mind of his characters, but gives a tone and colour to the scenes he describes from the feelings of their supposed inhabitants."[14] If he was equal to the greatest things, he was not above an attention to the smallest. Thus the gallant sportsmen in Cymbeline have to encounter the abrupt declivities of hill and valley : Touchstone and Audrey jog along a level path. The deer in Cymbeline are only regarded as objects of prey. But with Jacques they are fine subjects to moralise upon at leisure, under the shade of meloncholy boughs."[15] Shakespeare's morality is introduced in the same simple, unobtrusive manner. Imogen will not let her companion stay away from the chase to attend her when sick, and gives her reason for it :

Stick to your journal course; the breach of custom

Is breach of all ! [16]

"Shakespeare has always been praised for his skill in creating vivid, individual and life - like figures. His portrait gallery is large and extensive, remarkable alike for the variety of the figures and the richness, complexity and beauty of the individual men, women and maids who compose it."[17] Enthusiastic admirers have compared him to nature herself, which creates profusely and never repeats herself. The magic of Shakespeare's art compels admiration becauuse he never oversteps the bounds of impersonality and of the legitimate dramatic resources, requisite for the purpose of characterization. It was not open to him to present an elaborate descriptive portrait in the manner of the novelist like Sir Walter Scott and Thomas Hardy or dramatists like G.B. Shaw. "There are only a few references to the physique and dress of certain characters, such as the hugee body of Falstaff and the inky cloak of Hamlet or the beard and gaberdine of Shylock and the distorted body of the crook-back Richard etc."[18]

"The usual means of dramatic portraiture are dialogue, thought, action, emotion and the manner of speech, all of which are fully exploited by Shakespeare, who has a couple of devices also to supplement them. The total impression, which emerges after due analysis, comparison and versification, constitutes the real essence of the character for us."[19] In dialogue the character is speaking with other characters and other characters are speaking about him and thus, light is coming from two different sources. Thus, Hamlet is speaking with his fellow watchers on the platform about the drunkenness of the Danes and his remarks clearly indicate his own habit and nature. Then Ophelia reports about his behaviour to her father who jumps to the conviction of his madness. In the court scene the whole talk turns on his black-dress and melancholy deportment. But this impression may be supported or contradicted by the actual thoughts and actions of the character. Thus Macbeth and Lady Macbeth are effusive in the expression of their hospitality and loyalty to King Duncan but we know that they have already planned his murder and the shadow of death is palpably, close to the doomed guest. This conflict between 'appearance' and 'reality' is crucial in the great plays of Shakespeare and the result is what Nicoll has called 'deception' and self-deception'. Thus Olivia wraps herself in the cloak of mourning for her brother's death but falls in love with the handsome page, who is a lady like her; and is eventually hurried through the rites of wedlock with the youth who is mistaken for his disguised sister. Iago is addressed as 'honest Iago' by all and sundry but has only hypocrisy as the hall-mark of his nature.

In the mature plays of Shakespeare the character act and are acted upon and they visibly grow and change under our eyes through the stress of circumstances and their own feelings and experiences.The best illustration is afforded by Macbeth and Lady Macbeth who, following different roads, arrive at the destined ends completely transformed from what they were at the start. The sensitive Macbeth of pictorial and paralysing imagination has forgotten the taste of fear, while the imperious woman capable of producing male children only is altered into a helpless victim of her own unnatural ambition and groans out of the utter despair of her heart in 'what is done cannot be undone.'[20] This dynamic process creates the impression that they are made of flesh and blood and are not moving statues. The device which came most handy to

Shakespeare in this respect is 'soliloquy' which sprang from the close proximity of the actor to the audience around him. 'Soliloquy' gives us entrance into the inner chamber of the speaker's heart and soul. So that we can clearly observe the main springs of his motive and action and the currents and eddies of his thoughts and the collision of contrary of passions and impulses. The whole inner history of Macbeth and Hamlet is continuously revealed in their soliloquies and so is the case with Iago and Edmund, the villians, who do not wear their heart on their sleeves but generously reveal them in all their sordid nakedness in their soliloquies. A single soliloquy changes, Claudius from a hardened villian and sensualist into a weak human creature constant in his love for the queen, and Prince Harry boon companion of Falstaff, into a politician as astute and unscrupulous as his own father.

For individualizing the creatures of his imagination the artist has at his disposal two effective instruments contrast and the tone of a living voice in the speech. Shakespeare has shown great skill in the handling of these instruments. His characters come in pairs, and their contrast intensifies their individuality, Banquo remains a foil to Macbeth in the early part of the great tragedy and makes us actually aware of his partners tainted nature. His Subsequent change, showing a parallel movement, blazes the process of Macbeth's own earlier movement towads criminal ambition. The juxtaposition of Gloucester and Lear confirms the strength of the latter and the dumb helplessness of the former. While Hamlet's peculiar procastination is brought into bolder relief by the characters grouped around him, Claudius, Horatio, Laertes and Fortinbras. But for individualizing his characters Shakespeare finally depends on their tone and manner of speech. Shaw has rightly observed that "Shakespearean delineation of character owes all its magic to the turn of the line which lets you into the secret of its utterer's mood and temperament, not by its common place meaning, but by some subtle exaltation or stultification or shyness or delicacy or hesitancy or what not in the sound of it."[21] This is true of his comic figures also with Falstaff towering above all in his mastery over prose, flexible, many sided and malleable under the touch of his quick-silver wit and humour. The great heroines have each the tone and voice which is audible in their utterances while the tragic heroes convey the subtle nuances of their passions and moods in their speeches. Their manner changes constanty under the pressure of the changing rhythm of their thought and emotion.

Shakespeare's great characters are larger than life and they live in the element of poetry which creates an aura around them. The remark of Halliday is quite emphatic - "poetry inseperable from characters, the poetry is the character. Hamlet, Othello and the rest of the tragic heroes and heorines and in a lesser degree characters in other plays, are what they are because of what they say, or rather because of how they say it, because of the poetry and some of the tragic heroes Macbeth and King John are tragic heroes at all because of their poetry, without which they Would be unable to retain our sympathy. It is the glamour of poetry emanting from Antony and Cleopatra which lifts their apparently immoral passion to the empyrean height till they are deified (in their death). Caliban, the lump of earth and sub-human creature, acquires a sort of dignity and vital human touch through poetry and the fairies, witches, Puck and Ariel are vivified to our imagination and gain distinct individualities by means of their speech which is mostly poetical with a touch of lyricism in many cases and a clear incantatory not in others."[22]

Shakespeare's characters are living and breathing persons amenable to psychological analysis. Verification has provoked critics like German Schucking and American Stoll to deny totally any consistency and psychological coherence to Shakespeare's characters, which they say, were concieved and brought into being in an age which was primitive in its out-look and on a stage which was much more interested in the emotional excitement and movement of action than in the deep probing into the springs of human action and motives. Judged in the light of cold logic and psychology, it has been argued, some of the greatest figures in Shakespeare will turn out to be a bundle of traits which refuse to cohere-Othe llo, an artificial union of civilized and savage of human-nature; Cleopatra a prostitute in the begining and a saint and martyr of love in the end, Leontes a good man suddenly and inexplicably transformed into a jealous cynic and tyrant and the hard-hearted and comical shylock, the Jew, raised to the height of tragic dignity. Thus, the apparently solid and life-like creatures of plastic imagination begin to dissolve and disintegrate under the first impact of realistic and psychological probe. While this line of approach to the characters of Shakespeare is a salutary antidote and corrective to the Romantic laudation of his God like creativity, it has run to the last limit of scepticism and evoked spirited defence from a number of critics and scholars, who have found a strong sanction for the essential consistency of the great Shakespeare figures in the finding of the Freudian depth-psychology. C.H. Herford emphasized this fact as far back as the year 1923. "Modern psychology by its disclosure of the phenomena of dual and multiple personality, has eased the path of those who find real inconsistency in any of Shakespeare's characters: their inconsistency need not detract from their psychological truth."[23]

The line has been explored by critics like J. I .M. Stewart author of *Character and Motive in Shakespeare (1949),* and many of the apparent contradictions have been convincingly resolved and made intelligible in the light of the new psychology which has proved helpful in explaining the apparently unaccountable birth and operation of jealousy and other abnormal passions related to the peculiar nature of the human psyche and its, functioning in terms of 'compensatiation', 'transference' 'displacement' and sublimation'. The upshot has been the discovery of a deep consistency in the character of Lady Macbeth and a medically just treatment of Lear's madness. But it should never be assumed that all characters of Shakespeare are consistent and have an independent life. The improbability is still there and has to be accepted as a postulate and in early plays at least characters are clearly sacrificed and suddenly changed to meet the demand of the happy ending, which creates a shock especially in the cases where the characters have acquired strong individualities and cannot be moved like puppets. Even in great tragedies secondary figures at least sometimes speak out of character in obidience to the demand of the situation. Thus Horatio, who is expected to be quite familiar with the customs and conventions of the Danish Court ignorantly enquires about the cause of the common fire at the dead of night. The information so sought is obviously necessary for the audience, not for the enquirer himself. The lyrical description of the circumstances connected with the drowning of poor Ophelia. Which is put in the mouth of Gertrude, is out of character but serves as a fit epitaph or tribute to that delicate victim of cruel chance. In the last plays, characters waver between symbolic and naturalistic conceptions and fail to come into full life and freedom. Prospero, for example, is a remarkable example of this fact and Hermione and Imogen are also placed in the same category.

But when all these facts have been fully reckoned with and accepted, the magic and mastery of Shakespeare in this vital field of dramatic literature can be doubted by no sane student of his plays. Whether they were human types, as Johnson believed or distinct individuals as Pope presumed or the combination of the two as Coleridge argued, they stand vivid and alive, with a will, movement, tone, speech and manner of their own. In the mature plays they are clearly distinguished, even though the distinction like that between Goneril and Regan or Gertrude and Ophelia is Sometimes very subtle. Nicoll has neatly summed up this aspect of Shakespeare's supreme art and his incomparable detachment without the least diminution of his uniform sympathy towards his creations. "We sense Shakespeare's presence beyond the actions of his plays, a god-like presence often shrouded in mystery beyond the reach of reason and nevertheless potently appreciated; and at the same time we feel his vitality and strength identified with and expressing itself through the individual characters."[24]

*Antony and Cleopatra* is the finest of his historical plays,that is of those in which he made poetry the organ of history, and assumed a certain tone of character and sentiment, in conformity to known facts, instead of trusting to his observations of general nature or to the unlimited indulgence of his own fancy. The play is full of that pervading comprehensive power by which the poet could always make himself the master of time and circumstances. It presents a fine picture of Roman pride and eastern magnificence.

The characters breathe, move and live. Shakespeare does not stand reasoning on what his characters would do or say, but at once becomes them, and speaks and acts for them. He does not present us with groups of stage-puppets or poetical machines making set speeches on human life and acting from a calculation of problematical motives, but he brings living men and women on the scene, who speak and act from real feelings, according to the ebbs and flows of passions without the least tincture of pedantry of logic or rhetoric. Nothing is made out by inference and analogy, by climax and antithesis, but everything takes place just as it would have done in reality, according to the occasion. The character of Cleopatra is a masterpiece. What an extreme contrast it affords to Imogen. One would think it almost impossible for the same person to have drawn both. She is voluptuous, ostentious, concious, boastful of her charms, naughty, tyrannical fickle. The luxurious pomp and gorgeous extravagance of the Egyptian queen are displayed in all their force and lustre as well as the irregular grandeur of the soul of Mark Antony. Take only the first four lines that they speak as an example of the regal style of love-making

Cleopatra: If it be love indeed, tell me how much?

Antony: There's beggary in the love that can be reckon' d.[25]

The rich and poetical description of her person beginning-

'Age cannot wither her, nor custom stale

Her infinite variety, other women cloy

The appetites they feed, but she makes hungary.

Where most she satisfies.'[26]

Cleopatra's whole character is a triumph of the voluptuous, of the love of pleasure and the power of giving it over every other consideration. Octavia is a dull foil and Fulvia a shrew and shrill - tongued. Few things in Shakespeare have more of that local truth of imagintion and character than the passage in which Cleopatra is represented conjuring what were the employments of Antony in his absence-

He is speaking now, or murmuring-

Where's my serpent of old Nile?[27]

or again when she says to Antony,

after the defeat at Actium, and his sumnoning up resolution to risk another fight.

It is my birthday; I had thought to have held it poor; But since my lord is Antony again; I will be Cleopatra.[28] She had great and unpardonable faults, but the grandeur of her death almost redeems them. She learns from the depth of despair the strength of her affections. She tastes luxury in death. It is worth while to observe that Shakespeare has contrasted the extreme magnificence of the description in this play with pictures of extreme suffering and physical horror, not less striking partly to place the effiminate character of Mark Antony in a more favourable light and at the same time to preserve a certain balance of feeling in the mind. Antony's headstrong presumption infatuated determination to yield to Cleopatra's wishes to fight by sea instead of land, meet a merited punishment, and the extravagance of his resolution, increasing with the desperateness of his circumstances, is well commented upon by Enobarbus.

-I see men's judgement are
A parcel of their fortunes,
And things outward
Do draw the inward quality after them
To suffer all alike.'[29]

The repentence of Enobarbus after his treachery to his master is the most affecting part of the play. He cannot recover from the blow which Antony's generosity gives him, and he dies broken-hearted,'a master leaver and a fugitive.'[30] Shakespeare's genius has spread over the whole play a richness like the overflowing of the Nile. Arthur Symons calls Antony and Cleopatra the 'most wonderful'[31] of all Shakespeare's plays because Cleopatra is the 'most wonderful of Shakespeare women.'[32] David Daiches calls it "the most magnificent and the most puzzling of Shakespeare's tragedies."[33]

While *Romeo-Juliet, Othello* and *Antony* and *Cleopatra* are the all tragedies of love, the cast of the characters, the circumstances and the shape of the pattern of catastrophes all differ from play to play. What divides and destroys Romeo and Juliet is the feud between their families and not any 'flaw' in either of the young lovers. In Othello, the love of the fair youthful Desdemona and the middle-aged Moor is the attraction of opposites, a challenge to 'reason'; and Iago exploits the situation to ruin the marriage. In Antony and Cleopatra both the lovers are past their prime; their love has perpetually to stand an inquis ition within themselves; and it is a daily war and a daily conquest -the honours however being evenly shared by the Roman General and the Egyptian Enchantress.

Comparing *Romeo and Juliet and Antony and Cleopatra*, Coleridge says - "This play should be persused in mental contrast with *Romeo and Juliet*; - as the love of passion and appetite opposed to the love of affection and instinct. But the art displayed in the character of Cleopatra is profound; in this, especially that the sense of criminality in her passion is lessened by our insight into its depth and energy, at the very moment that we cannot but perceive that the passion itself springs out of the habitual craving of a licentious nature, and that it is supported and reinforced by voluntary stimulus and sought for associations, instead of blossoming out of spontaneouse motion."[34]

The Cleopatra of history and tradition was a synonym for lust and duplicity (as illustrated, for example by a story Nights') who had like Gautier's 'One of Cleopatra's Nights') who had bewitched, among others, Pompey the Great and Julius Caesar before it came to Antony's turn. In the heat of jealous rage, Antony himself tells her in the play (III. xiii. 116);

I found, you as a morsel cold upon Dead Caesar's trencher.
Nay, you were a fragment of Cneuis Pompey's, besides
what Unregister'd in vulgar fame. You have hotter hours,
luxuriously pick'd out; for I am sure,
Though you can guess what temperance should be,
You know not what it is.[35]

But this is not the whole truth, for Cleopatra was also the regal and resplendent Queen of Egypt; she was a princess "descended of so many royal kings"[36] (V. ii. 325); She says of herself with pardonable pride, "The man hath seen some majesty, and should know"[37] (III. ii. 41); and even Ocatvius Caesar concedes that Cleopatra, "being royal, look her own way"[38] (v. ii. 333) As if her sluttery and her queenly magnificence are not extremes enough, the Cleopatra of history and tradition was also the loyal mistress who followed her Antony in death, proving by that brave act of taking off that her love was indeed - it had at last become more than calculation or self-indulgence, and also that for more than Fulvia or Octavia, she alone was Antony's wife. In his controversial, Character Problems Shakespeare's plays. Levin Suhucking draws a sharp contrast in between the Cleopatra- the chamelionic, vulgar, heartless, immoral harlot of the first part of the play and the "thoughtful and motherly woman" of the last Acts and concludes that the two physiognomies are irreconcilable. Actually the three physiognomies the harlot, the queen, and the Martyr to love - are included & harmonised in the play. She fascinates and tantalises no doubt, but her characterlzatlon is no jumble of Shreds and patches - she is alive in and because of 'Shakespeare's poetry, for the "poetry is the key - to Cleopatra's charater as to all else."[39]

If Cleopatra both dazzles and tantalises us, Antony too poses an almost insoluble problem. While the splendour of Shakespeare's poetry makes us accept the tragic fact. Like Cleopatra's fascination, Antony's greatness is one of the two Absolutes of the play; there are tributes by Lepidus (I. iv. 10), by Caesar (I. iv. 56) and more than once by Cleopatra (I. v. 23, V. ii. 82);

I must not think there are
Evils enow to darken all his goodness.
His faults, in him, seem as the spots of heaven,
More fiery by night's blackness...[40]

When thou once
was beaten from Modena, wher thou Slew'st
Hirituis and Pansa, consuls, at thy heel
Did famine follow; whom thou fought'st against,
Though daintily brought up, with patience more
Than savages could suffer ...[41]
The demi-Atlas of this earth, the arm
And burgonet of men...[42]

His legs bestrid the ocean; his rear'd arm
Crested the world. His voice was propertied.
As all the tuned Spheres, and that to friends;
but when he meant to quail and shake.
He was a rattling thunder, for his bounty, the orb,

There was no winter in't; and autum 'twas.

That grew the more reaping...[43]

We see Antony's bounty in action when he sends Enobarbus' treasure to him even though he has gone over to Caesar (iv. v. 12) In Iv. vii. and viii, we see the fighter in action. But we are constantly invaded by the force of Philo's words in the opening scene (I. i. 57)

... Sometimes when he is not Antony,

He comes too short of that great property.

Which still should go with Antony. [44]

Plutarch describes that the year after Philippi, Antony as one of the triumvirs sent for Cleopatra, and according to him there went a rumour in the people's mouths, that the goddess Venus was come to play with the god Bacchus, for the general good of all Asia.

Enobarbus, who is solely the creation of Shakespeare, describes the beauty of Cleopatra, when he is alone with Maecenas and Agrippa (II. ii. 195)

The barge she satin in, like a burnish'd throne,

Burn'd on the water. The poop was beaten gold;

Purple the sails, and so perfumed that

The winds were love-sick with them..."[45]

The winds are love-sick, the water is amorous, the air itself would fain gaze on Cleopatra. All Nature has fallen for Cleopatra; what chance, then, for Antony to resist manifest - Venus' charms? As against the lure of Cleopatra's waywardness and wantonness, her variety and contrariety, Octavia can offer "beauty, wisdom, modesty."[46] "Richard throws away a kingdom, while Antony squanders an empire.[47] There are 42 scenes long and short - some of 10 lines, 9 Iines, 5 lines and 4 lines. In the end Antony has deprived Caesar of his cheap personal (apart from the general political) triumph; he has won Cleopatra again, and for all time. A double personal victory, this for Antony. Caesar as is appropriate, speaks the last word.'

She looks like sleep

As she would catch another Antony

In her strong toil of grace ...

She shall be buried by her Antony;

No grave upon the earth shall clip in it

A pair so famous...[48]

Shakespeare set himself an impossible task when he wrote *Antony and Cleopatra*. The issue is supposed to be love against honour (orduty). For Cleopatra who has after a life time of coquetry, contrariety and sensuality learned at last the meaning of the Absolute that is Love, her death is a vindication of her whole variegated and maddening life: for in her end is all yesterdays, and the sérpent of the Nile has been tranformed into the phoenix, the rare Arabian bird!

*The Taming of the Shrew,* is almost the only one of Shakespeare's comedies that has a regular plot, and downright moral. It is full of bustle, animation, and rapidity of action.

Petruchio is a madman in his senses, a very honest fellow who hardly speaks a word of truth and succeeds in all his tricks and impostures. He acts his assumed character to the life with untired animal spirits and without a particle of ill-humour from beginning to end. The most striking and at the same time laughable feature in the character of Petruchio through out, is the studied approximation to the intractable character of real madness, his apparent insensibility to all external considerations and utter indifference to everythlng but the wild and extravagant freaks of his own self-will.

*Measure for Measure* is a play full of genius as it is of wisdom. The 'height of moral argument ' which the author has maintained in the intervals of passions or blended with the more powerful impulses of nature, is hardly surpassed in any of his plays. But there is general want of passion, the affections are at a stand, our sympathies are repulsed and defeated in all directions 'The only passion' which influences the story is that of Angelo; and yet he seems to have a much greater passion for hypocrisy than for his mistress. Neither are we greatly enamoured of Isabella's rigid chastity, though she could not act otherwise than she did. As to the Duke, who makes a very imposing and mysterious stage character, he is more absorbed in his own plots and gravity than anxious for the welfare of the state. Claudio is the only person who feels naturally, and yet he is placed in circumstances of distress which almost preclude the wish for his deliverance. Mariana is also in love with Angelo, whom we hate.

Shakespeare was in one sense the least moral of all writers, for morality is made up of antipathies, and his talent consisted in sympathy with human nature in all its shapes, degrees, depressions and elevations . The object of the pedantic moralist is to find out the bad in everything; his was to show 'there is some soul of goodness in things evil'[49] He was a moralist in the same sense in which nature is one. He taught what he had learnt from her. He showed the greatest knowledge of humanity with the greatest fellow feeling for it.

*The Merry wives of Windsor* is no doubt a very amusing play, with a great deal of humour, character and nature in it : but we should have liked it much better, if any one else had been the hero of it instead of Falstaff. We could have been contented if Shakespeare had not been 'commanded to shew the knight in love'.[50] Wit and philosophers, for the most part, do not shine in that character; and Sir John himself by no means, comes off with flying colours. Falstaff in this play is not the man he was in the two parts of *Henry IV*. His wit and eloquence have left him. Instead of making a butt of others, he is made a butt of by them. Neither is there a single particle of love in him to excuse his follies. He is merely a designing, bare - faced knave, unsuccessful one. Shakespeare is the only writer who was as great in describing weakness as strength.

In *The comedy of Errors* Shakespeare appears to have bestowed no great pain on it, and there are but a few passages which bear the decided stamp of his genius. He seems to have relied on his author, and on the interest arising out of the intricacy of the plot. The curiosity excited is very considerable, though not of the most pleasing kind. We are teased as with a riddle, which we try to solve. In reading the play from the sameness of the name of the two Antipholises and the two Dromios, as well from their being constantly taken for each other by those who see them, it is difficult, without a painful effort of attention, to keep the characters distinct in the mind. We do not think Shakespeare's forte would ever have lain in imitating or improving on what others invented, so much as in inventing for himself and perfecting what he invented not perhaps by the omission of faults, but by the addition of the highest excellencies, "His own genius was strong enough to bear him up and he soared longest and best on unborrowed plumes."[51]

*As you like It* is the most ideal of any of Shakespeare's plays, It is a pastoral drama, in which the interest arise more out of the sentiments and characters than out of the actions or situations. It is not what is done, but what is said, that claims our attention. Nursed in solitude 'under the shade of melancholy boughs'[52], the imagination grows soft and delicate, and the wit runs riot in idleness, like a spoiled child, that is never sent to school. The very air of the place seems to breathe a spirit of philosophical poetry. Never was there such beautiful moralising equally free from pedantry or petulance.

And this their life, exempt from public haunts.
Finds tongue in trees, books in the running brooks,
Sermons in stones and good in everything.[53]

Jacques is the only purely contemplative character in Shakespeare. He thinks and does nothing. His whole occupation is to amuse his mind and he is totally regardless of his body and his fortunes. He is the Prince of philosophical idlers; his only passion is thought; he sets no value upon anything but as it serves as food for reflection. He can "suck melancholy out of a song, as a weasel sucks eggs?"[54] The motley fool or Touchstone, "who moralises on the time"[55], is the greatest prize he meets with in the forest. And leaves the Duke, as soon as he is restored to his sovereignty, to seek his brother out who has quitted it and turned hermit.

out of these convertites
There is much matter to be heard and learnt.[56]

Rosalind's character is made up of sportive gaiety and natural tenderness : her tongue runs the faster to conceal the pressure at her heart. She talks herself out of breath, only to get deeper in love. The coquetry with which she plays with her lover in the double character which she has to support is managed with the nicest address. How full of with voluble, laughing grace is all her conversation Orlando-

In heedless mazes running
with wanton and giddy cunning .[57]

How full of real fondness and pretended
Cruelty is her answer to him when he
Promises to love heer 'For ever and a day![58]

Say a day without the ever: no, no, Orlando, men
are April when they woo, December when they
Wed : maids are May when they are maids,
but the sky changes when they are wives.[59]

The silent and retired character of Celia is a necessary relief to the provoking loquacity of Rosalind, nor can anything be better conceived or more beautifully described than the mutual affection between the two cousins-

---We still have slept together,
Rose at an instant, learn'd, play'd, eat together,
And wheresoe'r we went, like Juno's swans,
Still we went coupled and inseperable.[60]

The unrequited love of silvius for Phebe shows the perversity of this passion in the commonest scenes of life, and the rubs & stops which nature throws in its way, where fortune has placed none. Touchstone is not in love but he will have a mistress as a subject for the exercise of his grotesque humour, and to show his contempt for the passion, by his indifference about the person. He is a rare fellow. He is a mixture of the ancient cynic philosopher with the modern buffoon and turns folly into wit and wit into folly, just as the fit takes him. His courtship of Audrey not only throws a degree of ridicule on the state of wedlock itself, but he is equally an enemy to the prejudices of opinion in other respects.

There is hardly any of Shakespeare's plays that contains a greater number of passage that have been quoted in books of extracts, or a greater number of phrases that have become in a manner proverbial. Some of them are the account of Jacques moralising on the wounded deer, his meeting with Touchstone in the forest, his apology for his own melancholy, and his satirical vein, and the well known speech on the stages of human life the old song of 'Blow, blow, thou winter's wind',[61] Rosalind's description of the marks of a lover and of the progress of time with different persons, the picture of the snake wreathed round Oliver's neck while the lioness watches her sleeping prey.

In The *Merchant of Venice* Shylock being a Jew has constant apprehension of being burnt alive, plundered, banished, reviled and trampled on, might be supposed to sour the most forbearing nature, and to take something from that 'milk of human kindness' with which his persecutors contemplated his indignities. The desire of revenge is almost inseperable from the sense of wrong, and we can hardly help sympathizing with the proud spirit, hid beneath his 'Jewish gaberdine.' stung to madness by undeserved provocation heaped upon him and all his tribe by one desperate act of 'lawful' revenge, till the ferociousness of the means by which he is to execute his purpose, and the pertinacity with which he adheres to it, turns us against him.

Antonio, his old enemy, instead of any acknowledgement of the shrewdness and justice of his remonstrance, which would have been preposterous in a respectable catholic merchant in those times, threatens him with a repetition of the same treatment.

I am as like to call thee so again,

To spit on thee again, to spurn thee too.[62]

After this, the appeal to the jew's mercy, as if there were any common principle of right and wrong between them, is the rankest hypocrisy, or the blindest prejudice, and the Jew's answer to one of Antonio's friend's who asks him what his pound of forfeit flesh is good for, is irresistible.

"To bait fish withal, if it will feed nothing else, it will

feed my revenge.[63] He hath disgrac'd me, and hinder' d me of half a million, laughed at my losses, mock'd at my gains, scorn'd my nation, thwarted my bargains, cool'd my friends, heated mine enemies : and whats his reason? I am a Jew."[64] Hath not a Jew eyes; hath not a Jew hands, organs, dimensions senses, affections, passions' fed with the same food, hurt with the same weapons, subject to the same disease, healed by the same means, warmed and cooled by the same winter and summer that a Christian is? If you prick us, do we not bleed? If you tickle us, do we not laugh? If you prick us, do we not die? And if you wrong us, shall we not revenge? If we are like you in the rest, we will resemble you in that.[65] If a Jew wrong a Christians, what is his humility? revenge. If a Christian wrong a Jew, what should his sufferance be by Christian example? Why revenge. The villiany you teach me I will execute, and it shall go, hard but I will better the instruction'.[66]

The whole of the trial-scene, both before and after the entrance of Portia is a master-piece of dramatic skill . The legal acuteness, the passionate declamations, the sound maxims of jurisprudence, the wit and irony interspersed in it, the fluctuations of hope and fear in the different persons, and the completeness and suddenness of the catastrophe, cannot be surpassed. Shylock, who is his own counsel defends himself well and is triumphant on all the general topics that are urged against him and only fails through a legal flaw. The keenness of his revenge awakes all his faculties; and he beats back all opposition to his purpose, whether grave or gay whether of wit or argument, with an equal degree of earnestness and self-possession. His character is displayed as distinctly in other less prominent parts of the play, and we may collect from a few sentences the history of his life. His daughter, whom he loves next to his wealth, his courtship and his first present to his wife Leah.

Portia is not a very great favorite with us; neither are we in love with her maid Nerissa. Portia has a certain degree of affectation and pendantry about her, which is very unusual in Shakespeare's women, but which perhaps was a proper qualification for the office of a civil doctor' which she undertakes and executes so successfully. The speech about mercy is very well; but there are a thousand finer ones in Shakespeare.

The graceful winding up of this play in the fifth act, after the tragic business is dispatched, is one of the happiest instances of Shakespeare's knowledge of the principles of the drama.

The *Two Gentlemen of Verona* is little more than the first outline of a comedy loosely sketched in. It is the story of a novel dramatised with very little labour or pretension yet there are passages of high poetical spirit and inimitable quaintness of humour, which are undoubtediy Shakespeare's. Mr M. Pope observed that 'It is observable know not for what cause) that the style of this comedy is less figurative and morc natural and unaffected than the greater part of this author's, though supposed to be one of the first he wrote.'[67]

The tender scenes in this play, though not so highly written, as in some others, have often much sweetness of sentiment and expressions. There is something pretty and playful in the conversation of Julia with her maid, about Protheus. Her answer to

Lucetta, who advises her against following her lover in disguise, is a beautiful piece of poetry.

Lucetta: I do not seek to quench your love's hotfire
But qualify the fire' s extremest rage,
Lest is should burn above the bounds of reason
Julia: The more thou damm'st it up, the more it burns
The current that with gentle murmurs glides.[68]

If Shakespeare indeed have written only this and other would have passage in the *Two gentleman of Verona,* he deserved Milton's praise of his -

'And Sweetest Shakespeare, Fancy's child,
warbles his nature wood-notes wild'[69]

But he deserves rather more praise than this.

*Twelfth Night; or What You Will* is justly considered as one of the most delightful of Shakespeare's comedies. It is full of sweetness and pleasantry. It is perhaps too good-natured for comedy. It has little satire, and no spleen. It aims at the ludicrous rather than the ridiculous. It makes us laugh at the follies of mankind, not despise them, and still less bear any ill-will towards them. Shakespeare's comic genius resembles the bee rather in its power of extracting sweets from weeds or poisons, than in leaving a string behind it. This may be called the comedy of nature and it is the comedy which we generally find in Shakespeare. His Comedy is of a pastoral and poetical cast. Folly is indigenous to the soil and shoots out with native, happy unchecked luxuriance. The poet runs riot in a conceit, and idolises a quibble. His whole object is to turn the meanest or rudest objects to a pleasurable account. The relish which he has of a pun, or of the quaint humour of a low character does not interfere with the delight with which he describes a beautiful lmage or the most refined love. The clowns forced jests do not spoil the sweetness of the character of Viola.

Much as we like Shakespeare's Comedies, we cannot agree with Dr. Johnson that they are better than his tragedies, nor do we like them half so well. If his inclination to comedy sometimes led him to trifle with the seriousness of tragedy, the poetical and impassioned passages are the best part of his comedies. The great and the secret charm of *Twelfth Night* is character of Viola. We have a friendship for Sir Toby, we patronise Sir Andrew, we have an understanding with the clown, a sneaking kindness for Maria and her rogueries, we feel a regard for Malvolio, and sympathise with his gravity, his smiles, his cross garters, his yellow stockings and imprisonment in the stocks. But the best part is Viola's confession of her love. We have already said something of Shakespeare's songs. One of the most beautiful of them occur in this play -

'Come away, come away, death,
And in sad cypress, let me be laid,
Fly away, fly away breath,
I am slain by a fair cruel maid.

-----------------------------------------

Not a flower, not a flower sweet,
On my black coffin let there be strewn

-----------------------------------------

Lay me O! where
Sad-true love never finds my grave,
To weep there? [70]

who after this will say that Shakespeare's genius was only fitted for comedy? Yet after reading other parts of this play, and particularly the garden-scene where Malvolio picks up the letter, if we were to say that his genius for comedy was less than his genius for tragedy than it would perhaps be wrong.

In *King John* has all the beauties of language and all the richness of the imagination to relieve the painfulness of the subject. The character of King John himself is kept pretty much in the background. The crimes he is tempted to commit are such as are thrust upon aim rather by circumstances and opportunity than of his own seeking. He is here represented as more cowardly than cruel and as more contemptible than odious. The play embraces only a part of his history. He has no intellectual grandeur or strength of character to shield him from the indignation which his immediate conduct provokes. He stands naked and defenceless, in that respect to the worst we can think of him, and besides we are impelled to put the very worst construction on his meanness and cruelty by the tender picture of the beauty and helplessness of the object of it, as well as by the frantic and heart-rending pleadings of maternal despair. The scene in which King John suggests to Hubert the design of murdering his nephew is a master-piece of dramatic skill. But it is still inferior to the scene between Hubert and Arthur, when the latter learns the orders to put out his eyes. If anything was ever penned, heart-piercing, mixing the extreme of terror and pity, of that which shocks and that which soothes the mind, it is this scene.

Arthur:.... My uncle practises more harm to me.

He is afraid of me, and I of him.

Is it my fault that I was Geoffrey's son?

Indeed it is not, and I would to heav'n

I were you son, so you would love me Hubert?

Hubert: If I talk to him, with his innocent Prate, He will awake my mercy which lies dead....[71]

The excess of maternal tenderness, rendered desperate by the fickleness of friends and the injustice of fortune, and made stronger in will, in proportion to the want of all other power, was never more finely expressed than in Constance. She addresses the Cardinal in these words-

'Oh father Cardinal, I have heard you say,

That we shall see and know our friends in heaven.

If that be, I shall see my boy again,

For since the birth of Cain, the first male child,

To him that did but yesterday suspire,

There was not such a gracious creature born.

---------------------------------------------------------------

Therefore never, never must I behold my pretty Arthur more."[72]

The contrast between the mild resignation of Queen Katherine to her own wrongs, and the wild, uncontrollable affliction of Constance for the wrongs which she sustains as a mother, is no less naturally conceived than it is ably sustained throughout these two wonderful characters. The accompaniment of the comic characters of the Bastard was well chosen to relieve the poignant agony of suffering, and the cold cowardly policy of behaviour in the principle characters of this play.

This, like the other plays taken from English history, is written in a remarkably smooth and flowing style, very different from some of the tragedies Macbeth, for instance. The passage consists of a series of single lines running into one another. This pecularity in the versification, which is most common in the three parts of *Henry VI.* has been assigned as a reason why those plays were not written by Shakespeare.

But the same structure of verse, occurs in his other undoubted plays, as in *Richard II* and in *King John.* The following are instances-

That daughter there of spain, the lady Blanch,

Is near to England; look upon the years.

of Lewis the dauphin, and that lovely maid.

If lusty love should go in quest of beauty.

Where should he find it fairer than in Blanch?[73]

The *Richard III* of Shakespeare is towering and lofty, equally impetuous and commanding, haughty, violent and subtle, bold and treacherous, confident in his strength as well as his cunning, raised high by his birth, and higher by his talents and his crimes, a royal usurper, a princely hypocrite, tyrant and a murderer of the house of plantagenet.

But I was born so high:

Our airy buideth in the cedar's top,

And dallies with the wind, and scorns the Sun.[74]

The groundwork of the character of Richard that mixture of intellectual vigour with moral depravity, in which Shakespeare delighted to show his strength gave full scope as well as temptation to the exercise of his imagination. The character of his hero is almost every where predominant.

*Henry VIII* contains little action or violence of passions, yet it has considerable interest of a more mild and thoughtful cast, and some of the most striking passages in the author's works.

The character of Queen Katherine is the most perfect delineation of matronly dignity, sweetness and resignation, that can be conceived. Her appeals to the protection of the king, her remonstrances to the cardinals, her conversations with her women, show a noble and generous spirit accompanied with the utmost gentleness of nature.

Again the character of Wolsey, the description of his pride and of his fall are inimitable, and have besides their gorgeousness of effect, a pathos, which only the genius of Shakespeare could lend to the distresses of a proud, bad man, like Wolsey. There is a child-like, simplicity in the very helplessness of his situation, arising from the recollection of his past overbearing ambition. After the cutting sarcasms of his enemies on his disgrace, against which he bears up with a spirit conscious of his own superiority, he breaks out into that fine poetry -

Farewell, a long farewell, to all my greatness.

---------------------------------------------------------------

And when he falls, he falls like Lucifer,

Never to hope again!.[75]

The character of Henry VIII is drawn with great truth and spirit. It is like a very disagreeable portrait, sketched by the hand of a master. His gross appearance, his blustering demeanour, his vulgarity, his arrogance, his sensuality, his cruelty, his hypocrisy, his want of common decency and common humanity, are marked in strong lines. His traditional pecularities of expression complete the reality of the picture. He is of all the monarch's in our history the most disgusting, for he unites in himself all the vices of barbarism and refinement without their virtues.

In *Henry VI* during the time of the civil wars of York and Lancaster, England was perfect bear-garden and Shakespeare has given us a very lively picture of the scene. The three parts of *Henry VI* convey a picture of very little else, and are inferior to the other historical plays. They have brilliant passages, but the general ground-work is comparatively poor and meagre, the style 'flat and unraised.'[76]

We have already observed that Shakespeare was scarely more remarkable for the force and marked contrast of his characters than for the truth and subtlety with which he has distinguished those which aproached the nearest to each other. For instance, the soul of Othello is hardly more disinct from that of Iago than that of Desdemona is shown to from Aemilia's, the ambitions of Macbeth is as distinct from the ambition of Richard III, as it is from the meekness of Duncan the real madness of Lear is as different from the feigned madness of Edgar as from the babbling of the fool, the contrast between wit and folly in Falstaff and Shallow is not more characteristic though more obvious than the gradations of folly, loquacious or reserved in shallow and silence, and again the gallantry of Prince Henry is as little confounded with that of Hotspur and with the cowardice of Falstaff, or as the sensual and philosphic cowardice of the knight is with the pitiful and cringing cowardice of Parolles. All these several personages were as different in Shakespeare as they would have been in themselves, his imagination borrowed from the life and every circumstance, object, motive, passion, operated there as it would in reality, and produced a world of men and women as distinct, as true and as various as those that exist in nature. The peculiar property of Shakespeare's imagination was this truth, accompanied with the unconsciousness of nature. Indeed imagination to be perfect must be unconscious, at least in production.

The characters and situations of *Henry VI* and *Richard II* were so nearly alike, that they would have been completely confounded by a common place poet. Yet they are kept quite distinct in Shakespeare. Both were kings and both unfortunate. Both lost their crowns owing to their mis-management and imbecility; the one from a thoughtless wilful abuse of power, the other from an indifferece to it. The manner in which they bear their misfortune corresponds exactly to the cause which led to them. The one is always lamenting the loss of his power which he has not the spirit to regain, the other seems only to regret that he had ever been king, and is glad to be rid of the power, with thc trouble; the effiminacy of the one is that of a voluptuary, proud, revengeful, impatient of contradictions and inconsolable in his misfortune; the effiminacy of the other is that of an indolent, good-natured mind, naturally averse to the turmoil of ambition and the cares of greatness, and who wishes to pass his time in monkish indolence and contemplation. Richard bewails the loss of the kingly power only as it was the means of gratifying his pride and luxury; Henry regards it only as a means of doing right, and is less desirous of the advantage to be derived from possessing it than afraid of exercising it wrong.

*Henry V,* is a very favorite monarch with the English nation, and he appears to have been also a favorite with Shakespeare, who labours hard to apologise for the actions of the King, by showing us the character of the man, as 'the king of good-fellows.'[77] He scarcely deserves this honour. He was fond of war and low-company. He was careless, dissolute and ambitious, idle or doing mischief. In private he seemed to have no idea of the common decencies of life, in public affairs, he seemed to have no idea of any rule of right or wrong, but brute force, glossed over with a little religious hypocrisy and archiepiscopal advice. His principles did not change with his situation and professions. Henry because he did not know how to govern his own kingdom, determined to make war upon his neighbours. Because his own title to the crown was doubtful, he laid claim to that of France. He did not know how to exercise the enormous power, which had just dropped into his hands, to any one good purpose, he immediately undertook to do all the mischief he could.

The comic parts of *Henry V* are very inferior to those of *Henry IV.* Falstaff is dead and without him, pistol, Nym and Bardolph, are satellites without a sun.

In Henry IV if Shakespeare's fondness for the ludicrous sometimes led to faults in his tragedies, he has made us amends by the character of Falstaff. This is perhaps the most substantial comic character that ever was invented, Falstaff's body is like a good estate to his mind, from which he received rents and revenues of profit and pleasure in kind, according to its extent, and the richness of the soil, wit is often a meagre substitute for pleasurable sensation, an effusion of spleen and petty spite at the comforts of others, from feeling none in itself. Falstaff's wit is an emanation of a fine constitution; an exuberance of good humour and good nature; an overflowing of his love of laughter and good fellowship; a giving vent to his heart's ease, and over-contentment with himself and others. He would not be in character, if he were not so fat as he is : for there is the greatest keeping in the boundless luxury of his imagination and the pampered self-indulgence of his physical appetites. He manures and nourishes his mind with jests, as he does his body with sack and sugar. He is represented as a liar, a braggard, a coward, a glutton etc. and yet we are not offended but delighted with him, for he does all these as much to amuse others as to gratify himself. He openly assumes all these characters to show the humourous part of them. The secret of Falstaff's wit is for the most part a masterly presence of mind, an absolute self-possession, which nothing can disturb. His repartees are involuntary suggestions of his selflove; instinctive evasions of everything that threatens to interrupt the career of his triumphant jollity and self-complacency. His very size floats him out of all his difficulties in a sea of rich conceits.

The characters of Hotspur and Prince Henry are two of the most beautiful and dramatic. They are the essence of chivalry. We like Hotspur the best upon the whole, perhaps, because he was unfortunate. The characters of their fathers, Henry IV and old Northumberland, are kept up equally well. Henry naturally succeeds by his prudence and caution in keeping what he has got; Northumberland fails in his enterprise from an excess of the same quality, and is caught in the web of his own cold, dilatory policy.

The pecularity and the excellence of Shakespeare's poetry is, that it seems as if he made his imagination the hand-maid of nature and the nature the play thing of his imagination. He appears to have been all the characters, and in all the situations he describes. It is as if either he had had all their feelings, or had lent them all his genius to express themselves.

In *Richard II*, the weakness of the king leaves us leisure to take a greater, interest in the misfortunes of the man. After the first act, in which the arbitrariness of his behaviour only proves his want of resolution, we see him staggering under the unlocked for blows of fortune, bewailing his loss of kingly power, not preventing it, sinking under the aspiring genius of Bolingbroke, his authority trampled on, his hopes failing him, and his pride career of his triumphant jollity and self-complacency. His very size floats him out of all his difficulties in a sea of rich conceits.

The characters of Hotspur and Prince Henry are two of the most beautiful and dramatic. They are the essence of chivalry. We like Hotspur the best upon the whole, perhaps, because he was unfortunate. The characters of their fathers, Henry IV and old Northumberland, are kept up equally well. Henry naturally succeeds by his prudence and caution in keeping what he has got; Northumberland fails in his enterprise from an excess of the same quality, and is caught in the web of his own cold, dilatory policy. The pecularity and the excellence of Shakespeare's poetry is, that it seems as if he made his imagination the hand-maid of nature and the nature the play thing of his imagination. He appears to have been all the characters, and in all the situations he describes. It is as if either he had had all their feelings, or had lent them all his genius to express themselves.

In *Richard II*, the weakness of the king leaves us leisure to take a greater, interest in the misfortunes of the man. After the first act, in which the arbitrariness of his behaviour only proves his want of resolution, we see him staggering under the unlocked for blows of fortune, bewailing his loss of kingly power, not preventing it, sinking under the aspiring genius of Bolingbroke, his authority trampled on, his hopes failing him, and his pride crushed and broken down under insults and injuries, which his own misconduct had provoked, but which he has not courage or manliness to resent. Richard's resignation of the crown after the loss of all his power, the use which he makes of the deposed king to grace his triumphal progress through the streets of London and the final intimation of his wish for his death, which immediately finds a servile executioner, is marked throughout with complete effect and without the slightest appearance of effort. The steps by which Bolingbroke mounts the throne are those by which Richard sinks into the grave. His heart is by no means hardened against himself, but bleeds afresh at every new stroke of mischance, and his sensibility absorbed in his own person, and unused to misfortune, is not only tenderly alive to its own suffering, but without the fortitude to bear them. He is however human in his distresses for to feel pain, and sorrow, weakness, disappointment, and anguish, is the lot of humanity and we sympathize with him according.

The character of Bolingbroke, afterwards *Henry IV* is drawn with a masterly hand-patience for occasion, and then steadily availing himself of it, seeing his advantage afar off, but only seizing on it when he has it within his reach, humble, crafty, bold and aspiring, encroaching by regular but slow degrees, building power on opinion and cementing opining by power. His bold assertion of his own rights, his pretended submission to the king and the ascendancy which he tacitly assumes over him without openly claiming it, as soon as he has him in his power, are characteristic traits of his ambitious and politic usurper. But the part of Richard himself gives the chief interest to the play. His folly, his vices, his misfortunes his reluctance to part with the crown, his fear to keep it, his weak and womanish regrets, his tears, his fits of hectic passion, his smothered majesty, pass in succession before us, and make a picture as natural as it is affecting.

*King Lear* is the best of all Shakespeare's plays, for it is the one in which he was the most in earnest. He was here fairly caught in the web of his own imagination. The passion which he has taken as his subject is that which strikes its roots deepest into the human heart.

The mind of Lear staggering between the weight of attachment and the hurried movements of passion, is like a tall ship driven about by the winds, buffetted by the furious waves, but that still rides above the storm, having its anchor fixed in the bottom of the sea, or it is like the sharp rock circled by the eddying whirlpool that foams and beats against it. The character of Lear itself is very finely conceived for the purpose. It is the only ground on which such a story could be built with the greatest truth and effect. It is his rash haste, his violent impetuosity, his blindness to everything but the dictates of his passions or affections, that produces all his misfortune, that aggravates his impatience of them, that enforces our pity for him. The part that Cordelia bears in the scene is extremely beautiful. The indiscreet simplicity of her love, which, to be sure, has a little of her fathers obstinacy in it and the hollowness of her sister's pretension. Regan and Gonereil, they are so throughly hateful that we do not even like to repeat their names. Their deliberate hypocrisy adds the last finishing to the odiousness of their characters. The whole character of Edmund, the bastard's is careless, light-hearted villainy contrasted with the sullen, rancorous malignity of Regan and Gonercil, its connection with the conduct of the under-plot, in which Gloster's persecution of one of his sons and the ingratitude of another, form a counterpart to the mistakes and misfortunes of Lear. His double amour with the two sisters, and the share which he has in bringing about the fatal catastrophe, are all managed with an uncommon degree of skill and power.

"It has been said, and we think justly, that the third act of Othello and the three first acts of Lear are Shakespeare's great masterpieces in the logic of passion, that they contain the highest examples not only of the force of individual passion but of its dramatic vicissitudes and striking effects arising from the different circumstances and characters of the persons speaking."[78] We see the ebb and flow of the feeling, its pause and feverish starts, its impatience of opposition, its accumulating force when it has time to recollect itself, In the present play which aggravates the sense of sympathy in the reader, and of uncontrolable anguish in the swollen heart of Lear, is the petrifying indifference, the cold, calculating, obdurate selfishness of his daughters, His keen passions seem whetted on their stony hearts. The contrast would be too painful, the shock too great, but for the intervention of the fool, whose well timed levity comes in to break the continuity of feeling when it can no longer be borne, and to bring into play again the fibres of the heart just as they are growing rigid from over strained excitement. Lear may well 'beat at the gate which let his folly in,'[79] after as the fool says, `he has made his daughters his mothers.'[80] The character is dropped in the third act to make room for the entrance of Edgar as Mad Tom, which well accords with the increasing bustle and wilderness of the incidents and nothing can be more complete than the distinction between Lear's real and Edgar's assumed madness.

Shakespeare's mastery over his subject, if it was not art, was owing to a knowledge of the connecting links of the passions, and their effect upon the mind, still more wonderful than any systematic adherence to rules, and that anticipated and outdid all the efforts of the most refined art, not inspired and rendered instinctive by genius. The scene in the storm, where he is exposed to all the fury of the elements, grand and terrible. When he sees the misery of Edgar, he comments 'Nothing but his unkind daughter could have brought him to this'[81] are in a style of pathos, where the extremist resources of the imagination are called in to lay open the deepest movements of the heart, which was peculiar to Shakespeare. In the same style and spirit is his interrupting the Fool, who asks 'whether a madman be a gentleman or a yeoman,'[82] by answering 'A king, a king.'[83]

The meeting between Lear and Cordilia is by far the most affecting part of them. It has all the wilderness of poetry, and all the heart-felt truth of nature.

Cordelia: O, look upon me, sir,

And hold your hands in benediction o'er me

Lear: ... I fear I am not in my perfect mind

For, I am a man, I think lady

To be my child Cordelia.

Cordelia: And so I am, I am![84]

The concluding events are sad, painfully sad but their pathos is extreme. The oppression of the feelings is relieved by the very interest we take in the misfortune of others, and by the reflection to which they give birth. Cordelia is hanged in prison by the orders of the bastard Edmund, which are known too late to be countermanded, and Lear dies broken-hearted, lamenting over her

Lear: And my poor fool is hang'd! No, no, no, life:

Why should a dog, a horse, a rat have life,

And thou no breath at all? 0, thou wilt come no more,

Never, never, never, never, never !-[85]

"The greatest of Lear is not in corporal dimensions but in intellectual; the explosion of his passions are terrible as a volcano; they are storms turning up and disclosing to the bottom that rich sea, his mind, with all its vast riches.

It is his mind which is laid bare."[86]

In *Midsummer Nights* Dream Shakespeare's characters are constructed upon deep physiological principles. There is something in this play which looks very like it. Bottom a weaver, is a character, who takes the lead of

This crew of patches, rude mechanicals,

That walk for bread upon Athenian Stalls,[87]

follows a sedentary trade, and he is accordingly represented as conceited, serious and fantastical. He is for playing the tyrant, the lover, the lady, the lion. He declares that he will roar you an 'twere any nightingale'.[88] Snug the joiner is the moral man of the piece who proceeds by measurement and discretion in all things. We see him with his rule and compasses in his hand 'Have you the lion's part written ? Pray you, if it be, give it me, for I am slow of study'-[89] 'You may do it extempore'[90], says Quince, 'For it is nothing but roaring.'[91]

Puck or Robin Goodfellow, is the leader of the fairy band. He is the Ariel of the *Midsummer Nights Dream*; and yet as unlike as can be to the Ariel in *The Tempest.* No other poet could have made two such different characters out of the same fanciful materials and situations. Ariel is the minister of retribution who is touched with the sense of pity at the woes he inflicts, Puck is a mad-cap sprite, full of wantonness and mischief, who laughs at those whom he ; misleads -

Lords what fools these mortals be![92]

The reading of this play is like wandering in a grove by moonlight: the description breathes a sweetness like odours thrown from beds of flowers. But it is converted (the play) from a delightful fiction into a dull pantomime, when acted on the stage. All that is finest in the play is lost in the representation. The spectacle was grand, but the spirit was fled. Poetry and the stage do not agree well together. The attempts to reconcile them in this instance fails not only of effect, but of decorum. The ideal can have no place upon the stage, which is a picture without perspective; everything there is in the foreground. That which was merely an airy shape, a dream, a passing thought, immediately becomes an unmanageable reality. The board of a theatre and the regions of fancy are not the same thing.

*Hamlet* is the one of Shakespeare's plays that we think of the oftenest, because it abounds most in striking reflections of human life, and because the distresses of Hamlet are transferred by the turn of his mind to the general account of humanity. He is a great moraliser; he moralises on his own feelings and experience. He is not a common place pedant. If Lear is distinguished by the greatest depth of passion, Hamlet is the most remarkable of the ingenuity, originality and unstudied development of character. Shakespeare had more magnanimity than any other poet and he has shown more of it in this play than in any other.

The character of Hamlet stands quite by itself. It is not a character marked by strength of will or even of passion, but by refinement of thought and sentiment. He is young and princely novice, full of high enthusiasm and quick sensibility the sport of circumstances questioning with fortune and refining on his own feelings, and forced from the natural bias of his disposition by the strangeness of his situation. He seems incapable of deliberate action, and is only hurried into extremities on the spur of the occasion, when he has no time to reflect, as in the scene where he kills Polonius and again where he alters the letters which Rosencrantz and Guilderstern are taking with them to England, purporting his death. At other times when he is most bound to act, he remains puzzled, undecided, and skeptical, dallies with his purposes till the occasion is lost, and finds out some pretence to relapse into indolence and thoughtfulness again. For this reason he refuses to kill the king when he is at his prayers, and by a refinement in malice. Which is in truth only an excuse for his own want of resolution, defers his revenge to a more fatal opportunity, when he shall be engaged in some act 'that has no relish of salvation in it'.[93] He is the prince of philosophical speculators; and because he cannot have his revenge perfect, according to the most refined idea his wish can form, he declines it altogether. So, he scruples to trust the suggestions of the ghost, contrives the scene of the play to have surer proof of his uncle's guilt and then rests satisfied with his confirmation of his suspicions, and the success of his experiments, instead of acting upon it. And this very speculation on his own infirmity only affords him another occasion for indulging it. It is not from any want of attachment to his father or of abhorrence of his murder that Hamlet is thus dilatory, but it is more to his taste to indulge his imagination in reflecting upon the enormity of the crime and refining on his schemes of vengeance, than to put them into immediate practice. His ruling passion is to think, not to act.

His conduct to Ophelia is quite natural in his circumstances. It is of assumed severity only. It is the effect of disappointed hope, of bitter regrets, of affection suspended, not obliterated, by the distractions of the scene around him. Amidst the natural horrors of his situation, he might be excused in delicacy from carrying on a regular courtship. When 'his father's spirit was in arms, it was not a time for the son to make love in. He could neither marry Ophelia, nor wound her mind by explaining the cause of his alienation, which he could hardly trust himself to think of. His conduct does not contradict what he says when he sees her funeral.

> I loved Ophelia, forty thousand brothers could not with all their quantity of love.
>
> Make up my sum.[94]

Shakespeare was thoroughly a master of the mixed motives of human character, and he here shows us the Queen, who was so criminal in some respects, not without sensibility and affection in other relations of life. Ophelia is a character almost too exquisitely touching to be dwelt upon. Oh rose of May, oh flower too soon faded ! Her love, her madness, her death, are described with the truest touches of tenderness and pathos. It is a character which nobody but Shakespeare could have drawn in the way that he has done, and to the conception of which there is not even the smallest approach. Her brother Laertes, is a character we do not like so well: he is too hot and choleric. Polonius is a perfect character in its kind. Not is there any foundation for the objections which have been made to the consistency of this part. It is said that he acts very foolishly and talks very sensibly. Again, that he talks wisely at one time and foolishly at another; that his advice to Laertes is very excellent, and his advice to the King and Queen on the subject of Hamlet's madness very ridiculous. But he gives the one as a father, and is sincere in it; he gives the other as a mere courtier, busybody, so it is officious & impertinent.

*Romeo and Juliet* is the only tragedy which Shakespeare has written entirely on a love story. It is supposed to have been his first play and he deserves to stand in that proud rank. There is the buoyant spirit of youth in every line, in the rapturous intoxication of hope, and in the bitterness of despair. It has been said of Romeo and Juliet by a great critic, that 'whatever is more intoxicating in the odour of southern spring, languishing in the song of the nightingale, or voluptuous in the first opening of the rose, is to be found in this poem. Romeo and Juliet are in love, but they are not lovesick. Everything speaks the very soul of pleasure, the high and healthy pulse of the passions, the heart beats, the blood circulates throughout. It is Shakespeare all over, and Shakespeare when he was young. He has founded the passion of the two lovers not on the pleasures they had experienced, but on all the pleasures they had not experienced. The only evil that even in apprehension befalls the two lovers is the loss of the greatest possible felicity yet. This loss is fatal to both, for they had rather part with life than bear the thought of surviving all that had made life dear to them. In all this Shakespeare has but followed nature, which existed in his time, as well as now. The modern philosophy, which reduces the whole theory of the mind to habitual impression and leaves the natural impulses of passion and imagination out of the account, had not then been discovered; or if it had, would have been little calculated for the uses of poetry. The feeling of youth and of the spring are here blended together like the breath of opening flowers. Images of vernal beauty appear to have floated before the authors mind, in writing this poem in profusion. The casual description is as full of passionate beauty as when Romeo dwells in frantic fondness on 'the white wonder of his Juliets hand.'[95]

It would be hard to say which of the two garden scenes is the finest, that where he first converses with his love, or takes leave of her the morning after their marriage, Both are like heaven upon earth, the blissful bowers of paradise let down upon this lower world.

Shakespeare is blamed for the mixture of low char acters. If this is deformity, it is the source of a thousand beauties. One instance is the contrast between the guileless simplicity of Juliets attachment to her first love, and the convenient policy of the nurse in advising her to marry Paris, which excites such indignation in her mistress. Ancient damnation! Oh most wicked fiend'[96] etc. And Romeo is Hamlet in love. There is the same rich exuberance of passion and sentiment in the one that there is of thought and sentiment in the other. Both are absent and self-involved, both live out of themselves in a world of imagination. Hamlet is abstracted from everything; Romeo is abstracted from everything but his love, and lost in it. Romeo's passion for Juliet is not a first love, it succeeds and drives out his passion for another mistress, Rosaline, as the sun hides the stars. The passage which Romeo speaks at the tomb of Juliet, before he drinks the poison, describing the loveliness of Juliet, who is supposed to be dead, have been compared to those in which it is said of Cleopatra after her death, that she looked 'as she would take another Antony in her strong toil of Grace.'[97] and a question has been started which is the finest, that we do not pretend to decide, We can more easily decide between. Shakespeare and any of the other author, than between him and himself. The character of Mercutio in this play is one of the most mercurial and spirited of the production of Shakespeare's comic muse.

... O my love ! my wife !

Death that hath suck'd the honey of thy breath,

Hath no power yet upon thy beauty.

Thou art not conquered... [98]

In *Coriolanus* Shakespeare has shown himself well-versed in history and state-affairs. *Coriolanus* is a store house of political common-places. The arguments for and against aristocracy or democracy, on the privileges Of the few and the claims of the many on liberty and slavery, power and the abuse of it, peace and war, are here very ably handled, with the spirit of a poet and acuteness of a philosopher. The whole dramatic moral of *Coriolanus* is that those who have little shall have less, and that those who have much shall take all that others have left. The people are poor, therefore they ought to be starved. They are slaves; therefore they ought to be beaten. They work hard; therefore they ought to be treated like beasts of burden. They are ignorant; therefore they ought not to be allowed to feel that they want food, or clothing, or rest, that they are enslaved, oppressed and miserable. This is the logic of the imagination and the passions; which seek to aggrandize what excites admiration and to heap contempt on misery, to raise power into tyranny, and to make tyranny absolute; to thrust down that which is low still lower, and to make wretches desperate: to exalt magistrates into kings, kings into Gods; to degrade subjects to the rank of slaves, and slaves to the condition of brutes. One of the most natural traits in this play is the difference of the interest taken in the success of Coriolanus by his wife and mother. The one is only anxious for his honour; the other is fearful for his life. Coriolanus himself is a complete character. His love of reputation, his contempt of popular opinion, his pride and modesty are consequences of each other. His pride consists in the inflexible sternness of his will; his love of glory is determined desire to bear down all opposition, and to extort the admiration both of friends and foes. His contempt for popular favour, his unwillingness to hear his own praises, springs from the same source. He cannot contradict the praises that are bestowed upon him; therefore he is impatient at hearing them. He would enforce the good opinion of other by his actions, but does not want their acknowledgements in words.

Pray now, no more: my mother,

Who has a charter to extol her blood,

When she does praise me grieves me[99]

His magnanimity is of the same kind. He admires in any enemy that courage which he honours in himself; he places himself on the hearth of Aufidius with the same confidence that he would have met him in the field, and feels that by putting himself in his power, he takes from him all temptation for using it against him.

In the title-page of Coriolanus, it is said at the bottom of the Dramatic Personae, 'The whole history exactly followed, and many of the principal speeches copied from the life of Coriolanus in Plutarch. Two of the principal scenes, those between Coriolanus and Aufidius and between Coriolanus and his mother, are thus given in Sir Thomas North's Translation of Plutarch, dedicated to Queen Elizabeth, 1579. Shakespeare has, in giving a dramatic form to this passage, adhered very closely and properly to the text. He did not think it necessary to improve upon the truth of nature. Several of the scenes in Julius-Caesar, particularly Portia's appeal to the confidence of her husband by showing him the wound, she had given herself, and the appearance of the ghost of Caesar to Brutus, are in like manner, taken from the history'[100] Coriolanus puzzles us sufficiently to provoke us into pushing it also among the problem plays. The hero's tragic flaw is supposed to be 'pride'. It is not any natural want of endowment, any hereditary defect, but defective upbringing that causes the 'flaw in Coriolanus' character. Shakespeare too makes it clear that Volumia is not a little responsible for the imbalance in her son's deportment. More than he, she is ambitious on his behalf. Volumnia is in no small measure the architect of her son's tragedy. She is her son's fate, just as Gertrude is her son's for the dominating good mother can ruin a son as much as the incestuous bad mother. The Tribunes, of course, are foxy creatures, willing to wound but afraid to strike they are Coriolanus' Rosencrantz and Guilderstern, but grown older, foxier and more unscrupulous and they take full advantage of Coriolanus' weaknesses (and weakness in his very strength to thwart and drive him to ruin.

As poetry, there is a falling off from *Macbeth* and *Antony Cleopatra*, but the verse is distinguished throughout and is often rhetorically brilliant and at least once (in climatic Volumnia scene: V. iii) reaches great heights. The play is dominated by the hero even more absolutely than Hamlet is by the Prince of Denmark. While Corilanus seen from one point of view, is "all masterpiece of construction."[101] for it is marked by a classical restraint and there are no distracting sub-plots, when we view it in relation to the hero's character alone it seems to be two plays uneasily joined in the middle. The scion of a noble house, a fighter, a patriot, how is it that Coriolanus becomes-as it were overnight -a fury, a scourge, an evil1 destiny?

In tragedies two problems taxed Shakespeare almost incessantly: sex and war, lust in the name of love and butchery in the name of war. One lunacy was as destructive as the other; one as common, and indeed as necessary, as the other. Duthie thinks that "the fundamental order-disorder theme is found in all the tragedies."[102]

In *The Winter's Tale* we wonder that Mr. Pope should have entertained doubts of the genuiness of this play. He was, we suppose, shocked at the chorus, Time, leaping over sixteen years with his crutch between the III and IV act, and at Antigonus' landing with the infant Perdita on the sea coast of Bohemia. These slips or blemishes however do not prove it not to be Shakespeare's for he was likely to fall into them as any body; but we do not know anybody but himself who would produce the beauties. The stuff of which the tragic passion is composed, the romantic sweetness, and the comic humour, are evidently his. Even the crabbed and tortuous style of the speeches of Leontes, reasoning on his own jealousy beset with doubts and fears, and entangled more and more in thorny labyrinths, bears every mark of Shakespeare's peculiar manner of conveying the painful struggle of different thoughts and feelings, labouring for utterance, and almost strangled in the birth.

The character of Hermione is as much distinguished by its saint like resignation and patient forbearance, as that of Paulina is by her zealous and spirited remonstrances against the injustice done to the queen and by her devoted attachment to her misfortunes. Camillo, and the old Shepherd and his son, are subordinate but not uninteresting instruments in the development of the plot, and though last not least, comes Autolycus, a very pleasant, thriving rogue; and what is the best feather in the cap of all knavery he escapes with impunity in the end.

*All's Well That Ends Well* is one of the most pleasing of our author's comedies. The interest is however more of a serious than of a comic nature.The character of Helena is one of great sweetness and delicacy. She is placed in circumstances of the most critical kind, and has to court her husband both as a virgin and a wife, yet the most scrupulous nicety of female modesty is not violated. There is not one thought or action that ought to bring a blush into her cheeks, or that for a moment lessens her in our esteem. Perhaps the romantic attachment of a beautiful and virtuous qirl to one placed above her hopes by the circumstances of birth and fortune, was never so exquisitely expressed as in the relfections which she utters when young Roussillon leaves his mother's house, under whose protection she has been brought up with him, to repair to the French King's Court.

Helena : ............ I think not on my father,

And these great tears grace his remembrance more

than those I shed for him. What was he like?

I have forgot him. My imagination

carries no favour in it, but Bertram's

I am undone, there is no living, none

If Bertram be away. It were all one

That I should love a bright particular star.[103]

The interest excited by this beautiful picture of a fond and innocent heart is kept up afterwards by her resolution to follow him to France, the success of her experiment in restoring the King's health, her demanding Bertram marriage as a recompense, his leaving her in disdain, her interview with him afterwards disguised as Diana, a young lady whom he importunes with his secret addresses, and their final reconciliation when the consequences of her stratagem and the proofs of her love are fully made known. The pressuring gratitude of the French King to his benefactress, who cures him of a languishing distemper by a prescription hereditary in her family, the indulgent kindness of the countess, whose pride of birth yields, almost without a struggle, to her affection for Helena, the honesty and uprightness of the good old Lord Lafeu, make very interesting parts of the picture. The wilful stubbornnesss and youthful petulence of Bertram are also very admirably described. The comic part of the play turns on the folly, boasting and cowardice of Parolles, a parasite and hanger-on of Bertram's the detection of whose false pretensions to bravery and honour forms a very amusing a episode. He is first found out by Lord Lafeu, who says 'The soul of this man is in his clothes'; and it is proved afterwards that his heart is in his tongue and that both are false and hollow.

In *Love's Labour's Lost* Shakespeare has set himself to imitate the tone of polite conversation then prevailing among the fair, the witty, and the learned, and he has imitated it but too faithfully. It is as if the hand of Titian has been employed to give grace to the curls of a full-bottomed periwig, or Raphael had attempted to give expression to the tapestry figures in the House of Lords. Shakespeare has put an excellent description of this fashionable jargon into the mouth of the critical Holofernes 'as too picked, too spruce, too affected, too odd, as it were to peregrinate, as I may call it.'[104]

The character of Biron drawn by Rosaline and that Which Biron gives of on the use and abuse of study, and on the power of beauty to quicken the understanding as well as the senses are excellent. The scene which has the greatest dramatic effect is that in which Biron, the King, Longaville, the Dumain, successively detect each other and are detected in their breach of their vow and in their profession of attachment to their several mistresses in which they suppose themselves to be overheard by no one. The reconciliation between these lovers and their sweethearts is also very good and the penance which Rosaline imposes on Biron, before he can expect to gain her consent to marry him, full of propriety and beauty.

In *Much Ado About Nothing,* Hero is the principal figure in the piece and leaves an indelible impression on the mind by her beauty, her tenderness, and the hard trial of her love. The passage in which Claudio first makes a confession of his affection towards her, conveys as pleasing an image of the entrance of love into a youthful Bosom as can well be imagined. In the scene at the altar, when Claudio, urged only the villian Don John, brings the charge of incontinence against her, and as it were divorces her in the very marriage-ceremony her appeals to her own concious innocence and honour made with the most affectingare simplicity.

The justification of Hero in the end and her restoration to the confidence and arms of her lover is brought about by one of those temporary consignments to the grave of which Shakespeare seems to have been fond. He has perhaps explained the theory of this predilection in the following lines-

Friar : She dying, as it must be so maintain'd,
upon the instant that she was accus'd
shall be lamented, pity'd and excus'd,
of every hearer : for it so fall out,
That what we have we prize not to the worth,
while we enjoy it; but being lack'd and lost,
why then we rack the value, then we find,
The virtue, that possession would not shew us
Whilst it was ours . - so will it fare with Claudio
When he shall hear she dy'd upon his words,
The idea of her love shall sweetly creep
Into his study of imagination;
And every lovely organ of her life
Shall come apparel'd in more precious habit,
More moving, delicate and full of life,
Into the eye and prospect of his soul,
Than when she liv'd indeed.[105]

The principal comic characters Benedick and Beatrice are both essences in their kind. His character as a Woman-hater is admirably supported, and his conversion to matrimony is no less happily effected by the pretended story of Beatrice love for him. The beauty of all this arises from the characters of the persons so entrapped. Benedick is a professed and staunch enemy to marriage and gives very plausible reasons for the faith that is in him. And as to Beatrice, she pesecutes him all day with her jests so that he could hardly think of being troubled with them at night She not only turns him but all other things into jest, and is proof against everything serious.

These are happy materials for Shakespeare to work on, and he has made a happy use of them. Perhaps that middle point of comedy was never more nicely hit in which the ludicrous blends with the tender, and our follies, turning round against themselves in support of our affections retain nothing but their humanity.

Dogberry and Verges in this play are inimitable specimens of quaint blundering and misprisions of meaning; and are a standing record of that formal gravity of pretension and total want of common understanding, which Shakespeare no doubt copied from real life, and which in the course of two hundred years appear to have ascended from the lowest to the highest offices in the state.

In *The Tempest,* there can be little doubt that Shakespeare was the most universal genius that ever lived. 'Either for tragedy, comedy, history, pastoral, pastoral-comical, historical-pastoral, scene individual or poem unlimited, he is the only man. Seneca cannot be too heavy, nor Plautus too light for him.'[106] He has not only the same absolute command over our laughter and our tears, all the resources of passion, of wit, of thought, of observation, but he has the most unbounded range of fanciful intention, whether terrible or playful, the same insight into the world of imagination that he has into the world of reality; and over all there presides the same truth of character and nature and the same spirit of humanity. His ideal beings are as true and natural as his real characters, that is as consistent with themselves, or if we suppose such being to exist at all, they could not act, speak, or feel otherwise than as he makes them. He has invented for them a language, manners, and sentiments of their own, from the tremendous imprecations of the witches in *Macbeth* when they do 'a deed withuot a name'[107], to the sylph like expressions of Ariel, who 'does his spiriting gently'[108]; the mischievous tricks and gossiping of Robin Good fellow or the uncouth gabbling and emphatic gesticulations of Caliban in this play."

*The Tempest* is one of the most original and perfect of Shakespeare's productions and he has shown in it all the variety of his powers. It is full of grace and grandeur. The human and imaginary characters, the dramatic and the grotesque, are blended together with the greatest art and without any appearance of it. The stately magician, Prospero, driven from his dukedom, but around whom, so potent is his art airy spirits throng numberless to do his bidding; his daughter Miranda, to whom all the power of his art points, and who seems the goddess of the Isle; the princely Ferdinand, cast by fate upon the heaven of his happiness in this idol of his love the delicate Ariel, the savage Caliban, half-brute, half demon; the drunken ships crew-are all connected part of the story, and can hardly be spared from the place they fill. Even the local scenery is of a piece and character with the subject. Prospero's enchanted island seems to have risen up out of the sea; the airy music, the tempest tossed vessel, the turbulent waves all have the effect of the landscape background of some fine picture.

The character of Caliban is generally thought to be one of the author's master-pieces. It is one of the wildest and most abstracted of all Shakespeare's characters, whose deformity whether of body or mind is redeemed by the power and truth to the imagination displayed in it. He has described the brutal mind of Caliban in contact with the pure and original forms of nature; the character grows out of the soil where it is rooted, uncontrolled, uncouth and wild, uncramped by any of the meannesses of custom. Schlegel, the admirable German critic on Shakespeare, observes that Caliban is a poetical character, and "always speaks in blank-verse. In conducting Stepheno and Trinculo to Prospero's cell. Caliban shows the superiority of natural capacity over greater knowledge and greater folly. The poet shows us the savage with the simplicity of a child, and makes the strange monster amiable. When it comes to Ariel, nothing was ever more finely conceived than this contrast between the material and the spiritual, the gross and delicate Ariel is imaginary power, the swiftness of thought personified. The courtship between Ferdinand and Miranda is one of the chief beauties of this play. It is the very purity of love."[109]

The *Tempest* is a finer play than the *Midsummer Night's* Dream which has sometimes been compared with it; but it is not so fine a poem. There are a greater number of beautiful passages in the latter. Two of the most striking in *The Tempest* are spoken by Prospero. The one is that admirable one when the vision which he has conjured up disappears beginning 'The cloud-capp'd towers, the gorgeous palaces'[110] etc, which has been often quoted. The other is that which Prospero makes in abjuring his art.

Ye eleves of hills, brooks, standing lakes & groves

And ye that on the sands with printless foot

-------------------------------------------------------------------

I'1l drown my book- [111]

Shakespeare has anticipated nearly all the arguments on the Utopian schemes of modern philosophy -

Gonzalo - I'the commonwealth I would by contraries.

Execute all things for no kind of traffic

would I admit; no names of magistrate.

-------------------------------------------------------------------

And women too; but innocent and pure:

No Soverignty.

Gon :- All things in common nature shall produce---[112]

*Troilus And Cressida* is one of the most loose and desultory of our author's plays. It rambles on just as it happens, but it overtakes together with some indifferent matter, a prodigious number of fine things in its way. Troilus himself is character. He is merely a common lover. But Cressida, and her uncle Pandarus are hit off with proverbial truth. By the speeches given to the leaders of the Grecian host, Nestor, Ulysses, Agamemnon, Achilles, Shakespeare seems to have known them as well as if he had been a spy sent by the Trojans into the enemy's camp to say nothing of their affording very lofty examples of didactic eloquence.

The character of Hector, in a few slight indications which appear of it, is made very amiable. His death is sublime, and shows in a striking light of the mixture of barbarity and heroism of the age. The threats of Achilles are fatal; they carry their own means of execution with them-

Come here about me, you my myrmidons,

Mark what I say - Attend me where I wheel.

-------------------------------------------------------

And when I have the bloody Hector found

Empale him with your weapon round about,

In fellest manner execute your arms;

Follow me, sirs, and my proceeding eye.[113]

He then finds Hector and slays him, as if he had been hunting down a wild-beast. There is some thing revolting as well as terrific in the ferocious coolness with which he singles out his prey: nor does the splendor of the achievement reconcile us to the cruelty of the means.

The characters of Cressida and Pandarus are very amusing and instructive. Shakespeare's Cressida is a giddy girl, an unpractised jilt, who falls in love with Troilus as she afterwards deserts him, from mere levity and thoughtlessness of temper. She may be wooed and won to anything and from anything at a moments warning; the other knows very well what she would be at, and sticks to it, and is more governed by substantial reasons than by caprice or vanity. Pandarus in Shakespeare has 'a stamp exclusive and professional'[114]: he wears the badge of his trade, he is a regular of Pandarus in Chaucer's story, is a friendly sort of go-between, tolerably busy, officious, and forward in bringing matter to bear. The difference of the manner in which the subject is treated arises perhaps less from intension, than from the different genius of the two poets.

Shakespeare never committed himself to his characters. He trifled, laughed and wept with them as he chose. He has no preudices for or against them. It seems a matter of perfect indifference whether he shall be in jest or earnest. According to him, 'the web of our lives is of a mingled yarn, good and ill together'[115]. His genius was dramatic, as Chaucer's was historical. He saw both sides of question, the different views taken of it according to the different interest of the parties concerned and he was at once an actor and spectator in the scene. If anything, he is too various and flexible : too full of transition, of glancing lights, of salient points. If Chaucer followed up his subject too doggedly. Shakespeare was too volatile and heedless. The Muse's using too often lifted him from off his feet. He often made infinite excursions to the right and the left. Shakespeare exhibited also the possible and the fantastical-not only what things are in themselves, but whatever they might seem to be, their different reflections, their endless combinations. He lent his fancy, wit, invention to others and borrowed their feelings in return. In Shakespeare the commonest matter of fact has a romantic grace about it, or it seems to float with the breath of imagination in the freer element. Shakespeare saw everything by intuition. What is most wonderful thing in Shakespeare's faculties is their excessive sociability and how they gossiped and compared notes together.

*Timons of Athens* has been written with as intense a feeling of his subjects as any one play of Shakespeare. It is one of the few in which he seems to be earnest throughout, never to trifle, nor go out of his way. He does not relax in his efforts, nor lose sight of the unity of his design. It is the only play of our author in which spleen is the predominant feeling of the mind. It is as much a satire as a play. The fable consists of a single event of the transition from the highest pomp and profusion of artificial refinement to the most object state of savage life, and privation of all social intercourse. The change is as rapid as it is complete, nor is the description of the rich and generous Timon bequeting in gilded palaces, pampered by every luxury prodigal of his hospltality, courted by crowds of flatterers, poets, painters, lords, ladies who -

Follow his strides, his lobbies fill with tendance,
Rain sacrificial whisperings in his ear;
And through him drink the free air - [116]

More striking than that of the sudden falling off of his friendds and fortune, and his naked exposue, in a wild forest, digging roots from the earth for his sustenance, with a lofty spirit of self-denial, and bitter scorn of the world, which raise him higher in our esteem than the dazzling gloss of prosperity could do. He grudges himself the means of life, and is only busy in preparing his grave. How forcibly is the difference between what he was and what he is. In this play Shakespeare has exposed the hollow friendship and shuffling evasions of the Athenian lords, their smooth professions and pitiful ingratitude. The lurking selfishness of Apemantus does not pass undetected amidst the grossness of his sarcasms and his contempt for the pretensions of others. An exception to this general picture of selfish depravity is found in the old and honest steward Flavius, to whom Timons pays a full tribute of tenderness. But while the sordid licentiousness of Apemantus, which turns everything to gall and bitterness, show only the natural virulence of his temper and antipathy to good or evil alike. Timon does not utter an imprecation without betraying the extravagant workings of disappointed passion, of love altered to hate. Apemantus sees nothing good in any object, and exaggerates whatever is disgusting. Timon is tormernted with the perpetual contrast between things and appearance, between the fresh, tempting outside and the rottenness within. Timon is here just as ideal in his passion for ill as he had been before in his belief of good. And Apemantus seems to be satisfied with his own ill-nature. One of the most decisive intimations of Timon's morbid jealousy of appearance is in his answer to Apemantus, who asks him,

What things in the world can'st
thou nearest compare with thy flatterers?
Timon. Women nearest: but men, men are the things
themselves.[117]

Timon neither loves to abhor himself nor others. All his vehement misanthropy is forced up-hill work. From the slippery turns of fortune, from the turmoil of passion and adversity, he wishes to sink into the quiet of the grave. He digs his own grave by the sea-shore contrives his funeral ceremonies amidst the pomp of desolation. Making the winds and his funeral dirge, his mourner the murmuring ocean seeking in the everlasting solemnities of nature oblivion of the transitory splendour of his life-time.

In *Othello*, the picturesque contrasts of character in this play are almost as remarkable as the depth of the passion. The Moor Othello, the gentle Desdemona, the villian Iago, the good natured Cassio, the fool Roderigo present a range and variety of character as striking and palpable as that produced by the opposition of costume in a picture. Their distinguishing qualities stand out to the minds eye, so that even when we are not thinking of their actions or sentiments, the idea of their persons is still as present to us as ever. These characters and images they stamp upon the mind are farthest as under possible, the distance between them is immense : yet the compass of knowledge and invention which the poet has shown in embodying these extreme creations of his genius is only greater than the truth and felicity with which he has identified each character withn itself, or blended their different qualities together in the same story. What a contrast the character of Othello forms to that of Iago. The making one black and the other white, the one principled, the other unfortunate in the extreme would answer the common purposes of effect, and satisfy the ambition of an ordinary painter of character. Shakespeare has laboured the finer shades of difference in both with as much care and skill as if he had to depend on the execution alone for the success of his design. On the other hand, Desdemona and Aemila are not meant to be opposed with anything like strong contrast to each other. Both are, to outward appearance, characters of common life, not more distinguished than woman usually are, by difference of rank and situation. The difference of their thoughts and sentiments is however laid open, their minds separated from each other by signs as plain and as little to be mistaken as the complexion of their husband.

The movement of the passion in Othello is exceedingly different from that of Macbeth there is a violent struggle between opposite feelings, between ambition and the stings of conscience, almost from first to last : in Othello, the doubtful conflict between contrary passions, though dreadful, continues only for a short time and the chief interest is excited by the alternate ascendancy of different passion, by the entire unforeseen change from the fondest love and most unbounded confidence to the tortures of jealousy and the madness of hatred. The revenge of Othello, after it has once taken thorough possession of his mind, never quit it, but grows stronger and stronger at every moment of its delay. The nature of moor is noble, confiding, tender and generous; but his blood is of the most inflammable kind; and being once roused by a sense of his wrongs, he is stopped by no considerations of remorse or pity till he has given a loose to all the dictates of his rage and despair. It is in working his noble nature upto this extremity through rapid but gradual transition, in raising passion to its height from the smallest beginnings and in spite of all obstacles, in painting the expiring conflict between love and hatred, tendernesses and resentment, jealousy and remorse, in unfolding the strength and weakness of our nature, that Shakespeare has shown the mastery of his genius and of his power over the human heart.

The third act of *Othello* is his finest display, not of knowledge or passion separately, but of two combined of the knowledge of character with the expression of passion, of consumate art in keeping up appearances with the profound working of nature, and the convulsive movements of uncontrolable agony, of the power of inflicting torture and of suffering it. Not only is the tumult of passion in *Othello's* mind heaved up from the very bottom of the soul, but even the slightest undulation of feeling is seen on the surface, as it arises from the impulses of imagination of the malicious suggestions of Iago. The progressive preparation for the catastrophe is wonderfully managed from Moor's first gallant recital of the story of his love, of his romantic success, the fond satisfaction with which he dotes on his own happiness, the unreserved tenderness of Desdemona and her innocent importunities in favour of Cassio, irritating the suspicions instilled into her husband's mind by the perfidy of Iago, and ranking there to poison, till he loses all command of himself, and his rage can only be appeased by blood. To begin with he cannot believe that his wife Desdemona can be unfaithful to him, though he lends his ears to the malicious scheming of Iago, Othello exclaims to himself,

If she be false, O then Heav'n mock itself:

I'll not believe it.[118]

But presently after, on brooding over his suspicions by himself, and yielding to his apprehensions of the worst his smoothered jealousy breaks out into open fury, and he returns to demand satisfaction of Iago like a wild beast stung with the envenomed shaft of the hunters. From this time, his raging thoughts never look back till his revenge is sure of this object. But in the scene immediately preeceding her death, the recollection of his love returns upon him in all its tenderness and force. And after her death, he all at once forgets his wrongs in the sudden and irreparable sense of his loss-

My Wife ! my wife ! what wife ? I have no wife.

Oh insupportable! Oh heavy hour!

This happens before he is assured of her innocence but afterwards his remorse is as dreadful as his revenge has been, and yields only to fixed and death like despair. His farewell speech before he kills himself, in which he conveys is his reasons to the senate for the murder of his wife, equal to the first speech in which he gave them an account of his courtship of her and 'his whole course of love.'[119] Such an ending was alone worthy of such a commencement. If anything could add to the force of our sympathy with Othello, or compassion for his fate, it would be the frankness and generosity of his nature. His character is beautifully confirmed by what Desdemona herself says of him to Aemilia after she has lost the handkerchief, the first pledge of his love to her.

Believe me, I had rather have lost my purseful of
cruzadoes
And but my noble Moor.
Is true of mind, and made of no such baseness,
As jealous creatures are, it were enough
To put him to ill thinking.[120]

In short s speech of Aemilia's, there occurs one of those side-intimations of the fluctutions of passion which we seldom meet with but in Shakespeare. After Othello has resolved upon the death of his wife, and bids her dismiss her attendant for the night, she answer,

I will my lord.

Aemilia, How goes it now? (He looks gentler than he did)[121]

Shakespeare has here put into half a line what some authors would have spun out into ten set speeches. The character of Desdemona predominates everywhere over her person. There is one fine compliment paid to her by Cassio, who exclaims triumphantly, when she comes ashore at cypress after the storm.

Tempests themselves, high seas, and howling winds,
As having sense of beauty, do omit
Their mortal nature, letting safe go by
The divine Desdemona.[122]

In general as is the case with most of Shakespeare' s females, we lose sight of her personal charms in her attachment and devotedness to her husband 'The extravagance of her resolutions, the pertinacity of her affections may be said to arise but of the gentleness of her nature. They imply an unreserved reliance on the purity of her own intentions, an entire surrender of her fears to her love, a knitting of herself heart and soul to the fate of another.'[123] It is certain that nothing but the genius of Shakespeare could have preserved the entire interest and delivery of Desdemona's part and have even drawn an additional elegance and dignity from the peculiar circumstances in which she is placed.

The character of Iago's one of the supererogations of Shakespeare's genius. Some persons more nice than wise, have thought this whole character unnatural, because his villiany is without a sufficient motive. Shakespeare, who was as good a philospher as he was a poet, thought otherwise. He knew that the love of power, which is another name for the love of mischief is natural to man. He would know this as well as better than if it had been demonstrated to him by a logical diagram, merely from seeing children paddle in the dirt or kill for sport. Iago in fact belongs to a class of character, common to Shakespeare and at the same time peculiar to him: whose heads are as acute and active as their hearts are hard and callous. Iago is a representation of diseased intellectual activity with the most perfect indifference to moral good or evil or rather with a decided preference of the latter. He is quite and nearly as indifferent to his own fate as to that of others.

*Macbeth* and *king Lear, Othello* and *Hamlet,* are reckoned Shakespeare's four principal tragedies. *Lear* stands for the profound intensity of the passion; *Macbeth* for the wilderness of the imagination and the rapidity of the action; *Othello* for the progressive interest and powerful alternations of heelings; *Hamlet* for the refined development of thought and sentiment. If the force of genius shown in each of these works is astonishing, their variety is not less so. They are like different creations of the same mind, not one of which has the slightest reference to the rest. This distinctness and originality is indeed the necessary consequence of truth and nature. Shakespeare's genius alone appeared to posses the resources of nature. *Macbeth* is like a record of a preternatural and tragic event. It has the rugged severity of an old chronicle with all that the imagination of poet can traditional belief. Shakespeare excelled in the opening of his plays. The opening of *Macbeth* is the most striking of any. The wilderness of the scenery, the sudden shifting of the situations and characters, the bustle, the expectations excited, are equally extraordinary. The castle of Macbeth round which 'the air smells wooingly' and where 'the temple-haunting martlet builds' 'the weird sisters' meet us in person on the blasted heath', the air-drawn dagger' moves slowly before our eyes, the 'gracious Duncan' the 'blood boultered Banquo' stand before us. Macbeth himself appears driven along by the violence of his fate like a vessel drifting before a storm. He reels to and fro like a drunken he staggers under the weight of his own purposes and the suggestions of others. He is not equal to the struggle with fate and conscience. He now bends up each corporal intrument to the terrible feat. His speeches and soliloquies are dark riddles on human life, baffling solutions and entangling him in their labyrinths. In thought he is absent and perplexed, sudden and desperate in act, from a distrust of his own resolutions. His energy springs from the anxiety and agitation of his mind. His blindly rushing forward on the objects of his ambition and revenge or his recoiling from them equally betrays the harassed state of his feelings. This part of his character is admirably set off by being brought in connection with that of Lady Macbeth, whose obdurate strength of will and masculine firmness give her the ascendancy over her husbands faultering virtue. She at once seizes on the opportunity that offers for the accomplishment of all their wished for greatness and never flinches from her object till all is over. The magnitude of her resolution almost covers the magnitude of her guilt. She is a great bad woman, whom we hate, but whom we fear more than we hate. She does not excite our loathing and abhorrence like Regan and Gonerill. She is only wicked to gain a great end and is perhaps more distinguished by her commanding presence of mind and inexorable self-will, which do not suffer her to be diverted from a bad purpose, when once formed, by weak and womanly regrets. The impression which her lofty determination of character makes on the mind of Macbeth is well described where he exclaims-

Being forth men children only;

For thy undaunted mettle should compose

Nothing but males![124]

She seems to have the same unshrinking fortitude in crime, that in other circumstances she would probably have shown patience in suffering. The deliberate sacrifice of all other consideration to the gaining for their future days and nights sole sovereign way and masterdom by the murder of Duncan. This solid substantial flesh and blood display of passion, exhibit a striking contrast to the cold, abstracted, servile malignity of the witches, who are equally instrumental in urging Macbeth to his fate for the mere love of mischief and a disinterested delight in deformity and cruelty.

The dramatic beauty of the character of Duncan, which excites the respect and pity even of his murderers has been pointed out. An instance of the author's power of giving a striking effect to a common reflection, by the manner of introducing it, occurs in a speech of Duncan, complaining of his having been deceived in his opinion of the Thane of Cawdor, at the very moment that he is expressing the most unbound confidence in the loyalty and services of Macbeth.

There is no art

To find the mind's construction in the face:

He was a gentleman, on whom I built

An absolute trust

O worthiest cousin (addressing himself to Macbeth)

The sin of my ingratitude e'en now

Was great upon me,[125] etc.

Another passage to show that Shakespeare lost sight of nothing that could in any way give relief or heightening to his subject, is the conversation which takes place between Banquo and Fleance immediately before the murder-scene of Duncan.

Banquo. How goes the night boy?

Fleance. The moon is down: I have not heart the

clock.

Banguo. And she goes down at twelve.

Fleance. I take't, 'tis later, Sir

Banquo. Hold, take my sword. There is husbandry in

heav'n,

Their candles are all out -

A heavy summons lies like lead upon me.

And yet I would not sleep Merciful powers,

Restrain in me the cursed thoughts that nature.

Gives way to in repose?[126]

In like manner, a fine idea is given of the gloomy coming on of evening, just as Banquo is going to be assassinated.

Light thickens and the crow

Makes Wing to the rooky wood.

------------------------------------------------------

Now spurs the lated traveller apace

To gain the timely inn.[127]

Macbeth is written upon a stronger and more systematic principal of contast than any other of Shakespeare's plays. It moves upon the verge of an abyss, and is a constant struggle between life and death. The action is desperate and the reaction is dreadful. It is huddling together of fierce extremes, a war of opposite natures which of them shall destroy the other. There is nothing but what has a violent end or violent beginnings. The lights and shades are laid on with a determined hand; the transition from triumph to despair, from the height of terror to the repose of death, are sudden and startling. Shakespeare's genius here took its full swing, and trod upon the farthest bounds of nature and passion. This circumstance will account for the abruptness and violent antithesis of the style, the throes and labour which run through the expression, and from defects will turn them into beauties. So fair and foul a day I have not seen, etc. 'Such welcome and unwelcome news together.' Men's lives are like the flowers in their caps, dying or ere they sicken.' Look like the innocent flower, but be the serpent under it.' The most outstanding feature of Shakespeare's characters is their individual distinctness, even when the broad-outlines are quite similar. For example Macbeth and Richard III. Both are tyrants, usurpers, murderers, both aspiring and ambitious, both courageous cruel, treacherous. But Richard is cruel from nature and constitution. Macbeth becomes so from accidental circumstances. Richard is from his birth deformed in body and mind and naturally incapable of good. Macbeth is full of the milk of human kindness, is frank, sociable, generous, He is tempted to the commission of guilt by golden opportunities by the instigation of his wife, and by prophetic warnings. Fate and metaphysical aid conspire against his virtue and his loyalty. Richard on the contrary needs no prompter, but wades through a series of crimes to the height of his ambition from the ungovernable violence of his temper and a reckless love of mischief. Shakespeare Julius Caesar is not equal as a whole, to either of his other plays taken from the Roman history. It is inferior in interest to Coriolanus, and both in interest and power to Antony and Cleopatra. It however abounds in admirable and affecting passages, and is remarkable for the profound knowledge of character, in which Shakespeare scarcely fail. Though in this play we do not admire the representation given of Julius Caesar. He makes several vapouring and rather pedantic speeches, and does nothing. Indeed he has nothing to do. So far, the fault of the character is the fault of the plot. The well known dialogue between Brutus and Cassius is a noble piece of high minded declamation. Cassius' insisting on the pretended effeminacy of Caesar's character, and his description of their swimming across the Tiber together, 'once upon a row and gusty day' are among the finest strokes in it. But the best scenes are those which follows the above scene when Caesar enters with his train -

Caesar : Let me have men about me that are fat, sleek-headed men, and such as sleep a - nights : Yon Cassius has a Lean and hungry look, He thinks too much, such men are dangerous.

Caesar : Would he were fatter; but I fear him not :

Yet if my name were liable to fear,

I do not know the man I should avoid

So soon as that spare Cassius. He reads much;

He is a great observer ; and he looks

Quite through the deeds of men.

Hc lovcs no plays.

As thou dost, Antony; he hears no music :

Seldom he smiles, and smiles in such a sort.

As if he mock'd himself, and scorn'd his spirit,

That could be mov'd to smile at anything.

Such men as he be never at heart's ease,

Whilst they behold a greater than themselves

And therefore are they very dangerous.

I rather tell thee what is to be fear'd

Than what I fear; for always I am Caesar.[128]

We know hardly any passage more expressive of the genius of Shakespeare than this. It is as if he had been actually present, had known the different characters and what they thought of one another and had taken down what he heard and saw, their looks, words, and gestures, just as they happened.

The character of Mark Antony is farther speculated upon where the conspirators deliberate whether he shall fall with Caesar. Brutus is against it-

And of Mark Antony, think not of him:

For he can do no more than caesar's arm,

When caesar's head is off.[129]

Shakespeare has in this play and elsewhere shown the same penetration into political character and the springs of public events as into those of everyday life. For instance, the whole design of the conspirators to liberate their country fails from the generous temper and overweening confidence of Brutus in the goodness of their cause and the assistance of others. Thus it has always been, those who mean well themselves think well of others, and fall a prey to their security. Cassius was better cut out for a conspirator. His heart prompted his head. His watchful jealousy made him fear the worst that might happen and his irritability of temper added to his negative purpose. The vices are never so well employed as in combating one another. Tyranny and servility are to be dealt with after their own fashion : otherwise, they will triumph over those who spare them, and finally pronounce their funeral, as Antony did that of Brutus.

All the conspirators, save only he,

Did that they did in envy of great Caesar:

He only in a general honest thought

And common good to all, made one of them.[130]

The quarrel between Brutus and Cassius is managed in a masterly way. The dramatic fluctuation of passion, the calmness of Brutus, the heat of Cassius, are admirably described. The scene between Brutus and Portia, where she endeavours to extort the secret of the conspiracy from him, is conceived in the most heroical spirit and the burst of tenderness in Brutus -

You are my true and honourable wife,

As dear to me as are the ruddy drops

That visit my sad heart -

is justified by her whole behaviour. The interest which Portia takes in Brutus and that which Calpurnia takes in the fate of Caesar are described in the nicest precision. Mark Antony's speech over the dead body of Caesar has been justly admired for the mixture of pathos and artifice in it: that of Brutus certainly is not so good.

In *Hamlet*, brother murder, also incest and usurpation, in *Othello*, wife-murder issuing from jealousy; *King Lear,* filial ingratitude-the rebellion of children against their father. In *Macbeth,* it will be regicide-killing one's King, a king who is also one's relation, benefactor and unsuspecting guest. All these are crimes "most foul, strange and unnatural."[131] The storm is both the meaning and mystery of the Tragedy of *King Lear.* The abnormalities in human relationships are matched by the aberrations in Nature. Goneril the 'mental monotrosity', Regan the heartless fiend and the angelic Cordelia. If *King Lear* was read as an allegory (as J.I.M. Stewart reads *Othello* as one), we might see in Lear's action a purblind impetuous violent rejection of the souls translucent reality and a suicidal embrace of the diabolic intellect of Goneril and the unbridled malice of Regan till - released from these monsters he reawakens to the immaculate sattwik glory of Cordelia, his true self. Again John F. Damby sees *King Lear* "as a play dramatising the meaning of the single word 'Nature'; and the word, 'nature', 'natural' and 'unnatural' seems to occur over 40 times in the play as against 28 in *Macbeth* and 25 in *Timon.* There is 'benignant' nature pitted against 'Malignant' Nature - Lear against his wicked daughters, Gloucester against his unnatural son. Just as the Nature is perverted, Reason is often perverted too. The whole community, the cosmos itself, is also torn in two."[132]

*Timons* of Athens has obvious points of similarity with *King Lear*. Both seem to hinge on the theme of ingratitude. As Lear is deceived in his two elder daughters, So Timons is deceived in his demonstrative friends, Timons moves out of Athens, and seeks refuge in a cave. We have a feeling that even in his worst extravagances Lear is 'more sinned against than sinning' Timons aberrations - both during the days of has affluence and the days of his self exile - seem to be imperfectly motivated. Timons 'fault is essential love, essential nobility, unmixed with any restraining faculty of criticism' says G. Wilson Knight and when the crash comes, as Timon's love had been universal "now his hate is universal, its theme embraces every grade, age, sex, and profession. He hates the very shape, the 'semblance' of man."[133] But where as both Lear and Gloucester having (like Timon) Purblindly caused their own misery, try to work out their salvation through patient sufferance. In *Timon* of *Athens* both the protagonists fight back, each deploying the utmost resources he can command. While Alcibiades would have Athens destroyed with his arms, Timon with his curses wishes that the city were indeed so destroyed. Timons disillusion is caused by sundary individuals refusing to honour the simple demand of friendship and the vials of his wrath are poured on all humanity. Alcibiades disillusion is occasioned by the senate (no doubt made up of individuals who have thrived on permits, licenses and war contracts' while Alcibiades has been fighting their wars). ignoring his pleas and adding injury to insult by banishing him, and his revenge takes the form of his marching against Athens, resolved to destroy it (as Coriolanus, banished from Rome, returns with the determination to bring her to her knees). Timon's misanthropy is so absolute that he will not respond even to Alicibiades friendship, music, art, love and polished conversation to the cave of loneliness, hashness, downrightness, hate and barking speech.

*Macbeth* is the shortest, yet the most awe-inspiring and essentially 'tragic' of the quartet, for the issue between Good and Evil - an interesting struggle - is nowhere else so sharply presented; and so vivid indeed is the evocation of Evil here that Wilson Knight has called Macbeth "the Apoclalypse of Evil".[134] "Macbeth is distinguished by its simplicity"[135] says Bradley, "by grandeur in simplicity, no doubt, but still by simplicity".[136] There is only one dominant character: Macbeth; and Lady Macbeth herself has her importance only in relation to him. While the theme of the play is, on a superficial view, Macbeth's 'crime' and its consequences, more than the physical action and the visible consequences it is actually the condition of Macbeth's mind-how it countenanced and willed the crime and persisted in the career of crime and how it reacted to the crime and its outer consequences - that constitutes the real centre of interest in the play. Doubtless both Hamlet and Macbeth present a spectacle of waste, and neither of course can plead - as a Lear or even an Othello could - that he is more sinned against than sining, but the causes that occasion the 'waste' are different. John Drinkwater said that Macbeth is "the tragedy of unchecked will destroying itself"[137], where as Hamlet is "the tragedy of unready will wasting itself."[138] Roy Walker states that - "If Hamlet is a study of moral man in an immoral society. Macbeth is a study of immoral man in a moral society."[139] The reason why the drama grips us is that Macbeth is pushed - or allows himself to be pushed over the abyess, partly by his own propensities and partly by circumstances; and once that happens his fall acquires inevitably an accelerating momentum till he crashes at the bottom at last, despairing yet defiant still. He becomes more and more the vehicle of evil, the terror and the pity he inspires in us make him the tragic hero in excelsis "Macbeth is a thoroughly representative human being"[140], says G.R. Elliot, and the plays, "in its whole design, bodies forth the essence of the tragedy of mankind."[141] He is in this prototypical of over-confident but self-destroying humanity that too often hugs the vain hope that it can somehow both eat the cake and have it. To quote Rossiter.

> It is a great poem because the powers of the mind that it invokes are in all human beings.... It's 'theme' is not ambition, or sin, or guilt merely; but rather the equivocal nature of Nature: Nature in which all things exist, whether we call them good or evil; which builds and destroys: which has a natural order, to which man feels he belongs and is blessed in that hope; and which seems also to be moved by forces as potent and chaotic as the witches. [142]

Like Satan, like Adam and Eve, Macbeth had the freedom to opt for evil; even as they couldn't, he too couldn't annual the consequences. After Duncan's death, neither Macbeth nor Lady Macbeth is the person they had been before. They have murdered themselves "The witches and his own ambition have conquered him."[143] Says Bradley. In Shakespeare Lady Macbeth is so fully identified with her husband that her ambition is only on account of him. "There is not a trace of self-seeking in Lady Macbeth"[144], says R.G. Moulton; "throughout the play she is never found meditating upon what she is to gain by the crown; wife like, she has no sphere but the career of her husband"[145] Macbeth hankers after the crown: knows that only through murder he could get it immediately: yet shrinks from the act from motives like gratitude for recent gifts and the possibility of losing the good opinion of "all sorts of people". Had Macbeth said "I won't do it, for it is morally wrong"[146], Lady Macbeth would doubtless have accepted the position, But his reasons are not so fundamental: they seem only to proceed from his timidity or sentimentality or fear of failure 'Hence Lady Macbeth thinks that it is her duty as wife to help him to overcome his timidity, buoy up his courage, and exorcise away his sentimental fancies. She is no more 'moral' than Macbeth, but neither is she arch villian.

From I.i. to III. iv. it is a single gigantic wave of psychic energy achieving glorious poetic transmutation: we are carried along the current of Shakespeare's passion and poetry carried us along, -and there is no parallel for this any where in Shakespearian tragedy.

Shakespeare obviously set himself an impossible task when he wrote *Antony and Cleopatra*. The issue or theme is supposed to be love against honour (or duty). Shakespeare dares to reverse the accepted priorities by giving his hero and heroine dimensions other than those of worldly wisdom, cool calculation or moral correctitude. Donald A. Stauffer declares that the writing of the play itself constitutes "a moral act of judgement", and he adds further :

> Deliberately he (Shakespeare) takes four steps:
>
> he must demonstrate that 'reason' is
>
> mistaken: he must belittle or blacken the
>
> cause of empire; he must make passion larger than
>
> the world; and he must-spiritualise and ennoble an
>
> historical liaison until it appears as the true quality
>
> of love. [147]

For Cleopatra who has after a lifetime of coquetry, contrariety and sensuality learned at last the meaning of the Absolute that is Love, her death is a vindication of her whole variegated and maddening life : for in her end is all her yesterdays, and the serpent of Nile has been transformed into the phoenix, the rare Arabian bird who has gone up in a tongue of mutual flame, her Antony.

'Shakespearian Tragedy' may be made to cover the four supreme tragedies *Hamlet, Othello. King Lear, Macbeth* and four Roman plays - *Titus Andronicus, Julius Caesar, Antony* so and *Cleopatra* and *Coriolanus*, the two History plays - *Richard II* and *Richard III*, and the two Mediterranean tragedies - *Romeo* and *Juliet* and *Timon of Athens*.

Lily Cambell in her *Shakespeare's Tragic Heroes,* describes Hamlet as a tragedy of grief, Othello of jealousy, Lear of wrath and old age, and Macbeth as a study in fear. They all are a mirror of passion. Irving Ribnor, in his A 'patterns in Shakespearian Tragedy' describes - Hamlet as being built on the pattern of growth, Othello & King Lear on that of moral choice and regeneration respectively. Timon and Macbeth as patterning the operation of Evil, and the last two Roman plays as embodying the final paradox that what destroys is also what confer uniqueness or greatness. Duthie thinks that "the fundamental order disorder theme is found in all the tragedies."[148] *Hamlet* is the play of the introspective intellect, disillusionment and release *Macbeth* is the play of the Dark, it's dissipation and a transcendence. *Lear* is the play of the dualities of gratitude and ingratitude, a disillusionment and a release. *Othello* is the play of deception, its dissolution and a transcedence into Truth.

Ever since the chronology of Shakespeare plays defined itself with sufficient clarity to push *Pericles, Cymbeline. The Winter's Tale, The Tempest and Henry VIII* to the last few years of his active career as a dramatist.

The recurring theme in most of the plays in royalty lost and recovered, order destroyed and restored. There is breaking up and ultimate re-making- of intimate family ties; 'Kith and Kin' are Sundered, torn far apart, and are finally reunited. 'Sorrow is' - as poignant as in the tragedies but beyond the dark tunnel there is sun at last the clear light of a new dawn. The themes of the last plays have no doubt a superficial resemblance to those of some of earlier plays : 'Jealousy' figures in *Cymbeline* and *The Winter's Tale*, as it does in *Troilus And Cressida* and *Othello*, though with a difference. Never the less, those last plays have a happy ending; the shortcomings of the past are made good in the present, and the future seems to open out endless vistas of possibility. The supposed dead are brought back to life, the enemies of yesterday are happily reconciled for pardon is the word to all and joy is offered to everybody. Since these plays seem to be neither tragedies nor comedies properly speaking, they have been variously called as Tragi-comedies, Romances, or Reconciliation plays. Tragi-comedies because the plays seem at first sight to move perilously towards tragic climaxes, but changing the direction suddenly and making briskly towards the heaven of comedy. Dramatist does seem to be "occupied with forgiveness, reconciliation, the adjustment, under Heaven, of goodwill among men."[149] In the last plays, grace becomes an active participant in human affairs. The preservation of Mariana, Imogen, Perdita and Miranda form imminent of death-their deliverance from death or dishonour to new life and joy the twilight glory of reconciliation following the fury and frenzy of the severances and feuds the triumph of innocence over its enemies, of Good over Evil-Exemplify the operation of the grace of Grace. In his last plays, Shakespeare seems to ask himself whether crime or injury, instead of being punished should be followed by repentance, forgiveness and reconciliation. For example the saintly King in *3 Henry VI* who is prepared to pardon even his murderer. Richard Isabella too, schooled in the christian ethic during her noviciate, is willing to plead for Angelo's life, though her first reaction is to pluck out his eyes. Absolute love also as in Desdemona can forget the injury and forgive the person who has just insulted and injured beyond repair. But Shakespeare felt, as we all feel, that for average humanity forgiving at the very moment of the injury is impossible. An eye for an eye, a tooth for a tooth is the more likely and more normal reaction. Time is the infallible healer of all wounds but it is essential that we should give Time a chance. The pattern here is : crime or injury an interval which facilitates repentance on the part of the injurer and re-thinking on the part of the injured and eventual disseverance and reconciliation. This is roughly the pattern followed in Shakespeare's last plays as well Cymbeline has injured Belarius, and Belarius has injured Cymbeline; Leontes has injured Hermione and all but killed her; Alonso has injured Prospero and Miranda. But there is a time gap between the causing of the injury and the next meeting. Circumstances have changed in the mean time, the mind is receptive to the invasion of grace, and so forgiveness, reunion and reconstruction follow as a natural course. Tragedy having received the impact of the grace of grace, remoulds itself into Divine comedy.

This close connection between the Tragedies and Romances have been noticed, and indeed emphasised by more than one critic Tillyard thinks that the Romances only "develop the final phase of the tragic pattern."[150] John Vyvyan also finds in these plays a pattern of regeneration."[151] *Hamlet* is thus contrasted with *Measure for Measure, Othello* with *The winter's Tale,* and *Macbeth* with *The Tempest.*

Sri Aurobindo's Career as a dramtist spans about twenty six years *The Witch of Ilni*, his fist attempt at drama was written in 1891 and *Vasavadutta*, his last play, in 1916 During this period, he produced eleven plays. Out of them, five are full length dramas and six are incomplete. Critics like S.K. Prasad, have gone to the extent of saying that Sri Aurobindo's dramatic genius "can be favourably compared with the Shakespearian as well as Kalidasa."[152] This is no mean tribute. When Sri Aurobindo began to write plays in English, Indian drama in English was yet to get recognition. Prof. M.K. Naik observes; "If Indian writing in English is the Cindrella of literature in English, Indian drama in English has always been, along with criticism, one of the twin Cindrellas of Indian writing in English."[153] Of the three forms of Indian English literature, that is, poetry, fiction and drama the last has registered the least progress till date. A perusal of Sri Aurobindo's own plays reveals that they do not merely depict life as it is seen on the surface. The picture of them is made richer by the vision and creative imagination of the dramatist. Sri Aurobindo's awareness of the dramatists role as a creator rather than a mere projector of gross forms of life is reflected in his Perseus the Deliverer, his most representative play. However, what he says here in the prefatory note of the play is applicable not only to it but, to a great extent, to the other plays as well. In the preface he says:

In this piece the ancient legend has been divested of its original character of a heroic myth; it is made the nucleus round which there could grow the scenes of a romantic story of human temperament and life impulses on the Elizabethan model.[154]

Sri Aurobindo adopted for his plays the Elizabethan model of drama perfected by the genius of Shakespeare. Modelling his plays exclusively on Shakespearean drama, Sri Aurobindo unfortunately imposed crippling limitations to his dramatic talent; while in 'Savitri' he boldly experimented with age old epic conventions. "In the large whispering gallery resounding with Shakespearean echoes which his plays in the main appear to be, Sri Aurobindo's distinctive voice is scarely heard as effectively as in other forms. It is said that even in handling purely Indian material in *Prince of Edur* and *Vasavadutta*, the dramatist could not throw off the yoke of Shakespeare, with the result that his characters seem to think, speak and act less like authentic Indians than like Elizabethan personages in Indian garb.[155] There is no denying that Sri Aurobindo adopts the Shakespearean model of drama but he cannot be charged with giving the go by to the Indian ethos just because he borrows the Shakespearean dramatic form. Prof. Naik, who somehow hears "persistent and loud Shakespearean echoes in character, incident, and even dialogue."[156] In Sri Aurobindo's plays, whether the influence of Shakespeare helped or harmed Sri Aurobindo, whether his plays should be dismissed as mere "pseudo Elizabethan drama"[157] or commended as entirely Shakespearean, is a debatable issue. But the fact remains that the influence of Shakespeare is there. As for the influence of the Indian classical tradition of drama, one influence at least is very obvious. In keeping with the Indian tradition, he gave happy ending to most of his plays. Scholars wonder why, with all his poetic gift and insight, Sri Aurobindo was not able to write a tragedy, for *Rodogune* is one. But his plays are predominantly happy ending plays. He seems to believe that "there can be dramatic creation of the greatest kind without a solution in death, sorrow, over whelming calamity or the tragic return of Karma-."[158] What he says below on Hindu Drama shows that this might have been the result of the influence of classical Sanskrit drama on him, which has demonstrated very well that, "in order to be great, it is not necessary for it to be tragedy.[159] He says: "The vital law governing Hindu poetics is that it does not seek to represent life and character primarily or for their own sake; its aim is fundamentally aesthetic: by the delicate and harmonius rendering to awaken the aesthetic sense of the onlooker and gratify it by moving and subtly observed pictures of human feeling; I did not attempt to seize man's spirit by the hair and drag it out into a storm of horror and pity and fear and return it to him drenched, beaten and shuddering. To the Hindu it would have been a savage and inhuman spirit that could take any aesthetic pleasure in the suffering of an Oedipus or a Duchess of Malfi or in the tragedy of a Macbeth or an Othello."[160]

He gives three reasons for it: first, "the divine tenderness of the Hindu nature; secondly, the influence of Budha; and finally, the principle that aesthetic and intellectual pleasure is the object of all poetic art."[161] Then he says: "The Hindu mind therefore shrank not only from violence, horror and physical tragedy, the Elizabethan stock-in-trade, but even from the tragic in moral problems which attracted the Greek mind; still less could it have consented to occupy itself with the problems of disease, neurosis and spiritual medicology generally which are the staple of modern drama and fiction. An atmosphere of romantic beauty, a high urbanity and a gracious equipoise of the feelings, a perpetual confidence in the sunshine and the flowers are the essential spirit of a Hindu play; pity and terror are used to awaken the feelings, but not to lacerate them, and the drama must close on the note of joy and peace; the clouds are only admitted to make more beautiful the glad sunlight from which all came and into which all must melt away."[162]

The analyses above though dispassionate, contains in the writer's choice of words subtle hints of his preference for the Hindu drama. His sympathies with it get reflected to some extent in his plays as well. Though they resemble the Elizabethan drama in form, in spirit they have greater affinity with the Hindu drama. It is worthwhile to notice that his stories deviate from their originals in an obvious attempt to attain greater kinship with Indian spirit by eliminating unnecessary violence and death. Sri Aurobindo says further while comparing the Hindu and the Elizabethan models of drama:

"It has been noticed that the Hindu drama presents many remarkable points of contact with the Elizabethan. In the mixture of prose and poetry, in the complete freedom with which time and scenery vary, in the romantic life-likeness of the action, in the mixture of comedy with serious matter, in the gorgeousness of the poetry and the direct appeal to the feelings, both these great literatures closely resemble each other. Yet the difference, though they do not strike us so readily as the similarities, are more vital and go deeper; for the similarities are of form, the difference of spirit. The Elizabethan drama was a great popular literature which aimed at a vigorous and realistic presentation of life and character such as would please a mixed and not very critical audience; it had therefore the strength and weakness of great popular literature; its strength was an abounding vigour in passion and action and an unequal grasp upon life; its weakness was a crude violence, imperfection and bungling in workmanship combined with a tendency to exaggeration, horrors and monstrosites. The Hindu drama, on the contrary, was written by accomplished men of culture for an educated, often a courtly audience with an eye to an elaborate and well-understood system of poetics."[163]

With such view of the Elizabethan drama, Sri Aurobindo, one would think, will be less amenable to the influence of at least its spirit than to the influence of the spirit of the Hindu drama. The view is likely to get added strength from his following observation on the two modes: "If we expect a Beautiful *White Devil* or a *Jew of Malta* from the Hindu dramatist, we shall be disappointed; he deals not in these splendid or horrible masks. If we come to him for a *Lear* or a *Macbeth*, we shall go discontented; for these also are sublimities which belong to cruder civilization and more barbarous national types; in worse crimes and utmost sufferings as well as happiness and virtue, the Aryans was more civilized and temperate, less crudely enormous than the hard earthy African peoples whom in Europe he only half moralised...."[164]

True to the Hindu tradition Sri Aurobindo scrupulously avoided creating scenes and characters that might have in any way polluted 'the moral atmosphere of the soul.[165] He represented not the cruder civilizations and more barbarous national types but the Aryan race which, according to him, was more civilized and temperate. This is one explanation for his deviation from the original story in *Rodogune*. In the original story Cleopatra kills her own husband and son to satisfy her lust for power and for revenge and instigates her sons to kill Rodogune, their beloved. Sri Aurobindo's typical Indian temperament would not permit such crude violence, such horror and monstrosity in his play. "To the sattwic turn of his temperament and imaginations studies of depravity or tragic endings of plays were less congenial than were stories of human life with a closing air of peace and calm."[166] So, his Cleopatra was made more humane and compassionate.

Sri Aurobindo combined in his temperament both tradition and contemporaneity. To him the myth and magic element in the *Kathasarit sagar* version of *Udayan-Vasavadutta* legend therefore, did not have much appeal As such, he trimmed off the parts of the story that were not likely to prove palatable to the modern taste.

A distinctive feature of the plays of Sri Aurobindo is that the dramatist in them revives or recasts old themes and legends instead of inventing new stories for them. This is no cover up for Sri Aurobindo's inability to invent his own stories. It rather emanates from his belief foreshadowed in his fragment of a play *The Maid in the Mill*. Antonio, one of the characters in the fragment, while putting forth arguments in favour of the choice of an old story for a play, says that an old story facilitates a quicker and better comprehension of the play where as a new plot hampers its appreciation:

— Then if the plot is new,  
The mind engrossed with incidents, omits.  
To take the breath of flowers and lingering shade  
In hurrying with the stream. But the plot known,  
It is at leisure and may cull in running  
Those delicate, scarcely-heeded strokes which lost  
Perfection's disappointed.[167]

He reiterates the same view, but from a different angle:

Being old besides  
The subject occupies creative labour  
To make old new, The other's but invention,  
A frail thing, though a gracious:[168]

So he concludes:

He's creator  
Who greatly handles great material,  
Calls order out of the abundant deep,  
Not who invents sweet shadows out of air.[169]

Not caring much for originality in respect of plots of his plays, he borrowed them from "the abundant deep"[170] of sources like the Greek mythology, the Kathasaritsagara, the Arabian Nights Entertainments etc. For him originality lay also in calling "order of the abundant deep"[171] , in carving out from the oceanic sources well-chiselled plots and impregnating them with new meaning and vision. 'Artistic economizing'[172] may be considered as another reason for Sri Aurobindo's practice, like that of Shakespeare, of stealing 'bodily his plots.'[173] Mr. K. Viswanathan points out on P.180 of letters.

Sri Aurobindo casually remarks that Shakespeare stole bodily his plots. It is said to be artistic economizing, Steal 'Muthos' and reserve your powers for the poetry. If you exhaust your powers on the invention of a plot you are a spent bullet when you come to the treatment of it... The stealing of the story does not diminish the poets' stature. The poets' excellence is revealed in what he does with the stolen property. If he-converts his theft into something rich and rare his crime is venial not venal. Just as in love and war stealing is no crime in poetic creation too. What we call originality, writes Prof. Lewes, then does not consist so much in the creation of something wholly new as in this repristination (to use Browing's word) of something old (convention and Revold, P.64)."[174] The last word on originality is implied in Anand Vardhanan's

Madhumasa iva drumah

"Genius is like the miracle of spring."[175]

Sri Aurobindo had read the best in many languages and had, it seems, developed a unique familiarity with different countries and peoples, and a capacity to identify himself with what ever people he chose to write about. So, unregardful of climes, cultures and people, he moved almost through the world in search of themes for his plays. It was only natural *In Perseus the Deliverer* he went to Greece, to Bagdad and *Bassora in the Viziers of Bassora,* to Norway in *Eric;* to Britain in *The House of Brut, The Birth of Sin, Achab* and *Esarhaddon* and *The Witch of Ilni,* and to Spain in *The Maid in the Mill.* For Vasavadutta and Prince of Edur he looked homewards. In fact, Sri Aurobindo is a dramatist depicting not only an age and culture, but a rainbow variety of ages and cultures.

The story of the play, The Viziers of Bassora was choosen from Sri Aurobindo's favourite book The Arabian Nights, his first full length dramatic creation. Another factor contrubuting to the choice seems to have been the amazing variety and novelty in the action of the tales as a result of which their dramatisation needed not "much of imaginative manipulation."[176] Though he borrows stories for his plays readymade for what he calls 'artistic economizing'[177], Sri Aurobindo incorporates changes in them with a view of bringing his themes into sharp focus. In the case of *The Viziers of Bassora,* the only change made in the original tale are a few alterations in names and their spellings and addition of some characters to the story to add to the dramatic effect. The creation of Fareed, son of the bad Vizier in the play is intended to provide a contrast to the character of Nureddene, son of the good Vizier. He serves also the purpose of accounting for the malignity of his father which seems rather motiveless in the original tale. The sub-plot in the original tale. The sub-plot involving Doonya and Murad is another addition to the tale which helps the growth of the main plot. If Doonya acts as a secret agent of love between Nureddene and Anice-Aljalice and as the artificer of the plan to unite them, Murad helps Nureddene at very critical moment, thus furthering the cause of good in the play. The other new characters born of the dramatist's imagination are Khatoon, wife of Almuene, Balkis and Mymoona, slave-girls, and Harkoos, the Egyptian eunuch in Ibn Sawy's household some of the characters of the original tale have been presented in the play in different light. Haroun al Rasheed, the Caliph, for example, is projected by Sri Aurobindo as a noble Virtuous man who, takes on himself the role of the protector of good and destroyer of evil. In a clear departure from the tale, he does not show Anice-Aljalice as living with the Caliph in Baghdad as his mistress, for this would not be in keeping with his fatherly image. Alzayni in the play conspires to kill the Caliph when the latter visits Bassora after issuing orders to depose the former and elevate Nureddene to Bassora's Kingship in persuance of his policy to punish the bad and protect the good. This is another change in the tale at the dramatist's hand.

A few other minor changes in the action of the play may be noted. Unlike his counterparts in the tale, Nureddene in the play does not go to Bassora as king. Similarly unlike in the tale, the main characters in the play do not set out to Bagdad, but the Caliph himself comes down to Bassora to settle all matters there. Then in the tale, the good Vizier falls ill and dies, exhorting his son to be faithful to Allah and Anis But Ibn Sawy, the Virtuous Vizier in the play does not die. He remains on the scene of Bassora throughout except for a brief period of stay abroad due to a royal assignment. This play depicts at least three sets of characters each set containing characters diagonally opposed in nature and disposition. There are the wild youths (Nureddene and Fareed), the old Viziers (Ibn Sawy and Almuene) and the rulers (Caliph Haroun and King Alzayni). If Nureddene, Ibn Sawy and the Caliph represent virtue, Fareed Almuene and the king are representatives of vice. The inevitable struggle that goes on for quite some time between the bright and the dark natures appear to darken the atmosphere of the play only temporarily, for unlimitedly the forces of good are victorious over the forces of evil and the play ends with glad sunlight. Prof. K.R.S. Iyenger, holds a different opinion in the matter. He says: "For the rest, it is not necessary to discover in the play any deep 'purpose', except that youth, beauty, love, charity, poetry, wit, honour are among the great blessings of life, and to foster them, not misuse them is the way of wisdom... The story of the two Viziers, Ibn Sawy and Almuene, and of their sons, Nureddene and Fareed, can almost be read as a morality play; but no! the poetry of the play and the comic spirit that presides over it permit no such critical excrescence."[178] The story of the conflict of bright and dark natures in this play cannot be read as a Morality play. Morality play deals with ethical problems in which the chief conflict is between good and evil. From the view point of the clash of good and evil, the play may be regarded as morality play because in it the conflict has been presented with considerable sharpness. But the conflict here is not intended to highlight its ethical connotations so much as the outcome of the conflict and its significance. Sri Aurobindo writes this play without having any moral axe to grind. He writes it to give a religious message: the message of faith. It is this message that is contained in the numerous serious meaning passages in the play without which it will become "a funny romantic comedy glistening with a Shakespearean abandon of world-power".[179] The Play abounds in love, song and laughter due to which it may be considered as a brilliant Romantic comedy, but still it is a Romantic comedy of the Aurobindonian type where some liberty seems to have been taken with the tradition regarding purpose of such a play.

Even as Romantic comedy, it is not confined to "a love affair that involves a beautiful and idealised heroine"[180] in which the course of love "does not run smooth, but overcomes all difficulties to end in a happy union."[181] It is "full of youthful exuberance and gaiety."[182] has plenty of humour and song, but something in addition to that, and something more important. In a beautiful summing up of the play Jesse Roarke says:

"Set in Bassora and Bagdad, it potrays the conflict of good and evil in various contexts, manners and degrees. There is malignity, and there is good hearted indulgent weakness, there is deformity and scheming and corruption, and there is high mindedness and uprightness and faith in Allah, in his justice and in the wisdom of the acceptance of fate: a blind, conventional acceptance, and something more living and profound... There is evil in the play, and darkness; but all expressed in bright words and in a way that we cannot really believe in it, as a positive and dangerous force: God reigns, and his vicegerent is at work: all is eventually set right with the coming forward of the Caliph who is wandering and circulating in disguise, "the good Haroun al Rasheed."[183] Thus in the comic play Sri Aurobindo weaves a purpose which is not serious enough to be called "deep" but is a "purpose" all the same. This applies to Sri Aurobindo and his work also and it explains why even in a play like this, a play of youth, beauty, song and laughter, a religious truth is embedded. by the faith which is reiterated through the bulk of his literary works is faith in God, faith in man, in life and laws of the universe that must inevitably lead man to divinity, his ultimate goal and destiny. It is faith in the essential nobility of man, and in the ultimate victory of good over evil. It is this faith in its various shades that echoes through the entire work of Sri Aurobindo. In this play he pleads the case of Virtue as against that of vice by presenting in it contrasting Characters like Ibn Sawy and Almuene, Nureddene and Fareed, King Alzayni and the Caliph, and by showing that the dark nature are crushed under weight of their black deeds where as the bright natures, after temporary set backs, trials and tribulations, ride the crest to land in a world of peace and sunshine. A brief survey of character in those opposite sets may be instructive in the context, particularly if we also look at the proceeds of their respective actions and natures. But, whereas the miseries and failure in lives of noble characters should be seen as the fire purifying their personality, as the test of their faith in virtue, or as its price, the miseries befalling the ignoble characters must be viewed as the penalty for their vice. Alumene's arrogance, his dark and dangerous mind, his malice, jealousy, revengefulness and tyrannical manners, beget him only hatred, causing him to be called a satan or Iblis out of hell Even his wife is not happy with him and she makes no secret of her aversion for the man. Nureddene, the wild handsome roister, is Ibn Sawy's son who "repeats the father But with a dash of quicker, wilder blood"[184] His past time seems to be chasing girls and tasting different wines. But the inherent goodness of Nureddene gets full flowering after the experience of love. It "brings about a progressive chastening of his temperament and releases the noble virtues and gives them their full paly.[185] With admirable candour he admits to Anice how he has erred so far, and seems to resolve firmly not to wander any more. His subsequent behaviour shows that he has gained considerably in strength of character and is able to prove his mettle. His development from an "errant gadabout", "a vagabond scapegrace." and a wanton youth into a sober matured nature is largely as a result of love, the alchemist that can turn dross into gold. Precisely the same purpose is served by showing characters like Fareed getting their deserved punishment. Fareed is like Almuene "as the young baboon is to the adult ape".[186] "a misformed urchin full of budding evil."[187] He has been spoiled by his over indulgent father. Reckless, rude and wild, he is devoid of the touch of humanness. This Caliban like creature hankers after money, curses, and plans the murder of, his own parents, with his strange ideas about education Almuene only raises up the hell that lurks within his son when he urges him on to wickedness and villainy in the name of not killing the natural man but only cultivating on the plan that nature has mapped. Fareed and Nureddene are contrasting characters, each throwing the other in bold relief. The tragic end of Fareed is well contrasted with Nureddene's prosperity though it is attained after considerable travail and trauma, the usual price of virtue. So, by depicting such diametrically opposite temperaments with basically opposed orientations of energies of life and then showing their respective fates, Sri Aurobindo with his Messianic power here develops the theme to affirm faith in virtue and in man's essential goodness. As usual he shows that in "the clash of good and bad, good inevitably emerges victorius."[188] In fact, good himself sees to it that dark, forces are defeated and virtue is restored to its position of triumph and eternal glory.

The *Viziers of Bassora,* though a Romantic comedy, thematically has religious overtones A significant difference between Sri Aurobindo's *The Viziers of Bassora* and the comedies of Shakespeare is that the former is characterized by a religious atmosphere which is conspicuous by its absence in the latter. Mr. Seetaram in this regard says:

"His (Shakespeare's) play are characterised by the absence of religion. They have more of the Renaissance humanism and zest for life. But the Viziers presents in bold relief characters with a well defined mental love for God and acceptance of His will..."[189] The theme of faith in the play shows Sri Aurobindo's belief that the world is governed by God who is All powerful, All knowing, All Merciful, All loving. He has firm belief that man's future is secure and there is every hope for humanity for a happy and bright future. Sri Aurobindo is not particularly disturbed by the manifestations of Evil in the world. Pain and evil is in his opinion not so real as it appear to be. According to him, "the universal and overpowering instinct of self-preservation" is because of "the normal satisfaction of existence."[190] The theme in *The Viziers of Bassora* anticipates Sri Aurobindo's Philosophical work *The life Divine*."[191] Through its plot, characterization and the entire setting, the play unfolds the theme of faith. Sri Aurobindo suggests the cheers and tears are the warp and woof of man's life. To be able to over-come the difficulties and sorrows punctuating his life, man must plead for God's fatherly love and kindness, for these, rather than justice can bring him peace and harmony. The play has another theme of love, though a minor one. Love is presented by Sri Aurobindo, as a benevolent force which destroys evil and conflict and paves the way for harmony and peace. *Vasavadutta, Prince of Edur. Eric, The Viziers of Bassora,* etc., can be cited as specific cases. In *The viziers of Bassora Anice-Aljalice,* like the other women in the play, contributes to harmony, sweetness and light to life around her through the radiation of love. The queen among all female characters there, she is a "nonpareil" in beauty, wit and all other accomplishments. A glance at her and Nureddene, the handsome wanton youth falls in love with her. More than her matchless beauty, what characterises Anice truly is sweetness of her temper. Sri Aurbindo sets out the all conquering influence of love through the conversion of Nureddene Significantly, Nureddene is perhaps the only character in the play, with the possible exceptions of Murad and Ajebe, who is shown undergoing changes with the development of the theme of love. All other character are flat. In this play the theme of evolution is conspicuously missing. The explanation of this fact may be that it is the first complete play of Sri Aurobindo written when he was not very conscious of the idea of evolution as he gradually became. In other plays conflict leads to transformation of character, suggesting evolution. Here Sri Aurobindo is preoccupied with the theme of victory of good over evil.

Anice - Aljalice's character assumes great significance also in view of her songs in the play. These songs have a profound significance as they are closely related to the inner meaning of the play. As Mr. Seetaraman points out: "The interpretative vision in a Romantic comedy reveals itself in and through love, laughter and song which are its warp and woof".[192] This is very true of *The Viziers of Bassora.* The song here reflect the theme of the play and underline its interpretative vision. Apart from their 'romantic ardour', they are to be valued also as the mirror of the playwrights view on "love, life and god."[193] one of the songs of Anice is about its power to ennoble man, to make him grow in God's image. Such love should rise above the pure physical level. True love helps man transcend his ego and teaches him surrender and self-sacrifice which eventually lead to self-knowledge of his true divine self, he is lead to divinity, Nureddene, Ajebe and Murad, are three lovers in The Viziers of Bassora, they are better human beings than Almuene, Fareed and Alzayni because the formers dissolve to some extent their egoes in their vital love for their beloved Anice, Balkis and Doonya, where as the latters are centred in their ego. The nobility of Ibn sawy and the Caliph may again be scribed to love, though of a different kind - it is the love of God. There is another song which highlights a fact interwoven in the story of the play. Good triumphs over evil, but only after a fierce struggle resulting into a lot of pain and suffering. Pain and suffering however are preconditions and price of man's growth in the divine image. So, from the fire of suffering alone one emerges pure gold of a man. Anice sings;

Heart of mine, oh heart impatient,
Thou must learn to wait and weep.
Wherefore wouldst thou go on beating
When I bade thee hush and sleep?
Thou who wert of life so fain,
Didst thou know not, life was pain?[194]

The way to peace in life is an attitude of "patient resignation" to God's will, immense unshakable. Faith in His Justice and Mercy. These give man strength and courage to meet any challenges.

*Perseus the Deliverer* is the only play of Sri Aurobindo to appear in his life time. It was published in 1942. It was in order to project the problems of his slave motherland and its aspirations for the future, that Sri Aurobindo wrote on themes like that of *Perseus the Deliverer*. When Sri Aurobindo chose Perseus Andromeda myth for his play, he wanted to weave into it a new meaning, make it a vehicle for his philosophy and give it an immediacy of purpose. While treating the theme afresh Sri Aurobindo has taken liberties with the locale, action and spirit of the existing myth In the prefatory note to the play he himself says;

> In this piece the ancient legend has been divested of its original character of heroic myth; ... The country in which the action is located is a Syria of romance, not of history... the creative imagination is its sole disposer and arranger; fantasy reigns sovereign; the names of ancient countries and peoples are brought in only as a fringe of a decorative background; anachronisms romp in ..., ideas and associations from all climes epochs mingle: myth, romance and realism make up a single whole.[195]

Sri Aurobindo changes names, characters and places, creates fresh scenes, introduces life-like, full-blooded characters and strings cosmic visions and dimensions in such a way and to such an extent that "nothing but merely the outline of the old story remains while everything else becomes completely Aurobindonian"[196]

The Playwright does not intend to make the play the story of

Perseus, "the heroic miracle-worker"[197] and Andromeda, "a paragon of passive sufferance."[198] His purpose is to transmute into "a romantic story of human temperament and life impulses on the Elizabethan model."[199] With the shift in emphasis in the play from the heroic deeds of Perseus to the drama in the inner world of man's mind, a recasting of the play on the Elizabethan model is not uncalled for. As Dr. Prema Nandkumar says: "Sri Aurobindo had no doubt desired to render anew the myth (of perseus and Andromeda) but had to avoid the pseudo-romantic stance of kingsley, consciously he chose the Elizabethan model, for the five act structure affords the greatest scope for the imaginative recreation of an age that is now past."[200] Another change of consequence to be noticed in the play is the character of Andromeda. Due to an altogether different conception of her character and its presentation in a different light, the story of Perseus becomes, in Sri Aurobindo's play, "Primarily the story of Andromeda whose deliverer he (Perseus) eventually becomes,"[201] Unlike in the Greek legend, where she is a passive figure, "a patient sufferer", Andromeda in Sri Aurobindo's plays is full of individuality-loving, compassionate, bold, self sacrificing, ready to revolt against the dire gods of dire cult. The "paragon of passive sufferance" in the old myth in transformed into a paragon of love and self sacrifice, into pity incarnate.

The Purpose with which Sri Aurobindo's mind was preoccupied at the time of writing *Perseus the Deliverer* lies a suggestion for one of its prominent themes deliverance from captivity. The other conspicuous theme in the play emantates from his philosophy of man's evolutionary destiny, his rising above the lower self and manifesting the higher divine self. Sri Aurobindo's choice of theme of deliverance for his play in the opening decade of the present century was of great relevance to the then conditions of India. The unique relevance of Andromeda myth, embodying the theme of deliverance from capitivity, to the political situation of India, when *Perseus the Deliverer* was being written, seems to be the most probable and a valid reason for the choice of the myth for the play. The political implications of the theme to be projected dramatically through the play were obviously great and far reaching for the capitive India and her people.

The symbolic signifance of the story of Andromeda and Perseus stands out due to the way Sri Aurobindo presents it in *Perseus the Deliverer.* Andromeda, the Syrian princes, has committed sacrilege in the eyes of the primitive people of Syria who believe in a primitive cult and worship dark gods like Poseidon. Moved by pity for Smerdas, a Babylonian victim of shipwreck to be sacrificed at the altar of Poseidon, she frees him and thus incurs the fiercest wrath of the Sea-God. According to Polydaon, the priest, she is responsible for all the havoc the furious god causes in Syria. Instead of showing mercy to helpless victims of shipwreck, the Syrians made them bleed to quench the blood thirst of their dark-violent gods. Tyranus is also one such Victim in the play. Praxilla as a typical Syrian has no mercy to show to people who die in Shipwreck if they are not Syrians. She rather enjoys the sight of their death. She also advises Andromeda not to waste her tears over the death of the foreigners. But Andromeda does not like it. She says-

I'll not be older!
I will not understand; I only know
That men are heartless, I only know
That men are heartless and your gods most cruel
I hate them![202]

She is moved to pity, her heart overflowing with compassion for the poor helpless men who are soon to be killed according to the cruel laws of Syria on dark Poseidon's altar.

They shall not die.
It is a shame, a cruel cold injustice

---

My sungod saved them, they belong to him
Not to your hateful gods. They are his and mine.
I will not let you kill them.[203]

Andromeda wants to save the life of the captives at any cost only to cool the anguish of pity in her heart. She will be at peace if she is able to save their lives. If in the act she dies, she will be still at peace. Nothing dissuades her from what she intends. She frees Smerdas, who was left to his fate even by her Sun-God, Perseus. She does not care a fig for the consequences for her action. She is accused of impious sacrilege, the penalty for which is death. Andromeda is chained to a rock to be devoured by sea-monsters. Polydaon gloats in his victory. Sri Aurobindo symbolically shows the plight of India with demons on her breast and sucking her life blood. The British rulers revelled like Polydaon in acts of mean cruelty and cold injustice to the suffering millions of India. Those, who, with their hearts fired by patriotic self-sacrifice, plunged into the national struggle for freedom, were subjected to means of torture cruel beyond words. Their crime, like Andromeda's was to rise in revolt against forces of barbarism that would not brook any attempt at freedom by those they have enslaved. Through his various characters Sri Aurobindo, Perhaps, wanted to inspire in the hearts of his countrymen the faith that India's freedom is a certainty, that even the gods will it and are ready to intervene to effect it sooner than later. When the play was written, for Sri Aurobindo "it was the time of 'country first, humanity afterwards and the rest nowhere'.[204] A Perseus to deliver Mother India also will soon come, the grisly foe will be killed, and she will be allowed to face the world with smiles as ever before this is the optimism *Perseus the Deliverer* was intended to generate in the heart of his readers of pre-Independence days. The readers of the play must have seen India in Andromeda.

Similarly, Perseus must have symbolised the forces of freedom represented by Indian political leadership. Polydaon and Poseidon for Sri Aurobindo's reader must have been symbols of the British Tyrannical forces and the British crown respectively. The ultimate fate of Andromeda must have suggested to the Indian people similar happy fate of their motherland too.

The theme of love has also been interwoven in the play though as a minor one. This is clear when we analyse the motivating force behind the act of Andromeda in freeing Smerdas and the act of Perseus himself in setting Adnromeda free. Perseus, no doubt, saves Smerdas and Tyranus, the hapless victims of shipwreck in the Syrian sea, from "the dead surges of the inhuman flood"[205]

But he refuses to defend them against Iolaus and his soldiers for the merchants are not prepared to fight in self-defence on the other hand Smerdas, an extremely greedy and cowardly creature does not fight to defend his life, but expects Tyranus or Perseus to do it for him. Some time after the two have been taken prisoners for being sacrificed at the altar of Poseidon, Perseus happens to meet them once again He is impressed by the self-composure of Tyranus. So he shears his chains, for his is a soul worth saving, But Smerdas to him is a "sordid treacherous thing of fear,"[206] trying to bribe him. Therefore, he does not feel inclined to sever his chains and leave Smerdas contemptuously to his lot. But Andromeda's attitude to weak and suffering human being is different. She takes it on herself to free Smerdas out of sheer compassion So, she frees Smerdas and rises higher, by the act, even than her sungod, Perseus. This is because of love overflowing her heart. Love is not born yet in the heart of Perseus. Though he is very powerful, his heart is seized by hate for men like Smerdas. But he is quick to rescue Andromeda even though the act means open defiance of the edicts of Syrian gods. The reason is clear. The response of his power to Andromeda's plight is markedly different because his heart has experienced love and he is now a transmuted man. It is his passionate love for her that is the motivating force behind his act of saving Andromeda from the jaws of the sea - monsters involving such a grand display of superhuman power that vanquished demonic forces of hate and mean cruel violence. Thus, it is one of the implicit purposes of the playwright to suggest the great strength of love through *Perseus the Deliverer.* This play has another theme which is equally important. The play being a work of more than contemporary relevance, it also deals with a subject that attracted wide attention both of philosophers and literary writers in Europe towards the end of the nineteenth century. It is the theme of evolution. *Perseus the Deliverer* suggest the same "circle of toil and hope and war and peace.."[207] the same "endless spiral of ascent and fall"[208] which ultimately brings us to and open the flood gates of Divine Light.

The play turns out to be what the prologue promise it to be a drama of conflict and change and progress. Not only *Perseus the Deliverer,* but all the dramas of Sri Aurobindo, according to Prof. K.R.S. Iyengar, are dramas of conflict and change.

> These are really dramas of life and love, of conflict and change: of conflict that is at the heart of life, of change that is the result of the dialectic of the conflicting opposites - of 'thesis' and 'anti thesis'..[209]

The play depicts the conflict inherent in life and also throw out suggestions, hint at possibilities, and invoke inspiring visions of the future. [210]

*Perseus the Deliverer* in particular is a play presaging man's evolutionary destiny. This play is a vindication of one of the important postulates of his own evolutionary philosophy namely, descent of the Divine to help man's progress on path of divinity, his movement towards self-realisation. Howsoever deadly might be the opposition of the nether forces to man's forward march, he must irresistibly move towards his higher self, to divinity, his ultimate destiny. This is the message of *Perseus the Deliverer,* where after the grim resistance, the dire primitive cult of Syria is shown as yielding place to a new religion of bright intellectualism and deep humanism, thus making for the reign of broader minds and kindlier manners, which in turn must ensure the growth of human, mild and merciful men, man's advance, in other words, to higher states of life.

*Rodogune* is the only tragic play written by Sri Aurobindo. In this play Sri Aurobindo makes no exception to his general practice according to which he prefers an existing theme to an invented one. For Syria Sri Aurobindo seems to harbour extra love. *Perseus the Deliverer* is about Syria, though the myth is Greek. Rodogune too is about Syria, but not the Syria of romance, but the Syria of history. To write about the historical Syria Sri Aurobindo goes to its history and finds in the page of Appian's accounts of the wars of Syria, a theme that catches his imagination as a fit one for his play. It is Cleopatra, the famous queen of Syria, which has been given in section 66, 67, 68 of the 'Syrian wars', must have been read in original by Sri Aurobindo for whom Greek was almost a mother tongue. It was reasonable conjecture that Sri Aurobindo borrowed the story of Cleopatra from the book of Appian, a Roman lawyer. Sri Aurobindo of course, made many changes in it to make the story suit his imagination and purpose.

"The Cleopatra of Appian's history is not the same as the cleopatra of Shakespeare's *Antony and cleopatra,* nor is she the Cleopatra of Dryden's *All For love,* as Dr. A.K. Sinha seems to believe."[211] The belief is not borne out by the account of Cleopatra available in the Encyclopaedia[212] The heroine of *Antony and Cleopatra* or *All for Love* seems to be Cleopatra VII Phelator (69-30 B.C.), the daughter of Ptolemy XII Auletes, who was personally attached to, and exercised considerable influence over, two of the chief Roman statesmen of her time Julius Caesar and Mark Antony. She was "by far the most famous bearer of the name."[213]

In Appian, Demetrius Nicanor, Cleopatra's first husband and the King of Syria, is made a captive in Parthia and is married to Rodogune, the parthian princess. As a result, Cleopatra grows jealous of Rodogune and hates Nicanor whom she kills after his return to Syria. Cleopatra's marriage with Antiochus, the younger brother of Nicanor, is a reaction to the latter's marriage with Rodogune. In Sri Aurobindo things are much different. Nicanor is not married to Rodogune who, unlike in history, is not king Phraates sister, but his daughter. So the question of Cleopatra's jealousy towards her does not arise Nicanor is not killed after his return to Syria by the craft of Cleopatra but dies miserably. A capitive, ...[214] in Parthia, "Cleopatra deeply in love with him, cherishes his memories even after his death."[215] Cleopatra, no doubt hates Rodogune. But the hatred has a different source Cleopatra says:

Parthian, you have born the hate
My husband's murder bred in me towards all your
nation.[216]

Even the hatred changes with the passage of time into motherly love and compassion. After her sons have joined her, Cleopatra is in no mood to live with the "cruel and unhappy thoughts" of revenge etc, which she hopes "to slay and busy with the past/which gave them birth."[217] Much better disposed to Rodogune she says:

Will you assist me, girl?
Will you begin with me another life
And other feelings."[218]

cleopatra's marriage to Antiochus is in her own words "a reason of state, an act of Policy."[219] (Ibid, P.340). She is full of contempt for her dead husband and exults over his death, for it was he who "exiled" her twins when they were still "babes". The two sons of Cleopatra born from Nicanor are Seleucus and Antiochus Gurupus in Appian. In Sri Aurobindo these become Antiochus and Timocles. As for Antiochus Cyzicenus, born from her second husband, he is altogether omitted in the play. The sons are changed here not only in name, but also in character. They differ from their counterparts in history and also from each other. In Sri Aurobindo Cleopatra and her sons are projected as better human beings. In order to do this Sri Aurobindo creates new characters, Phyllus and Cleone, the chancellor and his sister respectively. Phayllus is ever a trickster, an abhorred and crooked devil, the subtle Satan, the frame of evil, who with Cleone, the shrewd lipped, rose tainted harlot, keeps plotting and scheming to usurp power in Syria. As most of the evil machinations and villainy are attributed to Phayllus and Cleone, Cleopatra and her sons are rid of the evil action's that fall to their lot in Appian. Sri Aurobindo thus took from Appian, Justin and Josephus only the germinal idea for his play. He made in the history sweeping changes so that the play could embody his vision and philosophy. Sri Aurobindo's *Rodogune* differs in spirit and atmosphere from Corneille's play as well as Appian's history. It differs in action as well as the themes underlying their, respective action. Corneilles purpose in his play is to show Cleopatra's thirst for power as a career of crime and revenge. This is not so in Sri Aurobindo. Ambition in Cleopatra has not been denied. But it does not assume the proportions of the fatal flaw in her nor does it make her ruthless and violent. The jealous queen in Appian and Corneille gets transformed into a sorrowing mother in Sri Aurobindo. Unlike the characters in corneille, who are responsible for their actions, Cleopatra in Sri Aurobindo is not entirely so for all her sufferings part of the blame at least is to be shared by what has frequently been referred to as gods, Fate, Nature etc. This is so in the play because the playwright intends to project a different vision of life so unmistakable in the play As far as the changes Sri Aurobindo makes in history, they result from thematic considerations, from the requirement of projecting through the plays his own view of things or life-thought the visions expressed in his plays bear close resemblance with his philosophy. Interestingly, the play of Sri Aurobindo anticipate to a great extent, some of the important facets of his philosophy which he expressed years later in his purely philosophical works like *The Life Divine* and literary works like *Savitri*. The fact may be will treated as a corroboration of Sri Aurobindo's assertion that his philosophy is not the product of a thinking mind, but the statement of experience, realization. In common parlance a philosopher means one who derives conclusion from an intellectual exercise of the analysis of the external world.[220]

It is in this prospective that one has to look at *Rodogune* which has for its theme the Aurobindonian conception of Fate. In it there is frequent reference to fate, variously called 'Necessity', 'gods', etc., in the play, and implying some invisible powers which play important role in human affairs, So, in *Rodogune* in which Syrian history has been put in the mould of Shakespearean drama, Sri Aurobindo has embedded as its theme the truth discovered by the Indian Yogins. This is a venture quite in keeping with his universal vision. The truth forms part of the Hindu view of life and is the Indian answer to the question regarding man's freedom in relation to the Supreme Power governing the world. *Rodogune* may therefore be regarded as "an attempt to pour out upon the world India's light which in Sri Aurobindo's opinion is the need of the hour.[221]

It is this liberation from bondage to Nature which is the true progress of humanity and also the will of the Divine. The Divine will is behind Fate which works through Nature for man's progress. Life, according to Sri Aurobindo, is not chance or random incertitude."[222] It is rather "something forseen, planned in every detail".[223] Nature and fate have been working up to a secret purpose powerfully, persistently, through the ages, and ourselves are a part of it and fellow workers in the fulfillment of that invisible purpose."[224] The action of *Rodogune* embodies these facts of life, it hints at these truths about the workings of Fate and the purpose to which it works. So, Sri Aurobindo's view on Fate may serve as a background to the study of the theme of *Rodogune*. Through the plot, the characters and indeed the entire atmosphere of *Rodogune* he seeks to underline fatality as a truth of human life. Sri Aurobindo uses dramatic irony in this play to develop the theme of intervention of destiny. Instance of irony of fate in the lives of characters here are aplenty. But there is a wide gap between what is really done. For example, there is a strange contrast between Cleopatra's dreams and her achievements. She exults at the prospect of union with her long seperated sons and looks forward to the meeting with a lot of excitement but, as the crude irony of fate would have it, she is reduced to a woman who would refuse to be called mother by her own son Timocles, once so dear to her. The same Cleopatra who thought that her heart would break with joy at the meeting and believed that after her sons were restored to her, that "Never again can grief be born. In this glad world that gives me back my sons."[225] finds not joy, but quite different passions tugging at her heart-strings. She is too sick of war and hatred already, she chooses the younger Timocles for Syria's throne, instead of Antiochus, because the latter is war hungry, blood-thirsty and too ambitious, and might as a king embark upon a career of hatred and war to quench his insatiable thirst for a vast empire. Also Cleopatra suffers from an acute sense of loneliness which, she thinks, will only be intensified by Antiochus frequent trips out to battles, and she will find herself lonely in the crowded palace. Due to this possessive instinct, she wants to keep both her sons with her. It is another matter that Fate sees to it that the more she attempts to get rid of her loneliness the lonelier she becomes and cries in deep anguish; "I am alone, so terribly alone."[226] It is from Cleopatra's sense of loneliness that the tragic conflict of the play originates. For the sake of peace she would not hesitate even to elevate as queen Rodogune whom she hated so much for being the daughter of Phraates, the king of Parthia, who killed her first husband But, ironically, her efforts and sacrifices yield not glorious peace, but fratricidal civil war when she tries to take Mentho, the nurse, who knew the true precedence of the twins, into confidence about her plan for peace, the nurse refuses to be an accomplice to it and condemn it as 'cold, unmotherly and cruel plot".[227] "a wickedness beyond all parallel."[228] The wisdom and truth of Mentho's words dawn on Cleopatra, no doubt, but a little too late and only after she has fallen victim to cruel ironies to Fate. It was presumptuous on her part, to unmake, even though with a noble intent, what god had made. She is punished for her faults and she accepts the punishment. Mentho's words prove prophetic:

Dream not that happiness

can spring from wicked roots.

God overrules

And Right denied is mighty.[229]

But the warning is preceded by an advice, which may

be considered as the theme of the play-

What he has made strive not

to unmake but shun

The tragical responsibility

of such dire error. If from thy

act spring death And horror,

are thy human shoulders fit

To bear that heavy load?

observe his will;

Do' right and leave the rest to God above.[230]

In the Plays of Sri Aurobindo, most of the characters are either those who have faith in the rule of moral law in the world of a Force that far from being pitiless, blind, malignant, unjust and arbitrary is kind, benevolent and just, or those who through suffering come to recognize the existence of such a Force. If the Force bears us where it wills, not where we would, or if the invisible powers strike at every fault they see, the reason is different. It is a concern for man's perfection, his evolution from mortality to immortality, to divinity that is behind the apparent pitilessness or arbitrariness of the invisible powers. This is what Sri. Aurobindo means when he says: "God guides best when He tempts worst: loves entirely when He punishes cruelly, helps perfectly when violently He opposes."[231]

Sri Aurobindo emphatically rules out the part played by chance. He says: "chance, that vague shadow of an infinite possibility, must be banished from the dictionary of our perceptions, for of chance we can make nothing, because it is nothing. Chance does not at all exist; it is only a word by which we cover and excuse our own ignorance. Science excludes it from the actual process of physical law; everything there is determined by fixed cause and effect. But when it comes to ask why these relations exist and not others, why a particular cause is allowed to a particular effect, it finds that it knows nothing whatever about the matter ... and it is convinent then to say that chance or at most a dominant probability determines all actual happening, the chance of evolution ... But this is only a reading of our own ignorance in the working of the universe"[232] What governs the universe, in Sri Aurobindo's opinion, therefore is not chance a name only in fact of man's own ignorance but "the immortality that thinks" in us, "plans and reasons". So, the characters in Sri Aurobindo's plays are presented as engaged in unequal battle with forces they neither know of nor can ever control. They are at the best the playthings in the hands of these forces which often seem to work at cross purposes with human being, instilling in them awe and a sense of utter helplessness, and reducing them to baffled witnesses of spectacles of shattered dreams, mocked ambitions and vanquished hopes.

According to Sri Aurobindo, man will be able to transcend the limitations of his physical existence and live in the realm of eternal bliss as the growth of 'supramental conciousness' takes place. The character of Antiochus is an approximation to this ideal of Sri Aurobindo. So long as he is in the stage of 'Mind', he challenges and fights and takes pride in his victories, but, with the manifestation of patriotism, he is transformed into a man with a new knowledge and new vision. He is now above the feelings of earthly pleasure and pain. He is now a changed man for whom death is not an end but a beginning. He tells phyallus:

What were Death then but wider life than earth

Can give us to her Clayey limits bound?

Darkness perhaps! There must be light behind.[233]

Cleone's ruin is rooted in her own character. Her lustfulness and ambition and mad hatred for Rodogune turn her into "the good bitch" she is for Phayllus. She helps him in his wicked design and brings about her fall and frustration. The irony of Phayllus life is manifest when, in spite of his shrewdness, practical intelligence, cool calculations and cunningness, he realises with a rude shock the fortune is not his slave girl and that Fate is invincible for men like him. So, through his character again, the theme of the play is underlined. Like other charactes in the play, Timocles also is "thrown into the cauldron of passions, to learn and grow by hard fate."[234] and he too is a victim of irony of fate. Unlike Antiochus, who thinks "it is divinity on earth to be a King"[235] Timocles looks at Kingship of Syria as an epicure:

This is a paradise, a mother, friends

And Syria. [236]

Jealousy in him keeps smouldering, his loneliness and frustration intensify. Phayllus adds fuel to the fire and a stage comes when

Timocles seems to have lost all peace of mind and he thinks that he must have Rodogune at anycost. When Antiochus comes back to Syria giving up revolt, recovered amity seems to bind Timocles and Antiochus once more. But Phayllus, the fatal knave, who sits always whispering at Timocles ears, shatters the bonds once again. Working upon Timocles infatuation for Rodogune, he prevails upon the king to agree to the execution of Antiochus. when Antiochus has been killed, Timocles blames "only the dire gods And bronze Necessity"[237] for the murder. But Perhaps he, with his shapeless soul, the "clay for each passing circumstance to alter".[238]

He is highly combustible material

which Phayllus knows how to ignite."[239]

In Timocles' mind, heart and action we find "the coexistence of contraries- the noble sentiment and meanest of passion."[240]

Such a man is bound to suffer. But the suffering is purposive here too, so that the theme of the play is highlighted, once again. Fate has worked through his own passions and temperament. But his suffering has ennobled him. Rodogune in the play is presented as a pagragon of beauty, whose fair exterior is matched by a fairer interior. What attracts one's attention is a remarkable poise characterising her mind and spirit:

She is all silent, gentle, pale and pure,

dim-natured with a heart as soft as sleep.[241]

She seems to live in perfect peace with life. She has faith in Fate, and has acquiesced in it as the doer of all: "Nature and Fate do all."[242] As a result, she has calm and serenity, an ability to face even the worst in life without allowing her self-possession and harmony to be disturbed in the least. She knows no impetuous passions, but enjoys the placidity of deep emotions. She is-

monarch of a calm royalty within."[243]

The steadfastness of her character is exemplary. She is courageous, consistent and self sacrificing. She proves what she says by offering her all as sacrifice at the altar of true love when the need arises. Antiochus propose to her to go to Parthia, her country, as he sees Rodogune's life in danger along with his own. But Rodogune says:

I have no country, I have only thee,

I shall be where thou art; it is all I know

And all I wish for."[244]

When he dies, she goes to join him in death. Unable to stand the ghastly sight of Antiochus lying in a pool of blood, she falls down dead on his body. Rodogune after dying leaves behind a tale of pure and self sacrificing love. Through her character Sri Aurobindo seeks to project once again his favourite theme of the supremacy of pure and self sacrificing love, and its purifying and ennobling effect on man's soul.

The character of Antiochus is elevated and ennobled - as a result of Rodogune's pure love for him. Rodogune accepts him in the midst of danger and uncertainty effecting a change in the warrior's heart. He learns what love is and what love can dare. Antiochus comes to accept fate and looks at the greater truth and reality beyond which man moves through many lives, bound by fate, until he can overcome it. Sri Aurobindo believes that love is the supreme force on the earth. It can effect transformation of man's character and reawakening of his soul. That is why, Rodogune, who is the symbol of true love that enlightens and ennobles, lends her name to the play.

*Eric* from chronological point of view, is considered to be fourth of Sri Aurobindo's complete plays. Sri Aurobindo's preference for existing themes rather than the invented ones is apparent in *Eric* also. Dr. Prema Nandkumar who makes a scholarly attempt to trace the source of Eric's narrative is of the opinion that, keeping in view his fondness for re-charging existing themes and legends with new significances, one may reasonably suppose that Sri Aurobindo dived into the "abundant deep" of the sages of Norway and Sweden to get the story of Eric's rise to power. The main characters in the play belong to actual legend or history, though it has not been possible so far to identify Eric with any legendary or historical character.

The interest shown by Strindberg and Ibsen in Norse history, and the vogue of these dramatists among the intellectuals at the turn of the century, may have drawn Sri Aurobindo also to the same fountain-source. "In any case, he was deeply familiar with Norse history and legends before writing *Eric*, and he may have drawn upon them liberally."[245]

*Eric*, however is a new creation for, whatever his sources, Sri

Aurobindo transmutes and recreates the material to adopt it to his scheme of things and to project through it his vision of life. For him the truth of history is not so important as 'the truth of man's character.[246] He is interested mainly in delineating man's growth through the clash of circumstance and character, through the interplay of the one on the other. As such he does not feel obliged "to be historically accurate."[247] Sri Aurobindo has his own dramatic theories, contaning significant affirmations on the nature and function of drama. Referring to the object of drama he says that "it cannot serve its great purpose by the mere presentation of life and action and passions, however truly; vigorously and abundantly they may be potrayed. It must have an interpretative vision; the vision must have an explicit or implicit idea of life and the human being; the interpretative vision and the idea must appear to arise out of the inner life of characters through an evolution of speech leading to an evolution of action. According to him, the true movement that result in all great drama is really psychological and the outward action is only either its symbol or else its condition of culmination."[248]

From the view-point of interpretative vision, all the plays of Sri Aurobindo qualify to be considered as true dramas. They all interpret life and project a life vision. The life-thought they contain may pertain to his philosophy of evolution, or to love presented as "the great solvent of all varieties of evil"[249], and the "supreme truth and goodness and power."[250] It may be related also to Fate as the chief executive of Divine will. But though Sri Aurobindo's plays may be considered as almost dramatic renderings of his philosophic ideas, they are considerably interesting even as pure dramatic achievements. *Eric* contains a theme with which Sri Aurobindo remained almost as preoccupied as he was with the theme of evolution. Thy play is purported to be an exposition of the truth of love, the truth that finds expression in some way or the other in all his works, and the sublimest in *Savitri, Eric anticipates Savitri.* It points to the truth of which the great epic is a masterly exposition when he says:

Some day surely

The world too shall be saved from death by Love.[251]

The victory of Love over Death really takes place in Savitri, but it is not so in Eric. However it does form part of Eric's optimism which is inspired by his victory over – Aslaug. Motivated by the intensest feeling of hate, she fights against love with her whole might before finally yeilding to the imeratives of love. So Eric's victory over Aslaug is to be interpreted as Love's triumph over Hate and Eric is to be seen as dramatisation of the conflict between the two extreme emotions. Some sort of struggle between love and hate is to be witnessed in *Vasavadutta* also. It goes on for a time in Vasavadutta's heart. But ultimately, love gets better of hate. The resistance she offers to love which she feels for Vuthsa melts away with love reigning her heart sovereign. But the "mild struggle" between love and contempt in Vasavadutta can hardly be compared to the "agonising mental drama" it becomes in *Eric*. Here the action is more psychological than physical, so that the play fulfils another requirement of great drama as conceived by Sri Aurobindo. With the shift of emphasis from external to the inner action in the play, the conflict has naturally been delineated with greater intensity and vividness and on a larger scale.

Eric, a great warrior, is elected the King of Norway with the help of the people of the Northern Norway. But the South, claiming to be the real Norway, disputes Eric's right to Norwegian throne. Swegn, the Earl of Trondhjem, being the son of the late King Olaf Thorleikson, has hereditary right to Norway's kingship. Therefore, he refuses to yield to Eric, and a battle follows in which Eric emerges victorious. Swegn still refuses to owe allegiance to Eric who, for the first time in the country's history, has been able to conquer and unite it within a short period of three years. He is called "a mere usurper"[252], an "upstart"[253], and "fortune-fed adventurer"[254]. Aslaug, Swegn's sister, considers him not "an earl of Odin's stock"[255], but 'a pauper house of one poor vessel and a narrow fiord/ And some pine tree possessor."[256] This leads to the conflict on the physical level in the play. Eric is determined to maintain the newly forged unity of Norway and to put down with iron hand any attempt to disrupt it. Eric, therefore, confronts a problem. The unity he has attained through "the swiftness of his sword seems elusive, for it might not last when the sword is broken or when death proves swifter. So, he is in search of a power which proves more effective than "wisdom and force"[257] which he has. What can power be, he asks. Ready comes the reply to his question as it were, a reply which is also a very apt statement of the theme of Eric:

Love is the hoop of the gods
Hearts to combine.
Iron is broken, the sword
Sleeps in the grave of its lords;
Love is divine"[258]

Here is the answer to the problem Eric is faced with. From the "light lips and casual thoughts"[259] of Aslaug, Sri Aurobindo suggests, it is the gods who speak. This song, sung by Aslaug in all innocence, contains the whole truth Eric seeks to highlight. It epitomises the theme of the play. The real conflict in the play, however, is the one that goes on in the mind of Aslaug, the conflict on the psychological plane. Aslaug and Hertha, Swegn's wife, come to Eric's court disguised as dancing girls, to lure him into the trap of beauty and music and to do him to death at the earliest opportunity. They want to avenge their wounded family honour and pave the way for Swegns emperorship. Eric seems to have fallen in love with Aslaug at the first sight

"the girl with antelope eyes.
And the high head so proudly lifted up.
Upon a neck as white as any swan's.[260]

Aslaug's first reaction after seing Eric is like wise one of strong attraction towards his personal charms:

A mighty man!
He has the face and figure of a god, -
A marble emperor with brilliant eyes.
How come the usurper by a face like that?[261]

So far there is no real conflict in Aslaug's mind. Her natural attraction to Eric's beauty does not shake her in her resolve. Eric on his part is already bewitched by Aslaug's beauty. But ultimately the moves and counter moves of Eric and Aslaug bring the latter to a stage where she both loves and hates Eric. The game of see-saw between love and hate continues through tense moments and deep breath taking suspense for pretty long, till love emerges victorious in the end and the theme of love's supremacy and glory is underlined. The psyche of Aslaug which has been turned into a virtual battle-field, the warring forces are her love for Eric, a god wisdom and force and beauty, and her hatred for him for being the usurper of her brother's right. In the battle, Eric seems as much in control of himself as of the external situation, where as Aslaug seems to lose control over herself as well as over the situation. A character whose personality is centered in the vital, she keeps swinging to extremes from the passion of love to the passion of hate and thus appears caught in the intense inner conflict. Eric on the contrary fights a winning battle, his victory taking time only because he gives Aslaug a long rope. Aslaug, however, denies that she a "divided mind"[262] or is "heart-perplexed"[263] But the fact that she is getting less and less sure of herself, itself shows that she is fighting a losing battle against Eric and her love. The conflict between Aslaug's heart's desire and her mind's purpose, instead of ceasing as a result of her efforts, gains in intensity. The mind spurs to move forward to kill Eric, the heart holds her back:

A marble statue gloriously designed
Without that breath our cunning maker gives,
One feels in pain to break. This statue breathes!
Out of these eyes there looks an intellect
That claims us all; this marble holds a heart,
The heart holds love. To break it all, to lay
This glory of God's making in the dust!
Why do these thoughts besiege me? Have I then
No, it is nothing; it is pity works,
It is an admiration physical.
O he is far too great, too beautiful
For a dagger's penetration. It would turn,
The point would turn; it would deny itself
To such a murder.[264]

Aslaug, who once boasted, "There is/A trouble in my blood. I do not shake."[265] The reason is not far to seek. In spite of all her pretences and feignings, she fails to conceal her love for Eric. Eric knows the reality, so he says to her:

All is not lion-like and masculine there within.[266] At the very first use of force by the King, Aslaug seems to give in. When Eric holds her suddenly in his embrace and begins to kiss her, she exclaims:

O Gods! I love! O loose me![267]

The moment is most opportune for Eric to exhort her:

Sweetly, O Aslaug, to thy doom consent,

The doom to love, the death of hatred, Draw

No useless curtaining of shamed refusal

Between our yearnings, passionately take,

thy leap of love across the abyss of hate.

force not thy soul to anger. Leave veils and

falterings.

For meaner hearts. Between us let there be

A noble day light.[268]

Here the playwright subtly refers to another theme – the victory of heart over mind, suggested by Eric's "Think not! only feel!" In 'Eric', love seems to beget love; the barriers between the souls of Aslaug and Eric seems to assert its supremacy. The victory of heart over mind, however is not a smooth affair. Eric has, no doubt, been able to bring to surface the painstakingly concealed love of Aslaug for him. His "restrained violences" have drawn out her loving soul. But a gulf between her will and heart yet remains to be bridged.

Sri Aurobindo shows that fate and gods cannot play a negative role. They are for love, which is invincible and must prevail. Hertha in the play acts as Fate's instrument as does Eric. So, the two collaborate and are eventually victorious. This is suggestive of another major theme ie., Fate, To highlight it Sri Aurobindo writes one whole-play, *Rodogune*. It has been hinted at by passages scattered over all his plays. To accept Fate's invincibility as the Law of the world and as god's will, to collaborate with her rather than oppose her due to ignorance, is the way to peace. Eric and Hertha win, for they, unlike Aslaug, are free from egoistic pride and can see what Fate wills.

Hertha, after negotiating terms with Eric for peace of Norway with admirable ingenuinity and shrewdness, divulges to him the secret about her and Aslaug their identity, their treason and plots:

Thy enemies are here,

No dancing-girls, but Hertha, wife of Swegn,

And Aslaug, child of olaf Thorleikson,

His sister.[269]

This is a decisive step against Aslaug as she is now left alone with her plot which is bound to misfire. Eric grants Hertha all her three demond in return of her gesture of cooperation-life and liberty for Swegn, life and pardon for Aslaug and forgiveness for her own self. He, then, rightly rejoices in his victory which, indeed, is the victory of Freya, the goddess of Love ;

O Freya Queen;

Thou help' st me even as Thor and Odin did.

I make my Norway one.[270]

Eric feels that his victory has issued from a new knowledge which is the knowledge of his ownself. He has realised his "wide flaw" the lack of love in him. Without love "the trinity of glorious manhood"[271] remains incomplete In the beginning of the play, Eric says:

Wisdom and force I have; one strength behind

I have not; I would search it out. [272]

He has found it out now

Strength in the nature, wisdom in the mind,

Love in the heart complete the trinity of glorious manhood.[273] Hymns to love are quite in keeping with the main themes of the whole play which seems to have been written to celebrate love's power, grace and supremacy. Eric's triumph over Aslaug is made possible largely through love. As Alaug's heart is delivered from revolt and fierce hate, it is through the power of Love. Love tames an unruly heart, rids it of its waywardness, and liberate it from the violent impulses that trouble it and dissipate its energies. Aurobindo shows that love's powers are great and mysterious are its ways. This is well illustrated by the miracle it works in the play in the form of Aslaug's surrender. Eric knows that Fate is on his side and Aslaug is full of love for him and hence she cannot but surrender. He is right, for Aslaug surrenders to him. Sri Aurobindo through Eric lyrically expresses here his belief in the all conquering power of love:

Aslaug, the world's sole woman! thou cam'st here.

Aslaug, the world's sole woman! thou cam' st here

To save for us our hidden hopes of Joy

Parted by old confusion. Some day surely

The world too shall be saved from death by Love.[274]

The play, thus, has a predominant theme of love. It sets forth a celebration of the heart's triumph over the mind - "of the heart of love over the mind of hate"[275], of a calm royalty within over a passionate wayward heart. Love not only gets better of Aslaug's hate, but also of the rebellious, heart of Swegn. Swegn's aversion of Eric, his towering pride, his obtrusive sense of nobility, his rashness and obstinacy and narrow sense of loyalty do not allow him to a magnanimous surrender to the greater cause of Norway's unity and greatness, Eric however, holds it dearest to his heart and must achieve it irrespective of "pebbles" like Swegn obstructing his march, Full of sound and fury, Swegn is like the cloud that roars before it rains But Eric "is the thunderbolt that strikes/And threatens only afterwards".[276]20 Swegn is defeated and brought captive to Eric's court at Yara to submit to him, the "earth's mightiest man"[277] 21 He is already unnerved to know that Hertha and Aslaug are Eric's captives, that his "Fate has wandered into Eric's camp"[278]21 and that his "soul is made his prisoner."[279]22 Yet he does not surrender. Eric now understands that Swegn's submission can be effected "not by love only, but by love and force."[280]

This man must lower his fierceness to the fierce,

He must be beggared of the thing left, his pride

And know himself for clay.[281]

So, he decides to rob Swegn of his too lofty sense of honour and pride. Swegn cannot be allowed to oppose. His egoism, his pride and his desire against a country's fate, against the God's will. Eric's wisdom devises a plan to humble swegn. Hertha and Aslaug are asked to appear in their robes of dancing girls. This is a sight Swegn cannot bear. Hence he surrenders unconditionally to Eric to safeguard his family honour:

King, I have yielded, I accept thy boons.
Heir of a starveling Earl, I bow my head
Even to thy mercies. I am Olaf's son,
I shall be faithful to my own disgrace.[282]

The surrender may be unconditional, although not free from grief and shame. But the self abasement in Swegn's heart dissolves and yields place to happy surprise when he hears Eric grant him unexpected boons:

Four prisons I assign to Olaf's son.
Thy Palace first in Trondhjem, Olaf's roof,
Thy house in Nara, court-thy country,
To whom thou yieldest, Norway- and fit last
My army's head when I invade the world.[283]

Naturally over whelmed by the King's magnanimity,
Swegn says:

Eric enough! Have I not yielded? Here Let thy boons
rest.[284]

The victory of Eric over Swegn is thus complete. It serves the purpose in the play of reinforcing the theme of love, for Eric's victory is the victory of love over pride, of force and wisdom tempered with love over haughty pride of race, egoism and arrogance. Like his creator, Aurobindo, who was great champion of the nationalist cause, her will, her unity, integrity and peace, his mind is always full of "Norway's needs"[285]. Like Sri Aurobindo again, Eric feels that a unity attained through revolution, through "the swiftness of a sword"[286], may not last long. The warrior's sword can join, but it may fail to solder. Hence, the alternative is found in Love. To begin with Sri Aurobindo's nationalist politics was not very different from revolutionary terrorism. But by the time Sri Aurobindo was writing Eric, his political thinking had undergone changes. Here Sri Aurobindo's hero has discovered love as the most effective instrument for national unification, as the surest way to durable peace and unity.

Apart from the theme of love enshrined in the play, there is also in it the theme of Fate. If Aslaug is won through love and force, Swegn is won through love and grace. According to Sri Aurobindo, between Fate and man's soul, there is no contradiction whatsoever. "There is a divinity that sits in man"[287]. To harken to the soul's voice, therefore, is to heed God's voice. Fate is the mystic will, the heaven's secret, or the law Divine operating through the whole universe. As such faith in Fate means faith in God and vice-versa. As far as Sri Aurobindo is concerned he expresses through his plays faith in the Creator, faith in the Creation and faith in the law of the Creation. Eric exudes this faith in ample measure. The theme of evolution is also implied in *Eric*. As in the other plays of Sri Aurobindo, in Eric also characters are shown as growing - and developing and getting transformed through conflict into better human-being. Aslaug, the heroine of the play, is basically a character of the emotional type. She is thrown into the fire of conflict due to her own violent nature which knows only extreme emotions. Absolute and extreme in all things she must be, whether it is slaying or surrendering, hating or loving. A proud heart like that of Aslaug does not sink prostrate in surrender to force easily; and when it yields after all, it is filled with grief and shame. But: love washes it completely of all negative feelings so that a pure serene flame of love burns in the heart. Liberated from the agonising conflict between the warring passions in her heart, Aslaug now is happy that God has trapped her in the share of Eric's delight.

The transformation in the character of Swegn is equally conspicuous. He is a true representative of the Scandinavian traditions of heroism, culture and way of life, Swegn is ready to sacrifice all at the altar of his honour and pride. Regrettably for Eric, however, his sense of honour is too narrow to encompass the honour of the whole country. Like his sister, Swegn also is a violent spirit, impetuous and headstrong, stubbornness, arrogance, pride and egoism are the hallmarks of his personality. He takes greater pride in his race and blood than in his country. Eric says:

O narrow obstinate heart!

Had this been but thy country or a cause

Men worship, then it would indeed have been

A noble blindness, but thou serv'st thy pride.

-----------------------------------------------------

If from the ages he can buy this word,

"Swegn still was stubborn." That to him is all.[288]

But Swegn, the stoical hero, also changes. His abduracy and pride dissolve under the force of Eric's mighty personality, his terrible subtle mind and love, From the fire of his confrontation with Eric, Swegn emerges pure gold of a man. A brave honourable warrior, Swegn's is a fearless nature that cannot be cowed down to submission or purchased through offers of wealth, honour and state. His surrender to Eric adds to Swegn's stature, for it means raising above the narrowness of sticking only to one's racial honour to embrace the greater cause of the nations unity and honour.

*Eric* like Sri Aurobindo's other plays, presents the conflict of opposites, the resultant changes pointing to the possibility of a better and higher life for man Sri Aurobindo's experience of his own life had been that a crisis, a conflict, a dialectic means a change, a lurch forward, and a call to transformation. Eric in the play is shown as attaining the perfection of the three-fold nature: Strength in the nature, wisdom in the mind and love in the heart. This is the central idea of the play, the main thrust of its action. Chronologically, *Vasavadutta* may be considered the fifth and the last of the complete plays of Sri Aurobindo. It was written in 1915 when he had already completed *The Viziers of Bassora, Perseus the Deliverer, Rodogune* and *Eric.* It belongs to the Pondicherry period of Sri Aurobindo's creative activity. The play was completed in a remarkably short period of thirteen days. As is usual with him, "Sri Aurobindo borows the fable of this play also readymade, this time from a page of epic India ie... the legend of Udayana and Vasavadutta, which is quite popular in Indian literature. References to the legend are found in Buddhist and Jain works as also in works such as Kautilya's Arthashashtra, Patanjali's Mahabhasya etc."[289]

The story of King Udayana Vatsaraja, 'the Prince Arthur of Indian literature, has served as the source material for much literature - Brahmanical, Buddhist and Jain. In *Vasavadutta,* as usual, Sri Aurobindo handles great material - the Udayan Vasavadutta legend. He is faithful to his 'literary creed' and imparts novelty to the old theme through his "Creative labour". Hinting at some of the changes necessitated in the process of the legend's transformation by his creative genius, Sri Aurobindo in his Notes to Vasavadutta says:

> "... some of the circumstances, a great many of the incidents and a few of the names have been altered or omitted and others introduced in their palce."[290]

There are numerous minor changes regarding names of characters, places, etc. Sri Aurobindo decides in this play to do away with the 'myth and magic' part of the tale, perhaps keeping his modern audience in view. Sri Aurobindo's *Vasavadutta* has for its main theme celebration of heart's wisdom and power. "In the play the dramatist attempts to clinch the issue of superiority between the heart and the mind, the emotion and the reason, by presenting the story of love of Vasavadutta and Udayan in a way that shows the heart to be wiser and stronger than the mind."[291] One of the champions of the mind in the play is Yongundharayan, Vuthsa Udayan's minister. He is wise deep-seeing statesman capable of handling excellently well all the affairs of the state. As for Vuthsa, he is an admirer of nature, a seeker of beauty, an avid lover of music, a poet at heart, to whom "each petal is a thought".[292] He abhors statecraft and schemings and yearn for delight:

> My will is for delight. They are not beautiful,
> This state, these schemings.[293]

He is a champion of the heart and believes in doing what the heart desires. The clash of the heart and the mind has obviously started as the king does not heed the advice of his minister. Thus, the criss-crossing of the heart and the mind is introduced in the play through the clash between its two most important characters Vuthsa and Yougundharayan. The two hold exactly opposite positions as advocates of the heart and the mind respectively. However, they hold each other in high esteem. If Yougundharayan is treated by Vuthsa as his father. Vuthsa is treated by the minister as his son Vuthsa's friends Alurca and Vasuntha also seem to believe in acting according to the dictates of mind rather than be guided by the heart. They have reservations about his rather too generous attitude towards Gopalaca whom they find hard, stern, reserved and unresponsive even to the overwhelming love of Vuthsa. The

King Vuthsa, however, continues to show absolute faith in the Avunthian and with him he saunters towards the Vindhya ranges. Vasuntha warns him against walking far away from his safe capital with Gopalaca, but in vain. To Vasuntha's fear that if Vuthsa goes to Avunthie, his return from there may not be as easy as going there. Gopalaca, another champion of reason and cunning, has spread his snare well in the forest glade. The abduction takes place and Vuthsa is taken capitive to the Avunthian King. Vuthsa's abduction might be regarded as a setback to heart; intellectual wisdom might seem here to have an edge over heart's wisdom. In Avunthie, however, Vuthsa has many friends to help him. The theme of the play stands out in this background. What is victorious at last is the King's unsuspecting heart and not the suspicious minds of Youngundharayan; not the cold calculation, policy and statecraft, but "the promptings of the heart, the imperatives of love."[294] The promptings of the heart are superior to any other wisdom because of their origin in the Divine, for heart in fact is the representative of the Divine in the man. According to Sri Aurobindo, heart is the seat of the Guide with in us. Yougundharayan on his part is over whelmed with his Kings boldness and enterprise. He accepts his mind's defeat by Vuthsa's heart with remarkable grace. Such projection of heart in its triumphant glory, to bring the theme of the play into sharp focus is witnessed in the play when Mahasegn, the King of Avunthie, clashes with Ungarica his queen Both of them favour the marriage of Vasavadutta to Vuthsa, though for different reasons. The mother of Vasavadutta is in favour of the marriage because she thinks that Vuthsa is an ideal match for her daughter :

The first man of the age
will occupy her heart; the pride and love
That are her faults will both be satisfied.
She will be happy.[295]

The king's reason for the marriage is expressed
when he says to Vasavadutta:

...without thee
I have no hold on Vuthsa. Thou, my child,
Must be the chain to bind him to my throne,

Thou my ambassador to win his mind

And thou my viceroy over his subject will.[296]

Now that Vuthsa is his capitive, Mahasegn sees no difficulty in the marriage, but he wants to "teach" his daughter what she has to do. When Ungarica says that her heart will teach her what to do, Mahasegn reacts:

Oh, the heart; it is a danger,

A madness. Let thinking mind prevail.[297]

When Vasavadutta is summoned by the King, Ungarica satirically remarks:

Let royal wisdom tech a woman's brain

To use for statecraft's end her dearest thoughts.[298]

She is against Mahasegn's plans to use Vasavadutta for statecraft's ends. She would like her to follow the dictates of her own heart rather too frankly what his designs are and what she is expected to do to fulfil them. Vasavadutta is an obidient daughter of her father. She assures him:

Father, thy will is mine, even as 'tis fate's

Thou givest me to whom thou wilt.[299]

He hopes that now onwards Vasavadutta will be guided by her mind, not by her passions of the blood. A 'treaty' thus is struck between the king and his daughter. But it is meaning less, says Ungarica, Vasavadutta is still a 'babe' and can hardly understand the power of the heart. Ungarica is confident that ultimately it is heart that will prevail. Ungarica has no objection at the moment to Vasvadutta doing her father's will for she is confident that when the God of love awakes in Vasvadutta's heart, he will do his will and ultimately love will prevail. Ungarica is right to say that Vasavadutta does not understand at the moment her mother's words, when her mother has left her, Vasavadutta says to herself:

I love her best, but do not understand;

My mind can always grasp my fathers thoughts.[300]

In the conflict between the heart and the mind, the emotion and the reason, presented vividly in the play, the King is all for the mind and queen for the heart. The battle-ground for the war is Vasavadutta. She is drawn to Vuthsa right at the first encounter with him and feels compelled, in spite of her pride. She soon realises that she no longer governs her speech or action and is reminded of "the fire" her mother spoke of. Love is already born in her heart. But the resistance of the brain continues. The result is a fierce conflict:

His music is a voice that cries to me,
His songs are chains he hangs around my heart,
I must not hear them often; I forget
That I am Vasavadutta, that he is
My house's foe, and only Vuthsa feel,
Think Vuthsa only, while my captive heart
Beats in world-Vuthsa and on Vuthsa throbs
This must not be.[301]

While being irresistibly drawn to Vuthsa, Vasavadutta feels that she is growing 'a rebel' to her father's house. The victory of Vuthsa over Vasavadutta is the victory of heart over mind; it is the victory of love over statecraft and policy, over of heart's sincere passion mind's cool calculation. Vuthsa's marriage with the mind, the blending and harmonisation of the two into a perfect unity. Significantly, the integration is attained through love, which is divine and which can act as the best unifier. Because Vasavadutta presents love in this light, it may very well be regarded as a hymn of love. "Love" according to Mr Seetaraman, "is the great disentangler and the true diplomat."[302] In 'Vasavadutta', Manjoolica, Ungarica, Vicurna, and even Gopalaca all play into the hands of love and work to help the execution of Vuthsa's plan of escape with his beloved. Vasavadutta surrendering completely, Manjoolica working as Vuthsa's messenger and charioteer, Vicurna's car bearing forth his sister and he himself riding as her guard, Ungarica secretly helping the plan, Youngundharayan sending the messenger to Vuthsa at the ripest moment - all this is effected through love, the greatest manipulator. The King Mahasegn, reconciles with what has happened inevitably and tells Gopalaca himself to make the peace. He also asks him to go to Cowsambie with Vasavadutta's household, all her wealth etc. and stay there till she is solemnised as Vuthsa's queen. The King thus gives his final consent to the marriage of two loving hearts and yields at last to the powers of heart. All this happens not due to tricks or brains craft. It is effected by love, the alchemist. That is why, the play ends with the singing of love's anthem when all ends well Vuthsa to Alurca says:

Ride thou, Alurca, near us; Let thy harp
Speak of love's anthems and her golden life
To Vasavadutta. Love the storm is past,
The peril o'er.[303]

As in his other plays, Like *Eric, The Viziers of Bassora, The Prince of Edur,* etc in *Vasavadutta* also Sri Aurobindo presents the theme of love as a great benevolent force, capable of eliminating evil and dissolving conflict to make for harmony and peace. Whether it is Vasavadutta's vaulting pride or Mahasegn's blind political ambition, they not only prove ineffective before the imperative's of love, but are also destroyed. This is because love is divine force which, according to Sri Aurobindo, works to ennoble man by enabling him to rise above his base narrow egoistic self. Sri Aurobindo speaks of growth of Psychic conciousness, evolution of Psychicised Life-Spirit, Psychic transformation or psychicisation. These according to him, mean to remove the veil, by the power of Aspiration, Love, Bhakti, Surrender "Which covers and conceals the soul and bring forward the soul or PSYCHIC BEING to govern the mind, life and body and turn and open them all fully to the DIVINE, removing all that is opposed to that turning and opening."[304]16 Vuthsa, with his heart brimful with love and self-surrendering nature, is open to the influence of the Psychic to a great extent. He is essentially noble, loving, kind and bold and possesses all cultural accomplishments. He has an inner-self matching in beauty with his external personality. All these qualities of his inner and outer being grow in intensity as the play moves on. By the time it reaches the end, Vuthsa's mind, heart, senses and will are wholly integrated and he is close to being a psychicised man. The advent of love in Vasavdutta's heart and its gradual intensification till she knows nothing but love and her heart's desires, is in fact a near complete transformation of the princess who is initially too proud and prone to rule, and who understands her father's language of mind better than her mother's language of heart. Vasavadutta now heads fast towards being engulfed completely by the fire of love. From desiring to govern Vuthsa as his queen to yielding for perfect fusion of her entire being into that of her lover is not a long journey for Vasavadutta. Her proved heart ultimately yields. She does not remember anything now, not even her father's will, but only Vuthsa:

Have I a father or a house? O none,

O none, o none exists but only he.[305]17

This is a miracle, so easily wrought by love. Vuthsa's love for Vasavadutta knows no bounds and it begets in Vasavadutta's heart equally boundless love. Besides this there is Ungarica's love for her daughter. She sees to it that Vasavadutta's heart express itself and gets bound to the nobler loving self of Vuthsa. As a result, Vasavadutta learns that self-giving is a prerequisite of true love and hence surrenders to Vuthsa, her lord, body, heart and soul. Thus love purges Vasavadutta's being of the wavering and conflict, all her ego and pride, leads her to peace, harmony and bliss. The ultimate effect of love and self-giving is an integration of all her faculties: the concentration of her mind, heart, senses and will, and the eventual psychicisation of her being. The integration of her faculties, of her personality, takes place in the fire of love, the divine force. The victory of Vuthsa in the play is the victory of heart but not of the heart in the traditional sense of the term. Heart in common parlance denotes the seat of emotions. As such, the victory of heart would mean the victory of the emotion. However, as Sri Aurobindo points out, in Vedic Psychology, heart is "not restricted to the seat of the emotions; it includes all that large tract of spontaneous mentality, nearest to the subconscient in us, out of which rise the sensations, emotions, instincts, impulses and all those INTUITIONS and INSPIRATIONS that travel through these agencies before they arrive at form in the INTELLIGENCE.[306]18 This is what happens in Vasavadutta, where Vuthsa's intuitive wisdom overcomes the intellectual wisdom of Yougundharayan. Love takes possession of the heart of Vasavadutta too, and she also learns that self-giving is the supreme secret of peace and bliss in life. That is why, shedding all her false sense of pride and disregarding intellectual wisdom, she bows to Vuthsa in absolute self-surrender, saying:

Do with me what thou wilt,

for I am thine."[307]19

To conclude, the heart that prevails is the heart that loves. The victory of heart and the triumph of love in the play are not two different themes but one.

# REFERENCES

1. William Hazlitt, *The Round Table Characters of Shakespeare's Plays* (London: J.M. Dent & Sons Ltd., 1936), P. 171.
2. Ibid., P. 172
3. Ibid., P. 173.
4. Ibid.
5. Ibid., P. 177
6. Ibid., P. 180
7. Ibid.
8. Ibid., P. 181.
9. Ibid.
10. Ibid.
11. Ibid.
12. Ibid., P. 182.
13. Ibid., P. 183.
14. Ibid., P. 185.
15. Ibid.
16. Ibid., P. 186.
17. V.Rai, *William Shakespeare* (Varanasi : Bharatiya Vidya Prakashan, 1966), P.P. 246-47.
18. Ibid., P. 247.
19. Ibid., P.P. 247-48.
20. Ibid., P. 249.
21. Ibid., P. 250.
22. Ibid., P. 251.

23. Ibid., P. 252.

24. Ibid., P.. 254.

25. William Hazlitt, *The Round Table characters of Shakespeare's Plays* (London : J.M. Dent & sons, Ltd., 1936), P. 228.

26. Ibid., P. 229.

27. Ibid.

28. Ibid.

29. Ibid., P. 231

30. Ibid., P. 232.

31. K.R. Srinivasa Iyengar, *Shakespeare His work and His Art* (New Delhi : Sterling Publishers Private Limited, 1964), P. 520.

32. Ibid.

33. Ibid.

34. Ibid., P. 520.

35. Ibid., P. 521.

36. Ibid.

37. Ibid.

38. Ibid.

39. Ibid., P. 522.

40. Ibid.

41. Ibid., P. 523.

42. Ibid.

43. Ibid.

44. Ibid.

45. Ibid., P. 525.

46. Ibid., P. 526.

47. Ibid., P. 528.

48. Ibid., P. 535.

49. William Hazlitt, *The Round Table characters of Shakespeare's*

Plays (London: J.M. Dent & sons Ltd., 1936), P. P. 346-47.

50. Ibid., P. 349.
51. Ibid., P.P. 351-52.
52. Ibid., P. 338.
53. Ibid., P. 339.
54. Ibid.
55. Ibid.
56. Ibid.
57. Ibid.
58. Ibid.
59. Ibid.
60. Ibid., P. 340.
61. Ibid., P. 341.
62. Ibid., P. 321.
63. Ibid.
64. Ibid.
65. Ibid.
66. Ibid.
67. Ibid., P. 318.
68. Ibid., P. 319.
69. Ibid.
70. Ibid., P. 316.
71. Ibid., P. 308.
72. Ibid., P.P. 310-11.
73. Ibid., P. 312.
74. Ibid., P. 298.
75. Ibid., P: 304.
76. Ibid., P. 292.
77. Ibid., P. 285.

78. Ibid., P. 259.

79. Ibid., P. 260.

80. Ibid.

81. Ibid., P. 268

82. Ibid.

83. Ibid.

84. Ibid., P. 269.

85. Ibid., P. 270.

86. Ibid., P. 271.

87. Ibid., P. 244.

88. Ibid.

89. Ibid.

90. Ibid.

91. Ibid.

92. Ibid., P. 245.

93. Ibid., P. 234.

94. Ibid., P. 236.

95. Ibid., P. 252.

96. Ibid., P. 254.

97. Ibid., P. 257.

98. Ibid., p. 256.

99. Ibid., P. 217.

100. Ibid., P. 221.

101. K.R. Srinivasa Iyengar, *Shakespeare His world and His Art* (New-Delhi : Sterling Publishers Private Limited, 1964), P. 544.

102. Ibid., P. 549.

103. William Hazlitt, The Round Table characters of Shakespeare's plays (London: J.M. Dent & sons Ltd., 1936), P. 330.

104. Ibid., P. 333.
105. Ibid., P. 336.
106. Ibid., P. 238.
107. Ibid.
108. Ibid.
109. Ibid., P.P. 241-42.
110. Ibid., P. 242.
111. Ibid., P.P. 242-43.
112. Ibid., P. 243.
113. Ibid., P. 224.
114. Ibid., P. 225.
115. Ibid.
116. Ibid., P. 210.
117. Ibid., P. 213
118. Ibid., P. 202.
119. Ibid., P. 204.
120. Ibid.
121. Ibid.
122. Ibid., P. 205.
123. Ibid.
124. Ibid., P. 188.
125. Ibid., P. 190.
126. Ibid.
127. Ibid.
128. Ibid., P.P. 196-97.
129. Ibid., P. 197.
130. Ibid., P. 198.
131. K.R. Srinivasa Iyengar, *Shakespeare His world and His Art* (New Delhi : Sterling Publishers Private limited, 1964), P. 470.

132. Ibid., P. 490.
133. Ibid., P. 494.
134. Ibid., P. 502.
135. Ibid.
136. Ibid.
137. Ibid., P. 503.
138. Ibid.
139. Ibid.
140. Ibid.
141. Ibid.
142. Ibid., P.P. 503-504
143. Ibid., P. 507.
144. Ibid., P. 508.
145. Ibid.
146. Ibid., P. 509.
147. Ibid., P. 535.
148. Ibid., P. 549.
149. Ibid., P. 555.
150. Ibid., P. 561.
151. Ibid.
152. S.S. Jaiswal, *Sri Aurobindo's Plays - A Thematic Study* (New Delhi : Classical Publishing Company, 1993), P. 6.
153. Ibid., P. 6
154. Ibid., P. 11.
155. M.K. Naik, *A History of Indian English Literature* (Delhi : Sahitya Academy, 1982), P. 100.
156. Ibid., P. 99
157. S.S. Jaiswal, Sri Aurobindo's Plays - *A Thematic study* (New Delhi : Classical Publishing company, 1993), P. 17.

158. Ibid., P.P. 18-19.

159. Ibid., P. 19.

160. Ibid.

161. Ibid.

162. Ibid., P.P. 19-20

163. Ibid., P.P. 20-21

164. Ibid., P. 21

165. Ibid.

166. Ibid., P. 22.

167. Sri Aurobindo, *collected Plays,* B.C.L. Vol. 7 (Pondicherry : Sri Aurobindo Ashram, 1971), P. 826

168. S.S. Jaiswal, *Sri Aurobindo's Plays - A Thematic study* (New - Delhi : Classical Publishing company, 1993), P. 23.

169. Ibid.

170. Ibid.

171. Ibid.

172. Ibid.

173. Ibid.

174. K. Viswanathan, "Sri Aurobindo on Shakespeare", *The Banasthali Patrika,* Nos. 17-18 combined (July 1971 and Jan. 1972), P. 87.

175. Ibid.

176. Prema Nandkumar, *"The Viziers of Bassora : A study", Sri Aurobindo circle,* No. 23 (1967), P. 40.

177. S.S. Jaiswal, *Sri Aurobindo's Plays - Thematic study,*

(New-Delhi : classical publishing company, 1993), P. 32.

178. K.R.S. Iyengar and Prema Nandkumar, Sri Aurobindo : *A Biography and A History,* 4th ed. rev. (Pondicherry : Sri Aurobindo International centre of Education, 1985), P. 125.

179. Prema Nandkumar, "Sri Aurobindo's Dramatic Aesthesis" *The Banasthali Patrica,* Nos 17-18 combined (July 1971 and Jan. 1972), P. 66.

180. M.H. Abrams, *A Glossary of Literary Terms,* 3rd ed. (Madras : The Macmillan Co. of India Ltd., 1979), P. 26.

181. Ibid., P. 26.

182. Jesse Roarke, *Sri Aurobidno* (Pondicherry : Sri Aurobindo Ashram Press, 1973), P. 121.

183. Ibid., P.P. 121-122.

184. Sri Aurobindo, *collected Plays,* B.C.L. vol. 7, P. 579.

185. S.S. Jaiswal, *Sri Aurobindo's plays - A Thematic study* (New-Delhi : Classical Publishing company, 1993), P. 44

186. Sri Aurobindo, collected plays, B.C.L. vol. 7, P. 563.

187. Ibid., P. 566.

188. Sri Aurobindo, *collected plays,* B.C.L. vol 6,P. 225.

189. S.S. Jaiswal, *Sri Aurobindo plays - Thematic study,* (New - Delhi : Classical Publishing company, 1993), P. 44

190. Sri Aurobindo, *The life Divine,* B.C.L. vol. 18, (Pondicherry: : Sri Aurobindo Ashram, 1970), P. 93.

191. Vide Sri Aurobindo's *The Life Divine,* B.C.L. vol. 18, Chaps. XI, XVI.

192. S.S. Jaiswal, *Sri Aurobindo's plays - A Thematic Study* (New Delhi : Classical Publishing company, 1993), P. 49-50.

193. Ibid., P. 50.

194. Sri. Aurobindo, *collected plays,* B.C.L. vol. 7, P. 698.

195. Sri Aurobindo, *collected Plays,* B.C.L. Vol. 6, P.P. 2-3.

196. Sri Aurobindo, Perseus the Deliverer, *collected plays,* B.C.L. Vol. 6, P. 18.

197. S.S. Jaiswal, *Sri Aurobindo' plays - Thematic study* (New Delhi : classical publishing company, 1993), P. 62.

198. Ibid.

199. Sri Aurobindo, *collected Plays,* B.C.L. vol. 6, P. 1.

200. S.S. Jaiswal, *Sri Aurobindo's Plays - A Thematic Study* (New Delhi : classical Publishing company, 1993), P. 62.

201. Ibid.

202. Sri Aurobindo, Perseus the Deliverer, *collected Plays,* B.C.L. Vol. 6, P. 18.

203. Sri Aurobindo, *collected plays,* B.C.L. vol. 6. P. 35.

204. S.S. Jaiswal, *Sri Aurobindo's Plays - A Thematic study* (New Delhi, classical publishing company, 1993), P. 72.

205. Sri Aurobindo, *collected Plays,* B.C.L. Vol. 6, P. 161.

206. Sri. Aurobindo, collected plajes, B.C.L. vol. 6, P. 87.

207. S.S. Jaiswal, *Sri Aurobindo's plays - A Thematic study* (New Delhi : classical Publishing company, 1993), P. 77.

208. Ibid.

209. Ibid., P. 83.

209. Ibid., P. 83.

210. Ibid.

211. Dr. A.K. Sinha, *The Dramatic Art of Sri Aurobindo* (New Delhi : S. Chand & co., 1979), P. 120.

212. *Encyclopaedia Britannica* vols. V. 902, and XVIII, 811.

213. Ibid., vol. 902.

214. Sri Aurobindo, *collected Plays,* B.C.L. vol. 6, (Pondicherry : Sri Aurobindo Ashram, 1971), p. 340.

215. S.S. Jaiswal, *Sri Aurobindo's Plays- A Thematic study* (New Delhi : classical Publishing company, 1993), P. 97.

216. Sri Aurobindo, *collected plays,* B.C.L. vol. 6 (Pondicherry ; Sri Aurobindo Ashram, 1971), p. 354.

217. S.S. Jaiswal, Sri" Aurobindo's Play's - A Thematic Study." (New Delhi : classical Publishing company, 1993), P. 47.

218. Ibid.

219. Ibid.

220. Ibid., P. 102.

221. Ibid., P. 104.

222. Ibid., P. 107.

223. Ibid.

224. Ibid.

225. Sri Aurobindo, *collected plays,* B.C.L. vol. 6, P. 341.

226. Sri Aurobindo, *collected plays,* B.C.L. vol. 6, P. 420.

227. Ibid., P. 392.

228. S.S. Jaiswal, *Sri Aurobindo's Plays - A Thematic Study* (New Delhi : classical Publishing company, 1993), P. 115.

229. Sri Aurobindo, *collected plays,* B.C.L. vol. 6, P. 392.

230. S.S. Jaiswal, *Sri Aurobindo's Plays - A Thematic study* (New Delhi : Classical Publishing Company, 1993), P. 116.

231. Sri Aurobindo, *The Hour of God,* B.C.L. vol. 17, (Pondicherry : Sri Aurobindo Ashram, 1972), P. 108.

232. S.S.Jaiswal, *Sri Aurobindo's Plays - A Thematic study* (New Delhi : classical publishing company, 1993), P.P. 112-113.

233. Sri Aurobindo, *collected plays,* B.C.L. vol. 6, P. 423.

234. Jesse Roarke, *Sri Aurobindo* (Pondicherry : Sri Aurobindo Ashram Press, 1973) P. 122.

235. Sri Aurobindo, *collected plays,* B.C.L. vol. 6, P. 347.

236. Ibid., P. 351.

237. Ibid., P. 461.

238. Ibid., P. 438.

239. S.S. Jaiswal, *Sri Aurobindo's plays-A Thematic Study* (New Delhi : Classical Publishing company, 1993), P. 125.

240. Ibid., P. 126.

241. Sri Aurobindo, *collected plays,* B.C.L. vol. 6, P. 337.

242. S.S. Jaiswal, *Sri Aurobindo's plays - A Thematic study* (New Delhi : Classical Publishing Company, 1993), P. 127.

243. Sri Aurobindo, *collected plays,* B.C.L. vol. 6, P. 499.

244. Sri Aurobindo, *collected plays,* B.C.L. vol. 6, P. 430.

245. S.S. Jaiswal, *Sri Aurobindo's plays - A Thematic study* (New

Delhi : Classical Publishing company, 1993), P. 139.

246. Ibid., P. 140.

247. Ibid.

248. Sri Aurobindo, *The Future Poetry,* B.C.L. Vol. 9 (Pondicherry: Sri Aurobindo Ashram, 1972), P.P. 67-98.

249. K.R.S. Iyengar, and Prema Nand Kumar, *Indian writing in English,* 5th ed, rev, (New Delhi : Sterling Publishers Pvt. Ltd. 1985), P. 231.

250. Ibid.

251. Sri Aurobindo, *collected plays,* B.C.L. vol. 6. (Pondicherry : Sri Aurobindo Ashram, 1971), P 534.

252. S.S. Jaiswal, *Sri Aurobindo's Plays - A Thematic Study* (New-Delhi : Classical Publishing company, 1993), P. 142.

253. Ibid.

254. Ibid.

255. Ibid.

256. Ibid.

257. Ibid.

258. *Sri Aurobindo, collected plays*, B.C.L. Vol. 6, 471.

259. S.S. Jaiswal, Sri - Aurobindo's Plays - A Thematic Study (New Delhi : Classical Publishing company, 1993), p. 143

260. Sri Aurobindo, collected plays, B.C.L. vol. 6, P. 482.

261. Ibid., P.P. 483-84.

262. Ibid., P. 495.

263. Ibid.

264. Ibid., P. 503

265. Ibid., P. 501.

266. Ibid., P. 507.

267. Ibid., P. 506.

268. Ibid.

269. Ibid., P. 518.

270. Ibid., P. 521.

271. Ibid., P. 522.

272. Ibid., P. 577.

273. Ibid., P. 522.

274. Ibid., P. 534.

275. S.S. Jaiswal, *Sri Aurobindo's Plays- A Thematic Study* (New - Delhi : Classical Publishing company, 1993), P. 158.

276. Sri Aurobindo, *collected plays,* B.C.L. Vol. 6, P. 544.

277. Ibid., P. 543.

278. Ibid., P. 544.

279. Ibid.

280. Ibid., P. 546

281. S.S. Jaiswal, *Sri Aurobindo's Plays - A Thematic study* (New Delhi : Classical Publishing co., 1993), P. 159.

282. Sri Aurobindo, *collected plays,* B.C.L. Vol. 6, P. 554.

283. Ibid., P. 555.

284. Ibid., P. 556.

285. S.S. Jaiswal, *Sri Aurobindo's Plays - A Thematic study* (New Delhi : Classical Publishing company, 1993), P. 161.

286. Ibid.

287. Ibid., P. 163.

288. Sri Aurobindo, *collected plays,* B.C.L. Vol. 6, 549.

289. S.S. Jaiswal, *Sri Aurobindo's Plays - A Thematic study* (New Delhi : Classical Publishing company, 1993), P. 176.

290. Ibid., P. 177.

291. Sri Aurobindo, *collected Poems,* B.C.L. Vol. 5 (Pondicherry : Sri Aurobindo Ashram, 1972), P. 59.

292. Sri Aurobindo, *collected plays.* B.C.L. vol. 6, P. 217.

293. Ibid., P. 218.

294. K.R.S. Iyengar, "The Evolutionary Dialectic in Sri Aurobindo's Dramas", Indian Philosphical Annual, vol VIII (1972), P. 58

295. Sri Aurobindo, *collected plays,* B.C.L. Vol. 6, P. 251.

296. Ibid., P.P. 252-53.

297. Ibid., P. 251.

298. Ibid., P. 252.

299. Ibid.

300. Ibid., P. 255.

301. Ibid., P. 273.

302. M.Y. Seetaraman, *Studies in Sri Aurobindo's Dramatic Poems* (Annamalainagar, The University, 1964) P. 71

303. Sri Aurobindo, *collected plays,* B.C.L. Vol. 6, P. 329.

304. Glossary of Terms in Sri Aurobindo's Writings. (Pondecherry : Sri Aurobido Ashram, 1978), P. 123.

305. Ibid., P. 280.

306. Ibid., P. 48.

307. Sri Aurobindo, *collected plays,* B.C.L. Vol. 6, P. 294.

□

# *William Shakespeare*

## CHAPTER-IV

# Sonnets of Shakespeare and Sri Aurobindo

The sonnets were published perhaps in May, 1609 by Thomas Thorpe under the title 'Shakespeares Sonnets'. They were beset with vexed questions and have given rise to a fierce and prolonged controversy with confusing proliferations. We do not know for certain the various dates when they were composed, because they were written in parts over a number of years and have varying degrees of poetic and artistic excellence, with a strange mixture of mature and immature styles, thought and workmanship. The sonnets form a sequence of two main groups, one group is addressed to a young man of noble station and the other relates to a dark lady of voluptuous nature, who has seduced that friend. There is also a rival poet in the picture, who has managed to dislodge the author from the favour of his noble friend with the high 'swelling sail' of his Muse.

These sonnets represent Shakespeare's contribution to a poetic vogue which reached its full flowering in the 1590's. Sonnet as a form of poetry was first cultivated in Italy under the impelling inspiration of Dante and Petrarch, the latter being a more significant figure in this respect. The Italian influence, which was imported by Wyatt in the early Tudor period in England, proved short-lived, but a second wave which came from the French practitioners of the Italian tradition proved more lasting and fruitful and almost all the practising poets of England in this period, Spenser, Sidney, Drayton, Daniel etc. brought out their own sonnet - sequences. In most of these sequences the line of development, style, imagery, topics and themes are conventional. The story runs like a thread through the various sonnets, centres round love and courtship, whether the lady is real as in Spenser and Sidney or imaginary, a mere platonic idea.

She is represented as a fair charmer, white as snow so the lover, true to the tradition of chivalry burns with the flame of unrequited love, passes sleepless nights, appeals to the moon, courts sleep, sends prayers to the cruel goddess of love, drenched with the blood of his wounded heart, and in bitter anguish ransacks all the fields of nature, art and mythology to decorate the 'beautiful dame without mercy' with appropriate ornaments and figures of rhetoric. It was a common game played by the whole brotherhood of Sonneteers all over England, where real passion was totally lost in the cobweb of wit, fancy and Sidney, himself acknowledge in his apologie that these sonnets express love in a style so passionately cold that no reasonable woman can feel even the slightest tremor of heart under their impact.

The Shakespearean sequence consists of 154 sonnets, out of which no. 126, which comes at the end of the first group of 125 sonnets, is not a sonnet at all and the last two pieces (153-154) have nothing to do with the subjects. The first group of 125 sonnets is addressed to a friend of noble birth and great personal charms, whose friendship is a compensation to the poor poet for all the worldly gifts which fate has denied him. He seems to be averse to marriage and the poet is anxious to impress his mind with the paramount necessity of breeding fair copies of his beauty through his lawful union with a wedded wife. This is one way of perpetuating his beauty, the other being the celebration and perpetuation of the same beauty in the verses of the poet himself. Beauty after all is a tender flower easily destroyed by time, the creeping stealer of youth and freshness 'which makes dust of everything' and razes the proud monuments and tombs of marble and brass to the ground. It is, therefore, necessary to preserve and perpetuate it by all possible means, In this vein the poet is apt to pass into a contemplative mood and survey the predicament of our moral race and the natural paradox of the individul man, a compound of earth and spirit, a soul which is 'the centre of sinful earth', placed as a King or Judge among the wild passions prone to constant rebellion against its authority. Then there is a talk of absence and travel abroad and the change which the interval of time has wrought upon the mind of the friend, under the influence of a poet of prouder style and verse.

Was it the proud full sail of his great verse,

Bound for the prize of all too precious you,

That did my ripe thought in my brain in hearse,

Making their tomb the Womb in which they grew. [1]

Then comes the seduction of the fair youth by the 'dark lady', mistress of the poet himself, not the goddess of other sonneteers, but a circe of the world, always apt to drag men down into the bestiality of passion who deserve not an alter, but a whip:

Is't not enough to torture me alone,

But slave to slavery my sweet'st friend must be?

of him, myself, and thee, I am forsaken;

A torment thrice three-fold thus to be crossed.[2]

Another dose of his bitter cup has been added by the malicious slander of evil tongues wagging against the poet who registers a vigrous protest and stinging diatribe in sonnet no. 121.

I am that I am; and they that level
At my abuses reckon up their own.
I may be straight though they themselves be level
Unless this general evil they maintained:
All men are bad, and in their badness reign.[3]

This brief analysis of the contents of the sonnets is enough to demonstrate that the story contained in them is radically different from the one sanctioned by the established convention of sonnet-writing, initiated by the lovers of Beatrice and Laura. Here the centre is occupied by the young man, a sort of good genius of the poet, and the woman, in the background, is not only 'dark' of complexion, but also black of purpose, the poet's evil genius incarnate, the very fountain-head of his sin and degradation and corrupter of beauty and purity which he had prized in his friend as higher than 'the price of rubies'.

It seems that Shakespeare was not passively following the prevailing convention but trying to give a new orientation to it or to adopt it to his peculiar purpose. On other hand Sir Sidey Lee, one of the greatest Champions of Shakespeare's impersonality, has taken great pains to discover an impressive array of illustrations which go to prove that Shakespeare was steeped in convention and picked all its formal conceits and verbal turns of the stereotyped style. Yet the Champions of autobiographical elements in the sonnets are equally positive in their opinion and the clash of the two opposite view is best reflected in the brief conflict between Wordsworth and Browning. Wordsworth was convinced that 'with this key (sonnet) Shakespeare unlocked his heart,' To this Browning retorted, 'If so, the less Shakespeare he.' An attentive reader of these sonnets, however, cannot fail to be convinced, by many expressions of personal note of great intensity and realistic descriptions, of the fact that Shakespeare did unlock his heart in good many sonnets but with what modification of truth and mixture of fiction with fact, is well nigh impossible to disentangle from the real story unless we are quite sure of his biography, which is yet to be written. A via media has been suggested between the two views by a few critics headed by G. Wilson Knight, who have insisted upon the allegorical approach to them in order to find out, in the sonnets, Shakespeare's solution of a great problem which is at once personal and unique, and universal and human in its appeal. Shakespeare between his fair friend and false mistress, is like his own Prospero between Ariel and Caliban, between powers of light and darkness, love and lust, exaltation and degradation, and there is a movement towards an ideal which is above both. "The ideal of noble love 'Which looks on the tempest, but is never shaken', which defies death and lies beyond the 'bending sickle of Time' even though 'rosy-cheeks' and starry eyes are easily mown away".[4]

Starting with the brief analysis of the structure of the Shakespearean sonnet, which differs considerably from that of the Pertrarchan or Italian form. In an Italian sonnet the fourteen lines are broadly divided into two major parts, the first consisting of eight lines (1-8), is known as octave, and the second, of the remaining six lines, called sestet. In between the two sections, precisely speaking at the end of 8th line, there is a pause, generally indicated by a strong punctuation mark. A single aspect of thought develops continuously, like an advancing wave, through the whole length of the octave and stops at the end of this part. It is then followed by a second movement dealing with another aspect of the same thought, like the ebbing tide which closes on a note of repose at the end of the sonnet. The rhymes which bind together the lines in the two sections are also distinct. In the octave we have a fixed pattern, in which lines one, four, five, eight are connected together by one rhyme and two, three, six and seven by another-the formula for the octave, is abbaabba. In the Sestet the rhyme scheme varies, cd, cd, cd, or cde, cde, etc. As a rule, the number of rhymes should not be more than five in all.

In English form, which originated with Surrey and reached its perfection in Shakespeare, the fourteen lines are arranged in three quatrains rhyming alternately with an ending couplet. Sometimes however, as in sonnet no. 30 ('when to the sessions of sweet silent thought') the idea takes a sudden turn in the final couplet and the poem closes on a note of surprise. The rhyme scheme here is abab, cdcd, efef, gg.

Sonnets of Shakespeare have no uniform excellence or artistic and poetic quality and pieces mature in thought and style are strangely mixed with those which are quite patently faulty, frivolous and playful, as if the poet were simply playing with the subject. But the best of them are the finest specimens of genuine English poetry of the highest kind and the wonder is that this poetry is wrought out of the familiar stock of words bare of all ornaments, a natural and direct utterance without the least touch of any straining after effect. For example, a few of the best known sonnets, such as, 'Let me not to the marriage of true minds admit impediments;' 'Poor soul the centre of my sinful earth;' 'When to the session of sweet silent thought;' 'No longer mourn for me when I am dead' etc. The music which the poet wrings out of such plain words and the closeknit texture of the whole poem marks a tremendous advance upon the narrative poems. Perhaps the exacting discipline, sonnets scanty plot of ground with its rigid rules and rhyme-scheme taught the poet to be more careful in the selection of the right and effective words so as to reduce the surplusage to the minimum. But the maturity is also announced by the variety of the grave thought familiar themes and the speculative or meditative note which sounds in many of them.

In the great sonnets, as nowehere else in his works, we may hear the voice of the supreme master of English poetry opening his heart, revealing the profoundest thoughts and most poignant emotions in accents surer of immortality than the eternity promised to the beloved friend.[5] "They are among the greatest of all meditations on the mystery of human-nature, which is the mystery of a mortality which can never be content that the love and beauty it has known should be less than eternal.[6]

The sonnets have a further significance also, as they clearly anticipate the themes, conflicts and paradoxes of human life and contrasted types of characters, which are generally present in his plays. Thus the description of the femine grace and delicacy of the friend is reminiscent of Duke Orsino's description of Viola, disguised as his page, while the duty of leaving behind, copies of his fair face 'which the poet urges upon his noble friend is later repeated by Viola in her first encounter with Lady Olivia. The 'dark lady' has many incarnations in the plays from Rosaline in *Love Labour's Lost* to Cleopatra in the great Roman tragedy and the conflict between love and lust, in the theme of all the tragedies and dark-comedies, especially of *Hamlet* and *Troilus* and *Cressida*, *Lear* and *Timons of Athens*. A few sonnets also refer to the greatness of those who are the masters of themselves and with great strength that they have they are never inclined to hurt any body. This becomes a favourite sentiment in the plays and one can recall at random such famous illustrations as 'Hamlet's' 'Give me the man who is not. passion's slave' or Isabella's 'It is good to have a gaints strength but is tyrannous to use it like a gaint; and above all the character of Prospero, Shakespeare's superman, is standing embodiment of this ideal.

Mark Van Dorn has observed, "The great single subject of the sonnets is Time, swift-footed terrible time, that writes death on faces, roots out the works of masonry, fades roses, brings winter after spring, and makes in general, the music to which all the world marches groaning to its end."[7] This idea finds its final summation in Prospero's great speech on cloud-capped towers and great palace's which will fade and leave not a rack behind. So, the sonnets are the seed-plots of Shakespeare's plays.

In the 'sonnets' the speculations is wide and complex, so the friendship, love and its consummation in fruitful marriage, the evanescence of beauty, youth and love itself under the destructive touch of time, a bitter indictment of lust and a glance at the marriage of true mind's etc. are convassed by the poet in turn. In this last poem 'the marriage of true minds', is presented symbolically. The names of birds in the title have a long and complex mythical association. The phoenix is a legendary Arabian bird. Which was believed to live for five hundred years, the only specimem of its kind, at the end of which the old bird immolated itself and out of its ashes a new bird sprang into life. The bird is quite appropriately taken as a symbol of chaste love, untainted by the touch of flesh. Turtle on the other hand, the sacred dove of Venus, is the symbol of love. The union of the two is thus, described as 'married chastity; This love is a single mutual flame in bodies twain':

So they lov'd as love in twain
Had the essence but in one:
Two distincts, division none:
Number there in love was slain.[8]

The poem is at once a wail and a paean, the death of the lovers and the triumph of love:

Beauty truth, and rarity.
Grace in all simplicity,
Here enclosed in cinders lie
Death is now the phoenix' nest:
And the turtle's loyal breast
To eternity doth rest.'[9]

In this poem, therefore, body, soul, love and chastity, death and eternity have been harmonized in a higher unity, and time, the terrible agent of death, has been conquered by the constancy of spiritual love, a symbol of the union of human soul with the Divine Bridegroom, where all earthly loves and terror of death are resolved in the ecstasy of eternal union.

O Grave, where is thy victory!
O Death where is thy sting![10]

In style also the poem completes the curve, which starts with the luscious sweetness and flowers of rhetoric in the narrative poems, Passes through the 'Sonnets' with barer dignity, but not without occasional lapses into conceit and light-hearted word-play, and comes to rest in his poem where language has been reduced to its barest elements and Verbal surface to absolute transparency. This 'transparency' however, reveals clearly the gleaming facets of idea or meaning below it.

Shakespeare's 'Sonnets' were first published in 1609 and in 1966 came out Dover wilson's New Cambridge edition of these 'Sonnets'. For a very long time indeed they were regarded as habitual Elizabethan exercises in Sonnet form until Malone in his edition of *Shakespeare's Sonnets* (1780) brought out and emphassed their autobiographical character. Since then they have come to be increasingly accepted as intensely related to Shakespeare's life. Shakespeare's 'Sonnets', one hundred and fifty-four in number, stand broadly divided into two sections, the first section is written to or about a young man, while the second relate to a Dark Woman. The first section containing 1-126 and the second containing 127-54.[11]

In the first section, there is number of sonnets nos. 76, 78, 79, 80, 82, 86 which tells us about what is known as the Rival Poet. But identifying the young man and the Rival Poet has been a long drawn and difficult a game. It is generally maintained that the young man, Shakespeare's patron, is either Henry Wriothesley, Third Earl of Southampton or William Herbert of Pembroke. Dover Wilson and E.K. Chambers argue rather at length to build up the case of William Herbert of Pembroke as Shakespeare's probable young patron, or Wilson and E.K. Chambers argue rather at length to build up the case of William Herbert of Pembroke as Shakespeare's probable young patron. As for the Rival poet several names as those of Marlowe, Chapman, Nashe, Daniel, Constable and Markham are mentioned, but the choice ultimately falls on one of the two, Marlowe and Chapman. While Rowse goes all out for Marlowe and pleads for suspension of further speculations in this regard, Dover Wilson gives credence to the theory that the Rival poet is and could be none other than Chapman. The real point, however, is that while the identities of the young man and the Rival Poet have been frequently discussed and names mentioned in this connection, nothing very similar, definite or definitive, has ever been done to establish the identity of Shakespeare's Dark-Mistress. "The Dark Mistress in the 'Sonnets' has remained indeed in the dark so far: she has, perhaps been given up in despair."[12]

Shakespeare tells us about his Dark mistress in the second section of the 'Sonnets', that is, in sonnets 127-54. At the same time, we come across obligue references to her in what is called the Liaison-Sonnets, namely, Sonnet nos. 33, 34, 35, 40, 41, 42, 57, 58, 61, 92 and 93. But in spite of all that Shakespeare tells us about her she remains as strange and as elusive today as she has ever been. Dover Wilson says: 'beyond the fact that she was Shakespeare's mistress, that she had black hair and black eyes and that Shakespeare wrote a playful mocking sonnet to her beauty, nothing is known about her appearance. Nor has anybody ever made an even probable guess of her identity'.[13] It would be a natural temptation then to look upon this Dark Lady as no real being, but as only a 'literary' product, as a mythical character, as one of the series of Delias and Caelicas, Cynthias and Ideas, And yet it would be difficult to proceed with this tempting idea too far, for if the other two characters-the young patron and the Rival Poet in the 'sonnets' are real and identifiable, the Dark-Lady too would be real and identifiable as they are, because she does not stand related to the poet alone but to his young friend also. Moreover, of late a theory has been gaining currency that the person, from whom Thorpe received manuscripts for his 1609 collection of 'Sonnets', is neither Shakespeare nor his friend, for they would not have relished the publication of such personal and private poems, but the Dark Lady herself who, it is supposed, would have sold out the poems, if for nothing else, at least for ready monetary gain. It would, certainly be a timid escape to dismiss this lady as an imaginary being; in all fairness, she is to be accepted in fact, as one who accounted for happiness as well as misery in the poets life. The scattered, if scanty, details we are able to glean from the 'Sonnets' about Shakespeare's Mistress are that she had dark eyes, dark eyebrows and black hair, that she was possibly a gcntlcwoman, though not of noble-birth, and could play musical instruments and perhaps, sing also, that she was fond of witty conversation and was herself capable of it, that she was a married lady who broke her 'bed-vow' for Shakespeare's sake and was open to the charge of promiscuity, that she had had adulterous affairs with the poets young friend, and that for sometime the poet 'loved her dearly', but subsequently was shocked and disillusioned on account of her betrayal of his seemingly well-reposed trust.

For quite some time it was beleived that Shakespeare's Dark Lady was none other than Mary Fitton. Her case was championed by Tyler, and later it came to be accepted by other critics too. Miss Fitton has gone down in the private parlance of British history as a gay, wanton lady, as one who was rather of gentle birth, though not actually belonging to the ranks of nobility, who was interested in dancing and singing, who made herself suddenly notable as the leading lady in the masked dance before the Queen at the wedding ceremony of a cousin of William Herbert on June 16, 1600, who had an amorous affair with William Herbert which exploded into a scandal, and whom he refused to marry for which he incurred the Queens' wrath. Excepting that she was adulterous, ambitious and was associated with a young noble-man of Elizabethan England, Miss Fitton did not have even remote resemblance with Shakespeare's Dark-Lady, more particularly in physical features as she was a blonde. "Naturally the mystery of Dark-woman's identity remained as and where it was"[14]

The other guess that gained currency in this direction was that the Lady in question was Mistress Davenant, wife of a vintner in oxford and mother of Sir William Davenant, dramatist and stage-manager. The story goes that Sir William Davenant used to brag that he could well be Shakespeare's son, because the great dramatist, off and on, lodged at his father's inn in the course of his journey between stratford and London, and might, as he thought, have been drawn close, very close, to his winsome mother. It is difficult to say whether the game behind this guess was to make Sir Davenant look pathetic for his leaning towards an exalted, though assumed, paternity, or to reveal the identity of the Dark Mistress. "This could, however, have been a workable conjecture but for the fact that Sir William Davenant was born in 1606 while the Vintner did not open a shop in oxford before 1605 which makes him being Shakespeare's Son almost out of question."[15]

Yet another name, that of Elizabeth Vernon, figures, though it is admitted beyond doubt that she could never have been Shakespeare's Dark Lady. The only reason for her being mentioned in this connection is her association with the Earl of Southampton who married her sometime in 1598. The mystery of Dark Lady's identity is indeed deep, and though some of the sonnets in the first section stand written, as E.K. Chambers suggest to a woman, Elizabeth or Anna Hathaway, nothing definite can be said at the moment on this topic. The next of-course is a suggestion. "Could it at all be possible that the Dark Lady was a Negress, and not a native, who managed to stay in England, in London itself, and get into influential literary and social quarters by her intelligence, manners and 'natural' charms? The idea may be a little too far-fetched to find ready acceptance, but keeping in view the commercial and social traffic between England and Africa through Italy in the Elizabethan times, it should not sound preposterous or absurd."[16]

After reading the 'Sonnets' as the greatest love-poem in the language, and the mystery of the detail becomes as unimportant as to fade away. It hardly requires emphasising that in the whole corpus of Renaissance poetry the 'Sonnets' occupy a distinctive place of their own, they stand supreme as love poetry, as an expression of happiness and misery, of hopes and fears in love. But this could be possible only because of the Dark Woman for, in her absence or without her, these poems would have been something else, a merely insipid play on the theme of admired, adored friendship:

If I could write the beauty of your eyes
And in fresh numbers number all your graces,
The age to come would say, This poet lies:
Such heavenly touches ne'er touched earthly faces.'

(17. 5-8)

A woman's face with Nature's own hand painted
Hast thou, the master-mistress of my passion;
A woman's gentle heart, but not acquainted
With Shifting change, as is false women's fashion;
An eye more bright than theirs, less false in rolling,
Gilding the object whereupon it gazeth;
A man in hue, all hues in his controlling,
Which steals men's eyes and women's soul's amezeth.

(20. 1-8)

Lo, thus, by day my limps, by night my mind,
For thee and for myself no quiet find. (27. 13-14)
For thy sweet love remembered such wealth brings
That then I scorn to change my state with Kings.[17]
(29. 13-14)

The theme of idealised and unusully intimate friendship is so persistent and the poet's sense of self-effacement for the sake of his patron-friend is so pronounced that it is not unnatural to brand Shakespeare a paederast and the poems an ingenious exercise in paederasty. The young patron is the poet's 'fair friend (104.1), his 'beloved' (105.2), his 'saint' (144.7) his 'angel' (144.9), his 'rose' (109.11), his 'sweet thief' (99.2), his 'lovely boy' (126.1), his 'better part' (39.2); he is the 'world's fresh ornament' (1.9), the 'only herald to the gaudy spring' (1.10) the wonder and delight of the world. All this appears lavish and indeed perverse, if not shocking. It is the sheer presence of the Dark woman in the 'Sonnets' which gives them a different complexion and tone. The Dark woman has her relevance because she not only prompts poem but imparts to them a twist, a dimension, that is essentially, dramatic. The story of the two men, the poet and his friend, being involved with the same lady, Dark Woman, is dramatically presented : the phenomenon of the Eternal Triangle, with all its shifting moods and passions, its anguish finds a mighty moving expression in the 'Sonnets':

Even so my sun one early morn did shine
With all triumphant splendour on my brow;
But out alck! he was but one hour mine,
The region cloud hath masked him from me now. (33. 9-12)
Such civil war is in my love and hate,
That I an accessory needs must be
To that sweet thief which sourly robs from me.
(35. 12-14)

The Dark Lady did not infatuate the poet alone; she tempted and ensnared his friend also, causing natural jealousy and mistrust between the two. As Love-poetry the 'Sonnets', no doubt, cover a wide range, from happiness to despair, from comfort to agony, from togetherness to utter breach of relationship. The poet makes no secret of the fact that he is enamoured of the 'black' beauty of his mistress:

In the old age black was not counted fair,

Or if it were it bore not beauty's name;

But now is black beauty's successive heir,

And beauty slandered with a bastard shame: (127. 1-4)

She is his 'music' (128.1), his 'morning sun' (132.5) and 'that full-star that ushers in the even' (132.7), and to his 'doting heart' (131.3) she is indeed 'the fairest and most precious jewel' (131.4)

"In Sonnets after sonnets he speaks of her 'false-speaking tongue' (138.7), her 'unkindness' (139.2), her 'foul pride' (144.8), he runs her down as 'the wide world's common place' (137.10), 'the bay where all men ride' (137.6), as a faithless, inconstant, adulterous wench. He goes on to speak of the torment and torture, deep wound and 'the pity Wanting pain' (140.4) she causes to him. But though she is 'black as hell' (147.14) and 'dark as night' (147.14) his infatuation for her continues to burn: the poet in love is a poor victim of infatuation as also of an illusion of infatuation. His 'reason' pulls him one way, his 'heart' tosses him down to the other."[18] For some time he continues loving her, in the fond hope that his erring mistress would correct her ways. At times the mistress too does take pity on the poet:

... When she saw my woeful state,

Straight in her heart did mercy come,

chiding that tongue that ever sweet

Was used in giving gentle doom :

And taught it thus anew to greet,

I hate' she altered with an end,

That followed it as gentle day

Doth follow night, who, like a fiend,

From heaven to hell is flown away,

'I hate' from hate away she threw,

And saved my life, saying 'not you'[19].(145. 4-14)

She is past care, past cure, intractable, lost in the slush of sensual delight. And when the poets' 'honest faith in (her) is lost'[20] (152.8) this love relationship comes to a natural end. This story of love and hate is unfolded with striking realism, with a kind of honesty, frankness and candour that is disturbing. The poet is not an ideal lover, nor is his mistress a dream woman; both are real beings made of flesh and blood, open to all wordly taints, but this goes without saying that there is something personal, autobiographical about these love-poems; the love-tangle that is tackled in the 'Sonnets' is strictly private. Yet by sheer treatment the whole thing appears so general, so universal, so literary.

In the *Future Poetry* Sri Aurobindo demonstrated that even literature exhibits an evolutionary movement, passing through stages characterized by different sources of inspiration. He used the course of English poetry to illustrate this thesis. First there was a stage, exemplified by Chaucer, in which Englsh poetry was chiefly concerned with the depiction of the physical life. The next stage, typified by the Elizabethans, celebrated the life of the heart and will, the play of the emotions and the trials of passion. There followed an era of predominantly intellectual verse, noble in Milton, petty in Dryden and Pope. The so called romantic period was, in Sri Aurobindo's view, the first glow of the dawn of a higher, more spiritual inspiration. Blake, Wordsworth, and Shelley brough this new element into English literature but they failed to establish it there. The Victorians fell back to a mental inspiration and expression, prettified with a few romantic touches. The most significant trend in early twentieth centruy poetry, as Sri Aurobindo saw it, was a renewed attempt, most evident in Yeats and A.E. (Geoge William Russell), to give expression to a spiritual inspiration. The Post-war literary revolution belied his hopes that a higher sort of poetry might soon develop in England. Modern verse, with its repudiation of regular rhythm, was, he thought, an inadequate vessel for the mantra-like movement that characterized true spiritual poetry, which so far had found full expression only in the Vedas and Upanishads.[21]

Sri Aurobindo's first published volume was a collection of poetry; his last book, on which he worked for more than three decades, was an epic poem. Between the issuing of *Songs of Myrtilla* in 1898 and the partly posthumous publication of *Savitri*, he brought out nine volumes of verse and left unpublished enough for several more. His large body of poetry has never achieved the popularity of his prose writings, but he himself gave it special value for two reasons. First, he was by predilection a poet rather than a philosopher. Second, he considered poetry superior to prose as a means of expression. The truth that the mystic discovers are in their nature ineffable; finite words cannot convey the infinite. But poetry by making fuller use of the subtler resources of language, is better able to communicate the mystics 'intimations of immortality' than the more precise, less suggestive idiom of prose. In *The Future Poetry* Sri Aurobindo worked out a literary theory based upon this premise, in his poems he put this theory into practice.[22]

Sri Aurobindo wrote in all the four major poetic forms lyric, dramatic, narrative and epic. Sri Aurobindo's early lyric verse is conventional both in form and in subject matter. The poems in *Songs to Myrtilla,* most of which were written in England, deal with love, patriotism, nature, sorrow and death. All are rhymed, all arranged in familiar stanzas or couplet. The poems that he wrote in Baroda five to ten years later treat the same themes in verse that is at least outwardly of the same make. But the new poems show an increase in evocative power. Some of the poems written in Baroda contain hints of Sri Aurobindo's turn towards spiritual, and his 'longing... for new and lovelier things.' Three or four even deal frankly with spiritual subjects. (Rebirth) In some of his later Baroda verse he came close to spiritual philosophizing.[23] (In the Moonlight)

To understand what he meant by this we must familiarize ourselves with some of the ideas he developed in his critical writings. Poetry, he said, could be graded in two different ways, according to the source of its inspiration, and according to the degree of its rhythmic and verbal perfection. He felt inspiration could come from any 'plane': Physical, vital, psychic, mental, or those levels above the mind that he called 'overhead' planes. Poetry from each of these sources might be expressed with varying degrees of perfection adequately, effectively, or in an illumined, inspired, or 'inevitable' way. "Illumined poetry of a vital inspiration (that is expressive of the life energy), such as one finds often in Shakespeare"[24], was superior in poetic quality to adequate mental poetry or even to poetry that dealt with spiritual things in an ordinary way. The very highest poetry came 'from the overmind inspiration or from some very high plane of intuition. Sri Aurobindo called this supreme poetry 'the mantra', because he felt that the most perfect examples of it in world literature were mantras of the Vedas. His own attempt to develop a Supra-intellectual style was a concious effort to bring the power of the mantra into English poetry. [25]

Almost all of Sri Aurobindo's lyric poetry was written in traditional forms. He believed that form was of 'Supreme- importance' in the search 'for poetic perfection.' In particular he affirmed that metre was 'not only the traditional, but also surely the right physical basis for the poetic movement.' Most of his own poetry was written in familiar English metres and arranged in standard stanzas. 'Nirvana' demonstrates how even so conventional a form as the petrarchan sonnet could be used to express a very uncommon experience. In some of his later lyrics he experimented with classical quantitative metres. The Sapphics used in 'Descent' give the poem a rushing movement appropriate to the subject.[26]

Sri Aurobindo felt that free verse cut itself off from most of the aural resources exploited by metrical poetry. His attempts to find balance between free movement and measured rhythm are of considerable interest but compare unfavourably with his metrical successes.

Most of the lyrics that Sri Aurobindo wrote in Pondichrry treat explicitly spiritual themes; but he did not believe that spiritual inspiration had to be confined to 'elevated' subjects. His own dramatic poetry illustrate this well. Between 1906 and 1916 he wrote five complete verse plays and drafts of two others. His description of the first one to be published, 'a romantic story of human temperament and life impulses on the Elizabethan model' applies to the others as well. The plays are 'romantic' both in the literary and the popular sense: each deals with 'events and characters remote from ordinary life'; and in each the protagonist are a strong handsome youth and a beautiful resourceful girl who fall in love and (except in the tragedy *Rodogune*) eventually get married. Like Elizabethan dramas, Sri Aurobindo's are based on diverse literary sources (Greek myth, *The Arabian nights and Kathasarita Sagar*); are written in unrhymed iambic pentameter, with passages of prose; and are divided into five acts. In the *Future poetry* Sri Aurobindo commented on the hold that Shakespeare has had over later English poets, causing some of the best of them to turn out second rate verse dramas: Wordsworth's *Borderers*, Shelley's *Cenci*, etc. He felt that the main error of these poets was their unthinking acceptance of the Elizabethan notion of 'drama as a robust presentation of life and incident and passion.' It was not necessarily wrong for them to have adopted the Elizabethan dramatic form, for 'after due modification' it might 'still be used for certain purposes, especially for a deeper life-thought expressing itself through the strong colours of a romantic interpretation.' His own plays evidently were an attempt to introduce this 'deeper life thought' into English dramatic verse. The difficulties of such an experiment are obvious; for drama, by very nature, is bound down to outward speech and incident. Some of the dialogues of *Perseus the Deliverer* could only have been written by a poet having considerable yogic knowledge.[27]

Sri Aurobindo's other 'dramatic rommances' (as he called them) *The Viziers of Basora, Eric, and Vasavadutta* - contain no overt expression of occult or yogic knowledge. Like his plays, Sri Aurobindo's narrative poems are chiefly concerned with human love, but they regard it as a fall from more strenuous concerns. In *Urvasie,* Pururava's longing for the beautiful apsara causes him to abandon his duties as king of Aryavarta. 'Driven by a termless wide desire', he wanders 'over snow and countries vague'. Until he reaches the abode of Lakshmi in the high Himalaya's. The Goddess, knowing what he seeks, addresses him:

... Since thy love is singly great,

--------------------------------------------------------

Yields of barbarians from the outer shores.[28]

This poetic explanation of India's fall to foreign invaders was written just before the author tooks up the seemingly hopeless task of preparing his country for revolution. *Urvasie* at least partly a poetic working out of two opposed impulses: the search of beauty and delight, and the urge to act forcefully in the world. A similar conflict is at the centre of *Love and Death,* written in 1899. This narrative, briefer and poetically superior to *Urvasie* After completing *Love and Death*, Sri Aurobindo thought about adopting a number of Mahabharata episodes in English verse; but he wrote a canto or two of one such poem, *Uloupi*, a narrative based on Arjuna-Ulupi story. When he returned to narrative poetry a few years later, his increasing political commitment induced him to take as his subjects an incident from Indian History: the heroic stand of Baji Prabhu Despande, one of Shivaji's Lieutenants, against a vastly superior force of Mughals.

In 1909, while imprisoned in Alipore Jail, he began work on an epic that dervied both form and theme from classical Greece. Since his school days he had looked on Homer's dactylic hexameter as perhaps the most perfect metrical instrument ever devised. *Ilion,* the epic he started in jail, was on the technical side, an attempt to solve the problem of the hexameter in English. In 1915, be began another epic that would occupy him for the remaining thirty-five years of his life. The Subject of the new poem was the story of Savitri and Satyavan. Early versions of *Savitri* are similar to *Love and Death, Uloupi* in form and in treatment. In all three poems a story from the Mahabharta is presented in unrhymed iambic pentameter verse. The composition of *Savitri* was an endeavour to come in contact with the 'overhead planes' that are the native home of the mantra, and to give body to the knowledge and vision of those planes in revelatory speech. (Publised in 1950-57 Posthumously) (24000 lines).[29] But he did not create *Savitri* simply as a chart for the use of future explorers. He meant it as a rhythmical embodiment of his experience that could awaken sympathetic vibrations in those who read it. Sri Aurobindo stands as the creator of a new Vedic and Upanishadic age of poetry. The Vedic and Upanishadic inspiration constituting it is caught to a considerable degree in quantitative metres and to an even larger extent in blank-verse. Sri Aurobindo was a fine practitioner of blank-Verse, the quantitative hexameter and spiritual poetry resembling the Vedas and Upanishads and they aim at the flowering of the Divine in the human by a process of Yoga. His main poetic work lies along the line of potent synthesis of the outermost and the innermost. Besides, we must not forget the Sri Aurobindo was no scholar shut up in the past. He mixes wih his insight into vanished times a broad and multifarious knowledge of contemporary living and thinking and this would subtly impregnate any theme he might adopt. Hence to speak of Sri Aurobindo's poetic genius and not dwell upon the manner and technique and outer form of its activity is to shoot wide of the target.

Blank-verse is the hardest to infuse with poetic life, the inspiration has to balance to lack of the grace of rhyme by deft assonances and consonances, suggestive designs of stress and changing positions of the pause. A vital energy of most sensitive sound has to be at work in it if it is to pass that crucial test of poetry-exquisite enchantment or delightful disturbance by word-music. The creative pressure it demands for success is the proof of a genuine poet. Sri Aurobindo's being very striking in its music gives the lie, with quintessential force, to the charge that he is less a poet than Tagore or Iqbal or even Sarojini Naidu.

None of these has produced blank verse in English. And no other Indian has any thing to show in this 'tricky medium', which would bear comparison with the Aurobindonian afflatus, the blending continued through page after page of various colours and tones, the rich flexible beauty combined with the epic furor. And what English poet would not be proud to wield the wonderfully expressive style of that speech; In Love and Death, of the God of Love - Madan or Kama, as Indian Mythology names him when he manifests to help Ruru regain Priyumvada from the underworld? The young mourner doubts if the apparition is not just a dream of his "disastrous soul" :

But with the thrilled eternal smile that makes
The spring, the lover of Rathi golden-limbed
Replied to Ruru, "Mortal, I am he,
I am that Madan who informs tho stars
With lustre and on life's wide canvas fill
Pictures of light and shade, of joy and tears,
------------------------------------------------------------
------------------------------------------------------------
And passion blind as death and deaf as swords.
O mortal, all deep-souled desires, and all
Yearnings immense are mine.....[30]

While an alert eye converts the complete idea feeling to a concrete pictorial power of suggestion and each phase of it is given a perfectly representative rhythm to make it not merely glow and be seen but also vibrate and be heard in the heart of the aesthetic sense. A burst like this and it is one among many in the nine hundred and odd lines of *Love and Death* - sums up centuries of poetic evolution of the English language. There is the phrase of swift, felicity:

.... the thrilled eternal smile that makes

The Spring.

There is the phrase of tense grandeur:

And the young mother's passionate deep look,

Earth's high similitude of one not earth.

Last, there is the phrase of sweeping vehemence:

And passion blind as death and deaf as swords.[31]

But it is not alone these outstanding types of Verbal form that render the passage so memorable. Types which are less unexpected have also their unforgettable finality; they carry home to us with such a sure and moving touch what we have always known that they set the commonplace afire and by them the obvious attains a diamond crystallisation Nothing specially new is said in:

...... the husband's hungary arms and use

Unwearying of old tender words and ways,

Joy of her hair, and silent pleasure felt

Of nearness to one dear familiar shape.

And yet the conclusive and unpeachable word on the matter seems to be spoken with a happy effortless unassuming accuracy; the art is scarcely perceived, but it is present everywhere. The rhythm is flawlessly handled both as a subtle echo of the significance and as an instrument of timed music played by changing yet harmonising voice-weight and voice-lengths. The technique, like the style, reflects a genius most sensitively complex. He avoids the modern faults arising from a penchant for the colloquial : the flat and the anaèmic on the one hand, on the other the crudely impetuous. There is also a more careful harmonisation. Blank-verse artists of the twentieth century are frequently content to let just a faint touch of poetic form serve to lift the language from prose construction and prose pitch. The result is a spurious spontaneity. What it tries to cover up by its so called naturalness is lack of that intensity which confers on poetry its true distinction from prose and constitutes its true nature. Sri Aurobindo's later work has many dynamic moments of poetic thinking, but his young blank verse is seldom charged with intellectual values - it has no conscious philosophical atmosphere, it lays bare an idealism of emotion and character rather than of intellect and its thoughts are but glowing passions becoming mentally clear to themselves and forging arguments from that fiery self knowledge. The temperament that has fashioned it is akin to the Elizabethans and not to the Victorians or the poets of our century. Sri Aurobindo's blank verse hints the Indian in him and affines him to the genius of Kalidasa. He realised that in using a difficult instrument like blank-verse the born poet has to be an alert artist as well. His mind is more virile and that virile strength is not stark force alone. It has a suppleness which adapts itself to opulent no less than austere effects and often brings like Kalidasa's afflatus a sensuous and voluptuous sweep that makes him like Kalidasa a poet par excellence of Love. Love's countless moods colour the texture of *Urvasie*. In a brief quiet phrase like.[32]

And she received him in her eyes, as earth

Receives the rain.[33]

Sri Aurobindo can catch the whole of love's inner heart-the freshness, the surrender, the assuagement of a dream thirst, the transforming and creative penetration of the conciousness, the humble and happy gratitude as for a gift of the Gods.

In a sonnet Sri Aurobindo glorifies the 'form'-

Reject not form, what lives in form is He.

Each finite is the deep Infinity

Enshrining His Veiled soul of pure delight...

Form is the wonder-house of eternity. [34]

This is well in keeping with his integral vision where there is a harmonius blending of the spirit and the matter that he emphasises a perfect correspondence between substance and form. We have seen how great an importance Sri Aurobindo attaches to inspiration, vision and substance in poetry, but nowhere, in theory or in practice, he devaluates beauty or excellence of form or ignores its importance for poetic creation. "Poetry" he says in one of the letters, "is after all an art and a poet ought to be an artist of word and rhythm, even though necessarily, like other artist, he must also be something more than that, even much more."[35]

To Sri Aurobindo there is no confusion as to the meaning and relevance of technique in poetic creation. He considers technique to be indispensable. "certainly in all art good technique is the first step towards perfection."[36] But poetry is not merely a matter of correct and exquisite technique, for "technique is a means of expressin; one does not write merely to use beautiful words or paint for the sole sake of line and colour; there is something that one is trying through these means to express or to discover."[37] Poetry speaks directly to the mind through imagination and language. The best or the highest technique, he believes to be descending from above, from the Yogic conciousness. It is not a question of developing so much one's personal creative capacities as the capacity to receive. But the human instruments of verbal expression have to be perfected through knowledge, understanding and practice. And it is here that the technique enters. What Sri Aurobindo has contributed is the need of a proper balance between technique and substance of peotry. "The search for technique is simply the search for the best and most appropirate form for expressing what has to be said and once it is found, the inspiration can flow quite naturally and fluently into it. There can be no harm therefore in close attention to technique so long as there is no in attention to substance."[38] He says that "attention to technique harms only when a writer is so busy with it that he becomes in-different to substance. But if the substance is adequate, the attention to technique can only give it greater beauty."[39]

> "The Mantra" he says, "is possible when three highest intensities of poetic speech meet and become indissolubly one, a highest intensity of rhythmic movements, a highest intensity of verbal form and thought-substance, of style, and a highest intensity of the soul's vision of truth. All great poetry comes about by a unison of these three elements."[40]

Sri Aurobindo says that style is the amalgam, the fusion of all those constituents of a work of art which express the poets vision. It is really the exploitation by the poet of the formal devices language, thought, rhythm, imagery, mood and attitude - to give a faithful and sensitive expression of his vision. Style, Sri Aurobindo believes, is a living organism, "it is born and grows like any other thing"[41] Therefore really effective style, style with any life in it cannot be manufactured. He remarks, "I never manufactured my style..... of course, it was fed on my reading ...... for the rest it is yoga that has developed my style by the development of conciousness, fineness and accuracy of thought and vision, increasing inspiration and an increasing intuitive discrimination (self-critical) of right thought, word form, just image and figure."[42]

Poetry "opens to us by the word the doors of the Spirit,"[43] and seeks to recover the vivid and vital element of language, Sri Aurubindo distinguishes the style of prose from that of poetry. "While the first aim of prose style is to define and fix an object, fact, feeling, thought before the appreciating intelligence with whatever clearness, power, richness or other beauty of presentation may be added to that essential aim, the first aim of poetic style is to make the thing presented living to the imaginative vision, the spiritual sense, the soul-feeling and soul-sight."[44] The poet "sees beyond the sight of the surface mind and finds the revealing word, not merely the adequate and effective, but the illumined and illuminating, the inspired and inevitable word, which compels us to see also. To arrive at that world is the whole endeavour of poetic and illuminating, the inspired and inevitable word, which compels us to see also. To arrive at that world is the whole endeavour of poetic style."[45]

As a Seer poet and critic Sri Aurobindo penetrates the mystery of future poetic speech. With a sound optimism he points out that under the impact of spiritual concisousness and power, poetry will undergo a deep change not only in its forms and frames but also in its word and rhythmic movements. For "the poetic word is a vehicle of the spirit, the chosen medium of the soul's self-expression."[46] Therefore any profound change in the soul conciousness, in thought, in vision, in feeling reflects itself in the corresponding modification of the word and rhythm, which it has to use. For Sri Aurobindo, the greatest poets have always been those in whom the moments of highest intensity of intuitive and inspired speech have been of a frequent occurrence and in one or two like Shakespeare, of a miraculous abundance. For Sri Aurobindo language is a living throbbing reality having its body and its soul. The poet has to establish contact with its soul and has to obey its rules.

He says, "A language is like an absolute queen; you have to obey her laws, reasonable or unreasonable, and not only her laws, but her caprices-so long as they last-unless you are one of her acknowledged favourites and then you can make hay of her laws and (sometimes) defy even her caprices provided you are quite sure of the favour."[47]

Now, we can talk of diction, which is an integral part of style and implies choice and arrangement of words in a literary work. Sri Aurobindo points out that words in poetry serve a purpose which is different from that in prose. To quote him, "the poetic word is a vehicle of the spirit" itself and "it is the chosen medium of the soul's self-expression.[48] The poet deals with words like a magician at whose touch words move and act and become living, throbbing realities. For Sri Aurobindo rhythm and word-music are two indispensable things in the poetry. "Without an inevitable rhythm there can be no inevitable wording."[49] "Perfection of the language ---- perfection of the word-music and the rhythm, beauty of speech and beauty of sound."[50]

We find in his poetry the Elizabethan predilection for old and learned and romantic words, technical terms and unusual turn of speech like that of Metaphysicals, the epigrammatic and antithetical manner like that of Dryden and Pope. He wanted his language should have an Upanishadic charm and depth and a Kalidasian richness and concreteness. As a metrical craftsman Sri Aurobindo is without an equal in Indo-English poetry and as a master of blank-verse he ranks with the greatest English poets who have used it "Blank-verse" says Sri Aurobindo, "is the most difficult of all English metres; it has to be very skillfully and strongly done to make up for the absence of rhyme, and if not very well done, it is better not done at all...."[51] Many English poets have written successfully but Sri Aurobindo has admired and followed three, who have written great blank verse-Milton, Shakespeare and Keats. As K.D. Sethna points out, "the fusion of the early Milton with the late: this may be taken in general to characterize at its best the blank verse of Sri Aurobindo's twenties."[52]

Sri Aurobindo represents a new poetic consciousness which seeks to create a more refined instrument to express the new version and experience. So his poetry has a distinction of its own in its rhythm and language.

Most of Sri Aurobindo's later lyrics are sonnets and therefore are reflections of the highest terms of life, joy of being, delight of realisation and correspond in thought and substance to the philosophical concepts expounded by him in his *The Life Divine*. A glance at the contents of the poems will give us a fair idea of the poet's intuitive occupation in sonnets - 'The Kingdom Within', 'The Indwelling Universal', 'The Inconscient', 'Liberation', 'Cosmic Consciousness', 'Immortality', 'Evolution', 'Transformation', 'The Dumb Inconscient' and 'Nirvana' - to give only a few names. All these are marked by their increasing intensity and concentrated purity and fullness of the substance and language of intuitive expression. They fully illustrate the poet's conviction that "there is also a poetry which expresses things with an absolute truth but without effort, simply and easily, without a word in excess or any laying on of colour, only just the necessary."[53]

In 'Transformation' he reveals the subtle process of divine might filling the members of body;

I am no more a vassal of the flesh,
A Slave to Nature and her leaden rule;
I am caught no more in the sense's narrow mesh.
My soul unhorizoned widens to measureless sight,
My body is God's happy living tool,
My spirit a vast sun of deathless light."[54]

There are sonnets probing into the density of the inconscient– 'The conscious Inconscient', 'The Dumb Inconscient', 'The Inconscient Foundation' and 'The Inconscient'.

The fundamental concept of his philosophy finds expression in two sonnets 'Evolution'. In his first sonnets on 'Evolution' he addressed unfinished or transitional man-

All is not finished in the Unseen's decree.....

O Thou who climbedst to mind from the dull stone.

Turn to the miracled summits yet unwon.[55]

Another sonnets on the same subject is a mantric evocation of an epiphanic experience.

The fifty odd sonnets in which Sri Aurobindo expressed his spiritual realisation and occasionally, his moods of exquisite satire, are noted for their simplicity, directness and intensity of language. The sonnet called "A Dream of Sureal Science" speaks humorously of glands and harmones producing a Shakespeare, a Budha or a Napolean and ends with the couplet:

A Scientist played with atoms and blew out
The Universe before God had time to shout.[56]

The problem before Sri Aurobindo was not the construction of a dramatic diction, a diction like that of 'myriad minded'[57] Shakespeare, but a diction suited to a substance that was epic, lyric and dramatic in its inspiration. He desired that his diction should have an Upanishadic charm and depth and a Kalidasian richness and concreteness. For this "he drew upon the Elizabethan predilection for old and learned and 'romantic' words though he did not go to the length of Spenser, Sir Thomas Browne or the 'sugary' sonneteers of the period."[58] Similarly, in passages which express subtle states of the soul, he follows the romantic tradition in poetry from the time of Spenser and Shakespeare to that of Swinburne and Yeats.

We divide Sri Aurobindo's sonnets into three distinct periods. Sonnets that he wrote in the early period, that is from 1890 to 1892, they are five in number. They all are written in the Italian style or what we call the Petrarchan style of writting sonnets. The first one which he addresses to the bird cuckoo in, "To the Cuckoo" sonnet has the simplicity of style in abundance. Here he compares the melodies of Cuckoo bird to the heavenly showers which have the power to rejuvinate the earth and everything which has some kind of life in it and he further says that cuckoo bird and its singing has the power of bringing back the childhood, with its innocence, brightness and abundon into the heart of every human-being.

--- of Nature wakening her dead children moves,
But chiefly to renew thou hast the art
Fresh childhood in the obscured human-heart."[59]

But the vary next sonnets, all four of them are written in a different and more serious tone. In the sonnet 'Transiit, non periit', that he wrote in the memory of his grandfather, Rajnarayan Bose, who died in September 1899. In this sonnet he talks of death and after-life. He expresses his deep sentiments about his dear grandfather being a gift of the God and a blessing on this earth, that has been taken away by the God himself and definitely he has not been lost into the darkness of void. He expresses the faith that as the rivers, after running their course, joins the greater ocean, similarly the spirit of the departed soul has become one with the omnipotent God-

----As when a sacred river in its course

Dives into ocean, there its strength abide,

Not less because with Vastness wed and works

Unnoticed in the grandeur of the tides.[60]

In the next three sonnets, namely, 'What is this talk', 'To weep because a glorious sun', and in 'I have a hundred lives', in all these sonnets again he seems to be over-powered by the feeling and emotions of a person caught in the web of 'death' and the 'after-death' or a 'life beyond this life' kind of a feeling. Here he talks of the immortality of the soul and how no killer or slayer could kill it. He again expresses his faith in the 'after life' and advises human-being not to be terrified by the thought of death, as death welcomes us into a new and eternal life. To quote from his sonnet 'To weep because a glorious sun' :

---To shrink from pain without whose friendly strife

Joy could not be, to make a terror of death

Who, smiling beckons us to farther life."[61]

In his last sonnet of this period 'I have a hundred lives', he is very optimistic about meeting the almighty God in one of his births. He does not seem to be in any hurry because he seems to be completely convinced of his union with thc eternal and immortal spirit, even if he has to turn himself into a hunter and travel through all these hundred lives in his search, which eventually will lead him to his destination, somewhere in the stars -

----Until I lay my hands on thee indeed

Somewhere among the stars, as t'was decreed.[62]

In Sri Aurobindo's second phase of writting sonnets, that he penned from the years 1930 to 1950. He wrote fifty-nine sonnets out of which fourteen have been written in the Petrarchan tradition and rest have been written in the Elizabethan or Shakespearean style. The maximum number of sonnets are written in the Elizabethan style, with three quartrains and a couplet to round-off the the fourteen line sonnet. The Petrarchan or the Italian sonnet has its fourteen lines divided into the first octave of eight lines and the next sestet of the six lines. In the sonnets of this period, he again seems to be preoccupied with his and the human being's spiritual growth within. According to him all our out-ward trapping of this life and this world are not only transitory but also a means to achieve that ultimate bliss and ecstasy, by being united with that supreme power. In his sonnet 'The Kingdom within', he echoes similar sentiments-

.... A peace, a light, an ecstasy, a power.

Waiting at the end of blindness and the curse.

That veils it from its ignorant minister -

The grandeur of its free eternal hour.[63]

He repeats almost identical feelings and sentiments, but in different words and expressions in almost all of his sonnets of this period. He expresses his complete faith and trust in the immortality of man and the existence of that almighty, who would remove all our ignorance and cast upon us the light of the knowledge and remove all darkness, ignorance and pain from our life and bless us with the eternal and everlasting happiness and bliss. In his sonnet 'Evolution he says :

.......... I saw Matter illumining its parent Night.

The soul could feel into infinity cast

Timeless God-bliss the heart incarnadine.[64]

In the last five sonnets that are undated, Sri Aurobindo, seems to be again completely surrounded by the all-cousuming feeling of bliss, satisfaction and fulfilment at the thought of achieving one-ness with the God, and having successfully broken from the shackles of this earthly existence, having attained the final goal and destination of achieving the Nirvana, with its eternal peace, contentment and bliss. In his sonnet 'Transformation', he says that -

...... My body is God's happy living tool,

My spirit a vast sun of deathless light.[65]

In his sonnet 'Nirvana' he expresses his desire and hope of being one with the omni-present God, that union will release him from all the sadness, suffering and misery of this earthly life and attain a total release from all kinds of grief :.....All abolished but the mute Alone.

The mind from thought released,

the heart from grief

Grow inexistent now beyond belief;.....[66]

In the last three sonnets of this phase he writes about the discoveries of the science, though he does not seem to ignore the knowledge, even if superficial that is imparted by science. The knowledge that the science gives us is according to him absolutely cold, emotionless, without a spirit or a soul, only having the presence of practical intellect, which is capable of giving us only the outward, visible or the superfcial and incomplete knowledge. It lacks the depth and the penetrating gaze that can reveal to us the inner truth, the hidden, the invisible and the fathomless consciousness, which according to him is all important. He says in his sonnet 'Discoveries of Science III' -

Our science is an abstract cold and brief

That cuts its formulas the living whole.

It has a brain and head but not a soul:

It sees all things in outward carved relief.

But how without its depth can the world be known?

The visible has its roots in the unseen

And each invisible hides what it can mean

In a yet deeper invisible, unshown.......[67]

# REFERENCES


1. V.Rai, *William Shakespeare* (Varanasi : Bharatiya Vidya Prakashan, 1966), P. 74
2. Ibid.
3. Ibid.
4. Ibid., P.P. 76-77
5. Ibid., P. 78
6. Ibid., P. 79
7. Ibid.
8. Ibid., P. 81.
9. Ibid.
10. Ibid.
11. R.S. Varma, *Papers on Shakespeare* (New Delhi : S. Chand & Co (Pvt.) Ltd., 1973), P.P. 63-64.
12. Ibid., P.64.
13. Ibid., P. 65.
14. Ibid., P. 67
15. Ibid.
16. Ibid., P. 68.
17. Ibid., P.P. 68-69.
18. Ibid., P. 71.
19. Ibid., P. 72.
20. Ibid.
21. Peter Heehs, *Sri Aurobindo. A Brief Biography* (Delhi : Oxford University Press, 1989), P.P. 116-17.
22. Ibid., P. 118.

23. Ibid., P. P. 119-20.

24. Ibid., P. 120.

25. Ibid.

26. Ibid., P. 122.

27. Ibid., P. 123-24.

28. Ibid., P. 125.

29. Ibid., P. 126-27.

30. K.D. Sethna, *The Poetic Genius of Sri Aurobindo* (Pondichery : Sri Aurobindo Ashram Press, 1974), P.P.P. 9-10-11.

31. Ibid., P. 11.

32. Ibid., P. 12.

33. Ibid., P. 16.

34. Prem Tyage, *Sri Aurobindo. His Poetry and Poetic Theory* (Saharanpur : Ashir Prakashan, 1988), P. 147.

35. Ibid.

36. Ibid.

37. Ibid.

38. Ibid., P. 148.

39. Ibid.

40. Ibid., P. 149

41. Ibid.

42. Ibid.

43. Ibid.

44. Ibid.

45. Ibid. P. 150.

46. Ibid.

47. Ibid., P. 153.

48. Ibid.

49. Ibid.

50. Ibid.

51. Ibid., P. 168.
52. Ibid., p. 169.
53. Ibid. P.P. 49-50.
54. Ibid., P. 50.
55. Ibid.
56. V.K. Gokak, *Sri Aurobindo. Seer And Poet* (New Delhi : Abhinav Publications, 1973), P. 19.
57. Ibid., P. 69.
58. Ibid.
59. Sri Aurobindo, *Collected Poems* (Pondicherry : Sri Aurobindo Ashram, 1972), P. 123.
60. Ibid.
61. Ibid., P. 124.
62. Ibid., P. 125.
63. Ibid., P. 129.
64. Ibid., P. 157.
65. Ibid., p. 161.
66. Ibid.
67. Ibid., P. 168.

# CHAPTER-V

## Dramatic and Poetic Devices

Shakespeare was a poet before he become a dramatist and his progress as a dramatist is a process of moulding his poetry into an effective and flexible instrument of drama. In this way, he become the greatest exemplary of the poetic drama of his age; even though a fair portion of his work is written in prose which will claim our attention in its turn. A poetic drama, as M.M Reese has pointed out, is not just a play written in verse; it is poetic idea conceived dramatically, with all the characters and incident imagined from within.[1]

Shakespeare's poetry is rooted in the tradition of the age which was created by Spenser and the sonneteers, the composer of lyrics and songs, and on the stage itself there was the precedent of highly rhetorical, sonorous and at times bombastic and inflated poetry of Marlowe's mighty plays, with heroes of superhuman height and high soaring imagination playing with stars and planets. The rhetorical tradition was strong and broad based, affecting the taste of the writers and hearers alike and even Shakespeare in his maturest moment was able only to chasten and subdue it to his increasing naturalism, without discarding it completely.

The nature of his rhetorical delivery has been finely described by F.E. Halliday : "The lines would be delivered with the extravagant stylized gestures of the orator, the action suiting the word, the word the action for the apron stage of the public theatres resembled the orators platform and encouraged the conception that drama was only another and more exciting form of public oratory. In this rhetorical verse line is piled remorselessly on line, question on question, and illustration on illustration, with little variety, and all the flourishes of rhetoric are displayed to astonish and impress the audience."[2]

In the early plays, comedies, histories and tragedies alike, the poetry is lyrical and rhetorical; has an independent interest, is marked by the richness and fine excess of language, ornaments and elaborate imagery. The characters are not distinguished and all speak alike; But slowly the characters emerge above the surface, acquire individualities and are subject to changing emotions, the impact of which is felt by the poetic medium which also changes accordingly. The monotony yields to variety, the speed quickens, the images become shorter, swifter and more various and the texture in general more and more enriched and diversified. In the middle period of mature romantic comedies, Shakespeare comes under the discipline of prose which foster in him a habit of thrift and economy in the use of words, greater care in the use of epithets, a more effective intergration of image and allusions, a blending of the rhetorical and natural speech and subordination of the utterance to the subtle nuances of the thoughts and emotions of the speakers. The tragic period brings storm and stress, the clash and conflict of passion and thought, powerful conclusion of heart and mind which find expression in appropriate poetry, giving it the vivid impress of their peculiar force and changing pitch. As Charles Lamb puts it, 'before an idea bursts its shell, another is hatched and clamours for disclosure', 'where language is stretched to the utmost limits and seems to be panting breathlessly to keep pace with lightening speed of thought, the swift turn and eddy of feeling and emotion'. In the last plays , this tension is lowered, the manner is relaxed, the characteristics of the early lyrical style return and lie side by side with the more strenuous manner of the tragedies and poetry itself is diffused all over the plays a magic atmosphere less obtrusive but seldom to be ignored or missed completely.

> Shakespeare was a lyrical poet before he was a dramatic poet, and it was only natural that when he took to the writing of plays in verse he should apply to this dramatic verse the kind of ornament with which e was familiar in the works of Spenser and other Elizabethans, a conventional and ready made imagery that was in the main symbolic and literary, derived from the precious stones and materials, from sun and moon from flowers and animals and classical mythology in which tears and pearls, lips coral, cheeks roses, the lily and

Diana emblems of chastity; Hebe of youthful beauty and the cankerworm of corruption.[3]

The manner survives in later period and shows itself triumphantly in such passages as Hamlet's description of his father to his mother. The imagery is not only conventional but developed at great length only to create purple patches of poetry which distract attention from the business of the play. A familiar aspect of this decorative imagery is the description of natural phenomena in terms of classical mythology in the manner of Spenser.

But all so soon as the all-cheering sun
should in the farthest east begin to draw
The shady curtain from Aurora's bed.

*(Romeo and Juliet)*

The tendency to spin out an image or use a succession of images to illustrate a single idea in the manner of Shelley, is a remarkable characteristic of early poetry. An idea is first stated briefly and then elaborated at length and quite ingeniously: first the picture of a young face - 'Small show of man was yet upon his chin', then came the elaboration :

His phoenix down began but to appear
Like unshorn velvet on his termless skin,
Whose base out-bragg'd the web it seemed to wear.

and so on. Slow movement is also the result of the undramatic use of pun or word play, 'the fatal Cleopatra of Shakespeare', and of personification in the manner of elaborate description, best illustrated by the Bastard's speech on, commodity in *King John* and *Richard II's* numerous personification of Death and other abstract notions. There are also long similies which are pretty numerous even in such mature plays as *The Merchant of Venice*.

In the early plays "his mind delighted in coloured and decorative extravagances, and his ear responded to all the commensurate devices of sound. One can see the image of this fresh and glowing creation of words in his own description of Armado.

A most illustrious wight
A man of fire-new words fashion's own knight.

In this early exercise it is the enjoyment that is supreme,
the breathless playfulness; almost
as if language were intoxicating merriment."[4]

The advance towards mature poetic style will mean the discarding of the old conventional mythological and decorative imagry in the interest of images, original and daring, their increasing subordination of character and integration into the texture of the plays, a tendency to use images in cluster to create the appropriate atmosphere, the reduction of long similies into brief comparisons and their frequent replacement by metaphors and, above all, the progressive reduction of the superfluity of epithets and use of more pregnant and significant terms and phrases.

"The typical image of the lyrical plays is concentric; expanding like a bubble about its centre; the imagery of the next period is linear, a progress of well defined and lively figures which, however, do not compete unduly for attention; but *Hamlet's* imagery is centrifugal, flying off from the centre like sparks from a catherine wheel, splitting and creating new images in the process."[5]

In the tragedies the images tend to be briefer, sharper and are often packed in single words like Macbeth's snarling query - "was the hope drunk in which you dressed yourself ?"

> Most of Shakespeare's imagery is taken from nature, but much is also taken from the arts, palaces and monuments and pyramids are common images through out the plays. From Romeo's 'Palace of dim night' to Prospero's 'Cloud-capped towers and gorgeous palaces'. In addition to painting and sculpture, dancing, weaving metal-work, carpentry and other applied arts are drawn upon, and music, in all its forms, vocal and instrumental, and the instruments themselves are among the commonest of the images.[6]

Images are connected with various senses, with the easy dominance of those which appeal to the eye, the most precious sense in Shakespeare. Domestic images also abound - images of dress, of sport, indoor game and articles of toilet and luxury-lady Macbeth's perfume of Arabia etc. This brings us to what Miss Spurgeon has called 'iterative imagery', i.e, images which are recurrent and create the unity of atmosphere. Thus, in the comedies images of precious stones and jewels, of music, dance and flowers. In histories kingship is symbolised as the 'Sun' treacherous nobles as beasts of prey, the unmasking of pomp and glory as a tree hacked and dismembered etc. In the tragedies where hell is let loose and human passions and wickedness rampant, the recurrent images are drawn from rottenness, disease, dirt and filth, from animals preying upon one another, from the violent processes of torture, dismemberment, tearing devouring and fastening of fangs or boar's tooth into the flesh. There are images of sex - nausea, disgorging, swarming of flies in the shambles, breading maggots and coupling like toads in the cesspool and feeding on offals. In the later plays there is a welcome return to nature and *mythology, In Antony and Cleopatra,* there are images of gold, light, (Sun, moon) splendour and music, though combined with those of falling and breaking of towers and huge statues. The romances abound in flower-imagery, in mythological allusion and comparisons in things growing and budding, in the fertility of April and wealth of Autumn, in precious jewels, Sun and moon, whiteness of snow, the sea of Joy and finally the vanity of all human pomp and fading away of all splendour into the emptiness of death and the silence of eternity:

> We are such stuff
> As dreams are made on, and our little life
> Is rounded with a sleep.
> The world is a stage and men and women are actors;
> they strut and fret for a brief hour and then,
> 'melt into air, into thin air';

G. Wilson Kinght, in 'The Shakespearean Tempest, has taken great pains to work out his thesis that throughout the entire dramatic work of Shakespeare there runs the fundamental opposition of conflict and disorder with concord and love symbolized by tempest and music. Tempests are related to rain, cloud, sfog, all dark or wintry effects; whereas music harmonized with spring, summer, light and warmth. Moreover, tempests are also associated with trees, especially cedar, oak and pine and rough beast, while gentle beast and birds suggest the opposite idea. In the final play music ultimately subdues the tempests and often rises from its very heart.'

It is generally believed that Shakespeare drew his images from life rather than from books. But J.E. Hankins has listed a number of derived images for which Shakespeare must have been indebted to the Bible and a good many seminal books of the period-English, Latin and French. In the course of Shakespeare's dramatic development, the early lyrical and rhetorical elements become closely associated with character, situation and sentiment without losing their beauty and magic. We may refer to Ophelia's lament for the derangement of Hamlet's mind; Cleopatra's moving utterance over fallen Antony and her later glorification of him; Portia's speech on 'Mercy' and Prospero's noble moralizing over the vanity of human life,. Othello speaks some of the grandest and most epical lines, but there is not a word either out of character or isolated and extraneous. But side by side there also grows the opposite element of simplicity and directness of style which reaches its most piercing beauty in Hamlets 'Absent thee from felicity a while', or Lear's 'this lady is my child Cordelia.' Shakespeare has written thousands of simple, bare lines of 'pellucid lyricism' in his plays and sonnets which give lie to the conventional charge of 'ostentatious pomp and extravagance of diction and imagery' in his plays.

This brings us to the problem of the verbal texture or the changing pattern of diction in his dramatic poetry. In the early plays, for example, nouns and adjectives, even verbs come in pairs and alliterative words are used decoratively - 'Whipped and scourged with rods; smooth and gental news, sweet Fortune's minion and her pride' Shakespeare in his progress, either drops this device or renders it more effective by making the pair a combination of general with particular, or the literal with the metaphorical terms: in this form the device is frequent in Hamlet: 'gross and scope of opinion, dead vast and middle of the night, shot and danger of desire, morn and liquid dew of youth'. Similarly alliteration is mostly replaced by assonance or made more complex and subtle:

Take but good note, and you shall see in him
The triple pillar of the world transformed
Into a strumpets' fool.

Puns and quibbles in Shakespeare have been commented upon by most critics, but none has condemned the practice so outright as Johnson :

"A quibble is to Shakespeare what luminous vapours are to the traveller, he follows it at all adventures, it is sure to lead him out of his way, sure to engulf him in the mire. It has some malignant power over his mind, and its fascinations are irresistible ... A quibble is the golden apple for which he will always turn aside from his career, or stoop from his elevation... A quibble was to him the fatal Cleopatra for which he lost the world and was content to lose it ?"[7]

This is at least a fair statement of Shakespeare's practice of using pun or 'play' on words, not only for producing the comic effect but even on the most serious occasions; the habit was rooted in the general practice of the age and its universal interest in and curiosity about the words and their mysterious ways. To the present writer Gaunt's punning sounds cheap and impertinent to the occasion, 'Gaunt am I for the grave; gaunt as a grave'; while Mercutio's 'if you meet me tomorrow you will find me a grave man' is more artistic and dramatic. Effective also is the comment on Cicero's utility to the conspirators in *Juluis Casear* his silver hair will purchase us good opinion' In his maturity, Shakespeare manages to conceal this device, which takes away its grossness and makes its use seem more spontaneous. George Rylands has emphasized another device in the mature art of Shakespeare which accounts for the swiftness and pregnancy of the style. It is the handling of the stock poetic device known as 'Personification' in a manner suited to the demands of intense drama ; "It is no longer the question of an abstract word with a capital letter and conventional attributes ; the effect is obtained by a qualifying phase, a verb or epithet. In Shakespeare desire vomits, concealment feeds, corruption bubbles, fate hides' in an auger-hole, accident is shackled, description beggared, reason furs gloves, distinction puffs, liberty plucks justice by the nose, ambition shrinks through bad weaving, friendships milky heart turns in less than two night, valour prey on reason impatience becomes a mad dog, injury is pity's gaoler, emulation has a thousand sons. In the lines: 'And silken dalliance in the wardrobe lies' or 'to lie in cold obstruction and to rot' we have the required reconcilement of the general with the concrete,of the idea with the image,"[8]

Shakespeare's development, like that of Chaucer, is "a process of general release from the astonishingly artificial and sophisticated art with which he began and the gradual replacement of formal rhetorical devices by methods of composition based upon close observation of life and excercise of the creative imagination"[9] F.E. Halliday has dwelt at length upon the distinction between the Elizabethan and Jacobean poetry, which in substance, is the difference between Shakespeare's early and late styles.

> "The Jacobean poetry is one of compression, and lacks the definition of the Elizabethan : diction becomes more personal, syntax more elliptical, there is a greater range of tone, of light and shade, a greater elasticity and variation of speed, and the structural outline loses its precision because of the increasing metrical irregularity, the disappearance of line as a rhetorical unit, and of the bracing frame - work that no longer has expansive image to support it. The more obvious poetry of line and phrase given place to onapparently more natural, yet more elusive, because of the extended compass of its verbal harmonies and rhythms; the texture of the verse becomes correspondingly complex, its colour at once richer and more sombre, the quality of its music richer and more sonorus.[10]

At last in the final plays a relaxation of tension and of high pressure of thought and emotion produces a poetry more lyrical and expansive, a music simpler but piercing, a movement like that of a sinuous rill and a verse - form so flexible and ductile that it quite easily descends to the level of prose and rises to the highest of rapture and solemn meditativeness.

In introducing prose as a dramatic medium in the plays which were poetically conceived and poetically executed, Shakespeare was following a well-established convention which he developed and enriched -and finally extended and transformed beyond the limits of expectation. It was naturally the medium fit for ordinary conversation to indicate a lowering of emotional tension and Shakespeare later showed a subtle skill in indicating the sudden rise into the emotional intensity by making a character abruptly change from prose to verse. The Practice can be best studied in tragedies like *Hamlet, Macbeth* and *King Lear.* In the same way he learnt to distinguish the ranks of the speakers, at times, by making those of higher rank use verse while the lower persons struck to prose.

Lyly has established prose as a fit medium for comedy where

emotion is excluded and the whole attention is fixed upon the intellectual agility as well as the light-hearted mirth. Shakespeare follows this practice and assigns prose a very large share in comedies like *As you like it* and *Much Ado About Nothing* and makes it the sole medium for all comic scenes in tragedy and comedy alike. Prose was also conventionally employed to express madness or derangement to mark the speaker off from the sane and healthy minded character. Comedy which is based on realism, wit and common sense naturally provided the best training ground for Shakespeare, the prose-writer, and this discipline helped him immensely in chastening his luxuriant poetic style and tightening the structure of his verse through the infusion of the racy and realistic Words, 'common speech artistically heightened.'[11]

The most obvious function of prose in Shakespeare is bound up with the element of contrast between the romantic and realistic world which he is at pains to emphasize. So, in *Henry VI*, the prose- world of Sir John Falstaff is automatically distinguished from the poetic world of Hotspur where emotions were running high and ambition is inflamed, similarly in *Twelfth Night,* the romantic world of the main plot has its counterpart in the realistic world of the underplot where emotion is subdued and intellect keen and pitiless. In *As you like it,* two figures, Rosalind and Touchstone use prose to expose the absurdity of the romantic love. The heroine laughs at it, though her heart is fully in its grip, while the comment of Touchstone are the expression of a penetrating and completely detached mind With Shylock Shakespeare introduces a new variety of prose, passionate, hard-hitting and sounding like a bark, as it were, as if the passion smouldering in his heart were forcing itself into verbal spasms and intermittent outbursts. The strings of rhetorical questions appear to be the spontaneous expression of his sincerest and accumulated bitterness. This prose was priate to tragedy than to comedy with the prose of Falstaff Shakespeare reaches the apex of the comic prose. The prose that he speaks is as vital, complex and many sided as his personality. It bubbles and sparkles with mirth, is warm and romantic, analytical, meditative and fluent, at times poetical. It abounds in images drawn from all sources, bookish, learned and of tavern and market place.

In tragedies Shakespeare introduces the prose of many Varieties-witty and bitter, consciously or unconciously earthy, even obscene and Vulgar- the prose of the Nurse in *Romeo Juliet*; Cascain *Julius ceasar*, of Thersites in *Troilus and Cressida*. All these Varieties are found together in *Hamlet*, who is an epitome of mankind, at once courteous and biting, light-hearted and meditative refined and vulgar most poetical and most brutal. In the play itself prose ranges from the comic colloquy of the grave diggers to the courtly speeches of Hamlet and Osric. But the height of its excellence is reached in the moving passage quivering with subdued passion, rhythmical through and through in 'what a strange piece of work is a man!' Which is matched by the vision of the world as 'an unweeded garden; sterile promontory.'

"The prose spoken by Lear, Edgar and Lady Macbeth in madness is subtly varied from character to character and its pathetic effect even is not the same in the utterances of the counterfeit Edgar and the heart - broken whisperings of Macbeth's imperious consort.[12]

This brief survey is quite inadequate to reveal the richness and variety of Shakespeare's prose meant for being spoken on the stage, where it is used not only to express the characteristics of the speakers and their changing moods and emotions. Shakespeare was writing in the golden age when literary prose was not much apart from the prose of the common speech, so that he draws freely upon both the sources and acquires great strength, suppleness, beauty and natural rhythm. His comic prose has constant echoes of the racy language actually spoken by men, redolent of their environment, business and pastime, pregnant with worldly wisdom and the common proverbial saying, puns and jokes and topical allusions. It has a rhythm of its own.

The Universal love of music and song in the age of Shakespeare was a common place of history, and how this element also became more and more closely integrated with the general dramatic plan. In *The Merchant of Venice* where Portia is agonized by real suspense about Bassanio's success in selecting the right casket which is the condition precedent to her union with him for which her heart burns with desire. So music summoned to allay this agitation and the song about fancy and love, the sentiment begun and ended in the eyes and the emotion which settles permanently in the heart, is well calculated to set the chooser on the right path to success.

Moreover it creates an appropriate setting for the romantic union of the lovers. In *As you like it*, the songs sung in the forest of Arden re-inforce the atmosphere of simple and carefree life and hint at the courtier's deliberate effort to soothe themselves with the sense of ample compensation for the banishment from the centre of art and culture into the solitude of the rural haunts, exposed to the fury of wind and weather, *The Twelth-Night* music and song abound to create the appropriate atmosphere of general mirth and luxuriant ease demanded by the Title, but "Feste's discrimination in suiting the song to the mood and character of the company makes the company makes the songs an effective instrument of characterization".[13]

In *Hamlet*, poor Ophelia sings snatches of old ballads in her madness, which give us a clear inkling into the nature of shocks which have reduced her to that plight. She harps upon the death of her father, the memory of her lover and sometimes the fear that the lover may violate her modesty and then leave her to her fate. It may be interpreted as the expression of a suspicion lurking in her heart, as a result of her father's schooling, that Prince Hamlet stands so high above her that her union with him in marriage is impossible and his love, therefore, is not honest and sincere and may lead to the loss of her honour and character. This latent fear finds expression in the obscene tags of the old songs which she must have heard in her sane moments. The songs open to us a dark and hidden corner of her heart into which she never admits us conciously.

In *King lear*, music is used as a cure for Lear's madness and the atmosphere created by it is so enchanting that Lear opens his eyes only to find Cordelia with an aura of heavenly grace around her, which clearly emphasizes her symbolic significance Lear is thus lifted from the hell of his misery and torture into the simplicity and innocence of childhood with his daughter as the role centre of bliss on this earth In *Othello* the song enters the tragedy at its darkest moment with the tender 'Willow-song' chanted by poor Desdemona before her cruel sacrifice. It adds deep pathos to her brutal murder and creates a strong sense of her purity and also her lamb- like helplessness and passivity in her unmerited suffering. "The song enhances the effect of the tragedy and sheds a heavenly light upon the Christ like figure of the heroine."[14]

In, *Pericles*, Pericle is subjected to a double dose of music preceding the double reconciliation, first with his lost daughter and then with his lost wife, towards the latter of which he is directed in his sleep induced by the music suddenly falling from the heavens on his ear alone. In *Cymbeline*, the elegy sung over the supposed death of Imogen emphatically brings out the beauty and pathos of her tragic life and is in perfect keeping with the trends of her story in the direction of reconciliation; while the vision which visits the sleeping Posthumus is accompanied with a solemn music befitting the occasion of the resurrection of his soul so necessary for the devoted wife and the wrongly suspicious and hard-hearted husband. In *The winters Tale*, the musical lyrics set the tone appropriate to the delicate atmosphere in which Perdita is beautifully wrapped, and naturally lead to the solemn incantation of the final scene in which Hermione gradually comes back to life from what appears to be a stone statue. The process is a symbol of the animating touch of love and harmony as contrasted with the icy and deadening effect of cruelty and hate.

In *The Tempest*, at last, "music and song envelop the whole play and becomes artistically fused with plot and character. The songs of Ariel are at once a part of the enchanted atmosphere and an affective instrument for the furtherance of action according to the design of the human Providence, Prospero. The masque and the solemn utterances of Prospero about its symbolic meaning constitute the most appropriate circumstances for the close of the play and also of the most fruitful and epoch-making dramatic career on the glorious Elizabethan stage."[15]

Blank verse as a vehicle of drama was first introduced in English tragedy by the authors of Gorboduc, who were probably influenced by the Earl of Surrey's translation of Virgil's 'Aeneid' in this measure. But blank verse in the first regular English tragedy is mostly static and wooden, a fit medium for long, stately rhetorical passages, which abound there. It was, then, taken over by Marlowe and Kyd who introduced a greater measure of flexibility, variety and mobility and there by showed the way to the further development which it achieved in the infinitely more skilled hand of Shakespeare who plumbed the depths of the human mind and passion and articulated the conflicting thoughts and emotions of a variety of characters in the numerous situations of life which are faithfully represented in his plays.

Shakespeare breaks the monotony through the introduction of the variation in the movement, tempo and pitch of the verse. This is achieved by changing the iambic foot through trochaic and other substitution by changing the pause in the successive lines and by permitting the sense to overflow from one verse to another for a number of lines, so that the unit becomes a 'verse-paragraph', as in Milton's epics. We may take an example from one of mature comedies *Twelfth-Night* :

I see what you are, you are too proud;

But, if you were devil, you are fair,

My lord and master loves you; O, such love could be but recompensed, though you were crown'd

The nonpareil of beauty![16]

The shifting of the pause is remarkable here, and so is the run-on movement but more remarkable is the middle-line pause in the third verse. Another remarkable devices which is adopted frequently in his mature verse is the lengthening and contraction of lines in response to the tempo of thought and emotion. The lenghtened line generally has an extra syllable which may come at the end and be known as 'feminine-ending' and also in the middle Feminine ending is 'light-ending' in the sense that it is generally some preposition or conjunction so closely connected with the word in the next line that we pass on without pause. This helps the flow of sense and interweaves the lines into a brief paragraph. Substitution of the prevailing iambic foot by 'trochee', 'spondee' and 'anapaest'creates variations in the pace and if carried too far, as in the last plays of Shakespeare it may result in a double rhythm, one movement imposed upon another. The interweaving of lines and sounds is also effected by means of alliteration and assonance, which increases in frequency and grow in subtlety in the later plays, till they produced an orchestration or the effect of symphony. F.E Halliday analyses Alanso's speech in *The Tempest III*, iii,

O, it is monstrous, monstrous !

Methought the billows spoke, and told me of it;

The winds did sing it to me; and the thunder,

That deep and dreadful organ pipe, pronounc'd

The name of Prospero: it did bass my trespass.

To show the full perfection of the medium which now with its complex contrapuntal rhythm and assonance, approaches music on the one hand, and on the other, the medium of the Sculptor and potter, so plastic it is that the verse gives the impression of having been modelled out of homogeneous material, not constructed after selection from a multitude of words.[17]

All these changes and variations in the medium were due to the growing complexity and individuality of his characters, who acquired a definite voice and tone, audible, in all its variation, in their utterances, clearly expressive of the currents and eddies of their passions and emotions. In the lyrical world of *The Merchant of Venice* the discord comes from the dark figure of Shylock, whose calculating mind is echoed by the lines he speaks :

Pray you tell me this :

If he should break his day, what should I gain

By the exaction of the forfeiture ?

In the tragedies the surface of the blank - verse is churned and the lines become jagged and broken, under the pressure of emotion : Here is Othello's cry of agony:

Whip me, ye devils,

From the possession of this heavenly sight!

Blow me about in winds ! Roast me in sulphur !

O Desdemona ! Desdemona ! Dead !

Oh! Oh! Oh.

By the time we reach the last plays the blank verse has become Protean and malleable with a music that gently falls upon the ear like the notes of the heavenly melody:

And like the baseless fabric of this vision.

The cloud - capp'd towers, the gorgeous palaces.

The solemn temples, the great globe itself

......Shall dissolve,

......We are such stuff

As dreams are made on, and our little life

Is rounded with a sleep

Sri Aurobindo, in his play, displays a very wide range of imagery. Most of the images are functional. His imagery on the whole displays a high flight of poetic imagination, wide range of experience, a deep study of man and Nature and a highly sensitive mind fully capable of transforming sensations into world pictures. Imagery, in his plays, has been mainly used for characterization, revelation of them and creation of atmosphere. Each leading character has been presented through one central image which very aptly delineates his or her personality, as for example Cleopatra is a 'Niobe', Timocles is a 'Pale-leaf.' Antiochus is 'The Sun / Brilliant alone in heaven' Andromeda is a 'human merciful divinity', and Perseus is a 'bright god'. Images are also used for the gradual unfolding of the play's theme. The image of 'the golden hoop of love' in *Eric* may be cited as an example. Images are also utilised by Sri Aurobindo for the evocation or creation of atmosphere best suited to the action in the play. For example in *Perseus the Deliverer,* such image as of 'the ocean in tumult', 'the Sky in storm' Phayllus gesticulating 'more wildly' etc are utilised by the dramatist to create the proper requisite atmosphere. Highly suggestive and evocation images are utilized in the three romances and Prince of Edur to create an atmosphere of romance, love, beauty, affection, sympathy and benevolence.

The term 'Imagery', however is one of the most ambiguous terms in literary criticism. Two uses of the term can immediately be noted.

Imagery signifies all the objects and qualities of sense perception referred to in a work of literature. This term is derived from the term 'image' in psychology where it means a revival percept. This revival percept may be visual, olfactory, gustatory, tactile or auditory that is pertaining to any kind of sensation "But it will be wrong to suppose that in a work of literature images have merely sensory qualities. The verbal image is of a relatively complex character as it endeavours to present certain emotional or mental event connected with the sensation it revives."[18]

Imagery signifies figurative language and covers all figures of speech used for purposes of analogy. The two objects which are compared in a verbal image have been called the 'major term' (ie, the idea underlying the image) and the minor 'term' (ie, the material illustrating the idea) This is to say that a poetic image endeavours to present an emotion connected with the sensation it revives.

In our times Shakespeare imagery has drawn the attention of some of the leading critics.CF.E. Spurgeon, W. Clemen and W. Knight have studied it from three different angles. The methods adopted by these critics merit elucidation here.

Spurgeon, in her work *Shakespeare's Imagery and what it tells us*, has studied extensively the sources from which Shakespeare draw his image She has classified the 'minor terms' or 'vehicles' in Shakespeare's images and with the help of her statistical data she throws light on the likes and dislikes, prides and prejudices and habits and interests of Shakespeare. She has based her work on the conception that 'the imagery he' ie.. An artist 'instinctively uses is thus a revelation, largely unconscious of the furniture of his mind , the channels, of his thought, the qualities of things, the objects and incidents he observes and remembers, and perhaps most significant of all those which he does not observe or remember' Clemen does not agree with Spurgeon. He believes that 'An isolated image, an image viewed outside of its context, is only half the image. Every image, every metaphor gains full life and significance from its context .. It appears as a cell in the organism of the play, linked with it in many ways'. He therefore, in his *The Development of Shakespeare's Imagery,* studies the images in the context of the plays and as an inseparable part of an organic whole. Clemen's 'method of studying imagery can be called organic as against the statistical method used by Supergeon. For Knight imagry is the symbolic medium through which an artist attempts to communicate his vision. He in his *The wheel of Fire,* studies some of Shakespeare's play as an extended metaphor'.[19]

"The imagery of Sri Aurobindo can be put under different heading. Such as 1. Religious 2. Nature 3. Mythological or classical 4. Celestial 5. Domestic 6. Fine Arts and so on."[20] of these the religious imagery dominates all his plays. In *Rodogune* alone references to god or the gods are made seventy times. Fate and heaven are referred to sixteen and seven times respectively, and there are six refrences to the Devil, to libation, sacrifice and one to the sanctuary. Here are few significant examples of religious imagery in Rodogune:

He rushes on ward like a god of war.[21]

He is all high and beautiful like Heaven.[22]

A red libation, 0 thou royal sacrifice![23]

what villians secret hand

Profaned with death this royal sanctuary.[24]

Silence thou tempter ! He is sacred to me.[25]

In *Perseus the Deliverer* may be counted 102 references to the gods or Fate: almost on every page there are religious images for example on page 31, which is only a random choice we find the following religious references:

Where is my Sungod ?[26]

I want my Sungod.[27]

Whose face is like the grand Olympian zeus. [28]

And him she calls her Sun-god. [29]

The great gods that visit earth .....[30]

My Sungod served them, [31]

They must be bound on the god's altar...... [32]

Even in Sir Aurobindo's romantic comedies we find religious imagery used rather abundantly. For example, in *Eric*, there are eighty one references to the gods ; twenty eight to Fate and four to Heaven. Here are some examples:

By Fate.

For she alone is prompter on our stage, [33]

He has the face and figure of a god,- [34]

They say the anarchy of love disturbs God's even, [35]

Beware, provoke not the fierce god too much:[36]

Then the gods too work. [37]

Thou art my Fate and I am in thy grasp. [38]

For that is heaven's secret. [39]

In *The Viziers of Bassora* references to religious imagery are made twenty one times. A few of them are quoted below :

God's great stamp

And heavenly image on his mind's defaced."[40]

O Allah , if it be at all Thy will.[41]

Bow to the will of God, my son ;[42]

References to God; the Gods and Fate are made twenty- one times in *Vasvadutta*. Some of them are quoted below:

Fear not the obstacles the gods have strewn. [43]

But many gods stood smiling at his birth.[44]

Do the gods whisper it ? [45]

It was a perilous race and in the end.

Fate won by a head. [46]

Like shakespeare's play's, Sri Aurobindo's plays as well make abundant use of religious imagery in support of the idea that there are super human powers that control and direct the destiny of man. This idea is again reinforced by the following direct statements :

Care not if thou resist or if thou yield;

They do their work with mortals

*(Rodogune)*

All this I have done, and yet not I , but one greater.

Such is Athene's might and theirs who serve her.

*(Perseus the Deliverer)*

Fate orders all and Fate I know

Have recognised all the world's mystic will

That loves and labours. *(Eric)*

Life is my own again and all I love.

Great are by thy mercies, o omnipotent !

*(The Viziers of Bassora)*

This world's puppet of a silent will

Which moves unguessed behind,

our acts and thoughts ;"[47] *(Vasavadutta)*

Next to religious imagery comes nature imagery. Like Shakespeare, Sri Aurobindo also has drawn his images abundantly from Nature In Sri Aurobindo animal imagery consists of references to lions, tigers, antelopes, cigals, jackals, polar bears, horses and dogs. Of these lion and antelope images are abundantly used in all his plays. Sri Aurobindo's bird imagery, comprises eagles, hawks, crows, doves, Swans and peacocks. Good characters are almost invariably compared to lions and eagles :

O my bright lion,
you are a splendid and a royal beast, [48]
*(Prince of Edur)*

I still hold in my strength,
Though it hungers like a lion for the leap.[49]
*(Eric)*

I'll bear thee far.
As Heaven's great eagle.[50]
*(Vasavadutta)*

How like a sudden eagle he has swooped.
Upon the terror, [51]
*(Perseus the Deliverer)*

And like the lion
Thou art my warrior, [52]
*(Rodogune)*

The wicked characters are compared to owls, jackal, crows, dogs and bitch etc.

Worry the conscience of the Queen to death
Like the good bitch thou art. [53]
*(Rodogune)*

There goes thou Almuene, the son of Khakan,
Dog's son, dog's father, and thyself a dog : [54]
*(The Viziers of Bassora)*

What a blind owl thou art that see'st the sun
And think'st it darkness ! [55]

*(Rodogune)*

They say he is as big as a polar bear. [56]

*(Prince of Edur)*

Season images comprise chiefly spring and summer season:

All spring walks her in blossoms
And strews the pictured ground. [57]

*(The Viziers of Bassora)*

a dream of greenness
with visions of the white and Vermiel spring. [58]

*(Prince of Edur)*

Soft as spring
Fair like a hunted moon in cloud swept skies, [59]

*(Vasavadutta)*

O brother cast the snows out of thy heart.
Let there be summer. [60]

*(Eric)*

this is a tender boy
As soft a summer dews......[61]

*(Vasavadutta)*

His landscape chiefly depicts the beauties and glories of the forest life as in *Prince of Edur* -

Coomood, from your green prison on the heights.
There spring shall wall you in with flowers and make
Her blossoming creepers chain for your bright limbs
Softly forbidding you, when you 'ld escape. [62]

*(Prince of Edur)*

or of the simple and pure village life as in *Perseus the Deliverer*:

Homes of delightful laughter, if you have streams
where chattering girls dip in their pitchers cool,
And dabble their white feet in the chill lapse

of waters, trees and green mantled earth,
cicales noisy in a million boughs.
or happy chirp of common birds...[63]

The 'flower imagery' comprises roses, lily and jasmine mainly:

'Nay you are twin sweet roses an one stalk.[64]

*(Prince of Edur)*

My little wind tossed rose Andromeda. [65]

*(Perseus the Deliverer)*

I mean our thorny rose Cleone too...[66]

*(Rodogune)*

O, see her walk ! A floating lily in moonlight was her sister. [67]

*(Rodogune)*

A thorn beneath the rose.
That from the heavens of desire was born
And men call Vuthsa.[68]

*(Vasavadutta)*

It had no trees, I'm sure, no jasmine - bushes.
no happy breezes ......[69]

*(Prince of Edur)*

References to the forces of Nature such as tempest, lightening thunder etc abound in these plays :

Messengers
Abridge the road with tempest in their hooves
To bring them to me. [70]

*(Rodogune)*

Now has this love like lightening leaped at me! [71]

*(Rodogune)*

Whose stroke is like lightening, silent, Straight,
Not to be parried. [72]

*(Eric)*

Go friend I follow

As swift as thunder presses on the lightening.[73]

*(The Viziers of Bassora)*

Descends upon us in a thunder and whirl-wind.[74]

*(Prince of Edur)*

'Mythological or classical references are also found in abundance in these plays. Niobe *(Rodogune)'* Urjoon, Dushyanta and Shakoontala *(Prince of Edur)* Gorgon's cavern, Gorgon's head *(Perseus the Deliverer)* the tailed god *(Vasvadutta)*, ogre Ghaneem, Ayoob, Zed *(The Viziers of Bassora)*, Thor, odin, Freya *(Erich)* may be listed as a few examples. 'Celestial imagery is likewise constantly used in these plays of these references to the Sun, the moon, the stars and heavens are found in abundance. Almost all the heroes are compared with the Sun or possess sunlike qualities. Thus Perseus is the Sungod, and Antiochus is the Sungod, and Antiochus moves like a bright Sun 'Brilliant alone in the heaven'. The heroine are compared with the moon or else have moonlike qualities.

Sri Aurobindo's music imagery comprises mainly harp, lyre, lute and guitar. Similarly 'doll' and 'puppet' images are Sri Aurobindo's favourite domestic images.

The doll,

The Parthian puppet whom she fondles so,[75]

*(Rodogune)*

This boy between

Like a girls Cherisehed puppet stroked and dandled .[76]

*(Vasavadutta)*

In Sri Aurobindo's plays imagery serves three main purposes:

1. Characterisation 2. Unfolding of the theme or meaning of the play, and 3. Evocation of atmosphere.

The Characters in the plays of Sri Aurobindo are not types but individuals. In *Rodogune* 'the key image' for Antiochus is of the Sun:

Look ! There he comes

Carrying himself as if he were the Sun

Brilliant alone in heaven

O Sun, thou goes rushing to the night

which shall engulf thee.[77]

'The key image' for describing the plight of Cleopatra is that of Niobe:

Even my own mother is a Niobe.[78] (Act III. Sc ii. P 91) The play is a study in Cleopatra's lonelineses. She feels happy at the death of her husband because she thinks that she will be able to get the company of her beloved children. But Fate wills her to shed tears over her sons murder and cry in anguish 'I am alone, so terribly alone' She is indeed a Niobe whose children were slain and who wept even when she was tansformed into a statue. Timocles, character is admirably presented through the image of a pale leaf :

There is Timocles

Whose light, unstable mind like a pale leaf

Trembles, desires, resolves, ronounces.[79]

Phayllus' character similarly is delineated through the image of an owl:

what a blind owl thou art that sees't the sun.

And think'st it darkness.

The owl image is highly suggestive as it nicely sums up all the features of his character such as his owlish treachery, his blindness to the reality and his love for dark deeds.

In *Vasavadutta* 'The key image' for Vuttsa Udayan is the cupid, or kamdeo :

I have seen the god of love.

Wearing a golden human body. [80]

And Vasavadutta herself is Prakriti, ie

human soul, always yearing for the love of Purusha:

I have loved thee always

Even when I knew it not.[81]

In the Prince of Edur the image of the goddess of the forest is 'the key-image for comol-cumary.'

I have been wondering in my woods alone

Imagining myself their mountain queen.[82]

I understood

Their leafy language

We'll set you under a bough, our goddsess of the spring.[83]

The image of a springing stem in used to delineate the character of Bappa:

O thou springing stem

That surely yet will rise to meet the Sun! [84]

This image beautifully symbolises Bappa's swift and certain rise towards the apex of glory. In *Perseus the Deliverer* the central image delineating the character of Perseus is that of a 'bright god'

My Sun was a bright god and bore a flaming sword.

To kill all monsters. [85]

Perseus indeed is a 'bright-god' who stands against the forces of 'that elder world' to which Poseidon and Polydaon belong and he kills all monsters symbolising superstitions and dark religion and establishes the realm of enlightened humanism on earth. Andromeda's character is similarly depicted through the image of a divinity, human and merciful

O human merciful divinity,

----------------------------------------------------------------

Where thou wert born, pure -eyed Andromeda,

There shall be some divine epiphany

of calm sweet hearted pity for the world, [86]

Elements of divine mercy and compassion are the central feature of Andromeda's characters and these are best delineated through the image of 'human merciful divinity' used for her. Polydaon is described as a priest of death:

Priest of Poseidon and of death.[87] (Act v. Sc.ii.P 125)

This 'priest of death' image beautifully sums the different traits of his characters and his prime ambition, after becoming the king of Syria to paint Syria gloriously with blood'.

Hundred shall daily die to incarnadine

The streets of my city and my Palace floor,

For I would walk in redness. I'll plant my garden

with heads instead of lilacs Hecatombs

of men shall groan their hearts out for my pleasure.

In crimson rivers. [88]

In *The Viziers of Bassora* the noble vizier is a man made in 'Gods image' while the wicked Vizier is a 'brutish amalgam of gorilla and Barbary ape'! Nureddene is a 'handsome roisterer' while Fareed is a 'half-devil' These images suitably sum up the respective characters they stand for. The images used by the characters in these plays reveal their mental make-up and differentiate them from other characters. Particularly Vuthsa Udayan, Eric, Bappa, Antiochus and Perseus mostly use metaphorical language full of literary imagery. Here are some examples-

Vuthsa Udayan :

See this strange flower I plucked below the stream !

Each petal is a thought.[89]

Eric :

They say the anarchy of love disturbs

Gods even, shaken are the marble natures,

The deathless hearts are melted to the pang

And raptures. [90]

Bappa :

Till then my antelope, range my hills and make them

An Eden for me with thy wondcrous beauty

Moving in grace and freedom of the winds,

Sweetness of the green woodlands;[91]

Antiochus : What were death then but wider life than earth.

Can give us her clayey limits bound ?

Darkness perhaps ! There must be light behind. [92]

Perseus :

The day shall come when men feel close and one.

Meanwhile one forward step is something gained.

Since little by little earth must open to heaven

Till her dim soul awakes into the light. [93]

The true nature of a character like Phayllus, Almuene, or Polydaon is revealed through the images he uses in his dialogues. We generally find recurrent use of animal imagery comprising generally snakes, dogs, bitch, and tiger etc.

Phayllus :

Women fein and lie by nature

As the snake coils,

Almune :

I know you dog ! When my back's turned you bark.

But whine before me. [94]

Poseidon :

Wake! Wake! Do you not hear Poseidon raging

Beneath the cliffs with tiger-throated menace. [95]

In Sri Aurobindo's plays imagery is also used for unfolding the theme of the play. Very often a single image is employed to convey the poet's vision as projected in a particular play. In *Rodogune*, for example, the image of the hunters and the hunted conveys the main idea of the play. As the tragic play *Rodogune* is mainly concerned with the problem of human suffering and the objective correlative which Sri Aurobindo uses as a formula for the idea of suffering is that of 'hunting'. It is note worthy that Shakespeare, too, uses this image of hunting to convey the idea of suffering. Antiochus is hunted by Fate and his unequal hunt is depicted through these words of Eremite:

... thou shalt not be king

But at they end shall yield to destiny

For all thy greatness, genius pride and force.

Even as the tree that falls. [96]

Timocles and Cleopatra are hunted by loneliness and the Furies:

Timocles :

My soul once more
Is hunted by the tempest. [97]

Cleopatra :

I am alone, so terribly alone ! [98]

Timocles :

What furies out of hell have I aroused
within, without me ?[99]

Cleopatra : Will the Furies stir
Because I hated grim Antiochus ?[100]
Cleone is hunted by lust :
Lust drives her, not ambition. [101]
and Phayllus by the desire to rise :
I have a need for growth;
I feel a ray come nearer to my brow,
The world expands before me. [102]

In *Eric* the theme of the play is conveyed through the image of the golden hoop.The divine golden hoop of love enables man to jump over the abyss of hate and achieve perfection. It completes the holy trinity of manhood, which demands 'strength in the nature', wisdom in the mind' and 'love in the heart' (Act III, Sci, p58) Another significant image which Sri Aurobindo uses in the play to convey his vision is the snow image:

How to sway men's hearts, rugged and hard
As Norway's mountains, as her glacier's cold...
O brother , cast the snows out of thy heart
Rubies of passion on a bosom of snow, [103]

The snow image represents the cold reasoning in man which does not respond to the warm and animating touch of love, The theme of the play is the conquest of hatred and indifference by love and friendship.

The theme of *Vasavadutta* is similar to that of *Eric*; it is the victory of love, of the heart over man's cold reasoning faculty ie, intellect Vasavadutta herself is the battleground and the victory of the heart over the head is very effectively presented through the powerful images of fire and flood Vasavadutta cries :

There is a fire within me and a cry.

My longings have all broken in a flood

And I am the tossed spray! [104]

Nor age nor custom pale my fire of love. (Act IV, Sc ii. P. 108)

In *The Viziers of Bassora,* the theme of the clash between the forces of good and evil, represented by the two Viziers is illustrated through a set of contrasting images. Animal, internal and disease images (evil characters are called gorillas, apes, dogs, baboons, kites, vultures, goblins, satan, and evil is compared with leprosy) are used to represent the evil forces and images from celestial phenomena, jewellery, music sunbeams, smiles and laughter are used to represent the noble characters and benevolent forces. The play has very rightly the predominance of bright and colourful imagery.

*Perseus the deliverer* is an allegorical play. Here Poseidon stands for 'a state of crude and evil religion based on fear and division' and Athene for a refind and enlightened religion based on love and compassion. Andromeda represents an almost Christian love for the suffering humanity and is an embodiment of the principle of charity and compassion Phineus represents gross materialism which denies the divine principle. But these characters symbolise other ideas also. Athene can be said to symbolise the triumphs of intellectualism ie, of the scientific spirit, over the untamed forces of nature represented by Poseidon further more Athene can be said to represent the anglic powers that raise man to divinity and Poseidon and his monsters may signify man's animal impulses and desires which spell disaster and ruin.

The theme of *Prince of Edur* is not quite clear. Inspired by the idea of Nationalism, Sri Aurobindo perhaps, intended to write a play on the legend of Bappa, a glorious figure of Rajasthan. But while writing the play, Sri Aurobindo might have decided to cast the play in a slightly different mould and introduced ideas which ran counter to the original plan. Thus in Act III the atmosphere of spring and gaiety runs counter to the idea of honour and chivalry presented in Act I & II As the theme of the play cannot be clearly defined , it will be idle to study the imagery of the play in relation to the theme.

Imagenry as a means of the evocation of atmosphere is best utilised by Sri Aurobindo in *Perseus the Deliverer* In this play 'the ocean in tumult' the 'sky in storm' 'the gods at work' a Phayllus gesticulating 'more wildly' a Perseus with 'Tasselled aegis' and 'winged sandals' and many more such images create the proper and requisite atmosphere. A beautiful atmosphere of romance, love, beauty, affection, sympathy and benevolence at times besieged by the forces of evil is created with the help of highly suggestive and evocative images in, *The Viziers of Bassora, Vasavadutta, Eric* and *Prince of Edur In Rodogune* imagery is successfully utilised in presenting the forehadow of the coming event The imagery of Furies by Timocles may be cited :

What furies out of hell have I aroused within, without me?[105]

Similarly Eremites words for Rodogune:

Who art thou rather, born to be a torch
To kingdom ? Is not thy beauty right seen
More terrible to men than monstrous forms
which only frighten ?[106]

and Eunice's quick reply :

What if kindoms burn,
So they burn grandly ?[107]

have premonitary effect and they mentally prepare the audience to await the event which will engulf the kingdom of Syria.

Imagery in Sri Aurobindo's poetry can be a study by itself. Broadly speaking, the whole poetry of Sri Aurobindo is concerned with images, since the poet is primarily the seer, the visualiser. When the vision dawns upon him, images come one after another pressing like pictures from a moving reel. They help in communicating the poet's vision and' we experience his world with force and clarity? 'We have innumerable images particularly in his narrative poems and in *Savitri* These images are of many kinds conventional experimental, sensous, Visual, aural kinetic, kinesthetic growing as direct impressions, or as similies or metaphors. All his images are luminious, deep and arresting , making us 'see and experience', opening up whole avenue of creative vision and imagination, They come from all quarters of life - nature, society, daily life, science, technology, cosmos itself. But it is the visionary, revelatory or intuitive perception that is the primary source for most of his images, and it is these that working like flashes communicate to the readers the poet's vision.

In the early poetry we find the poet's, imaginative sensibility revealing itself in sparkling images. The poems *songs* to *Myrtilla* draws our attention through its brilliantly picturesque images:

Sweet is the night, sweet and cool
As to parched lips a running pool;
Sweet when the flowers have fallen asleep
And only moonlit rivulets creep
like glow-worms in the dim and whispering wood. [108]

Then we have another picture

The blue sea dances like a girl
with Sapphire and with pearl
crowning her locks. [109]

then

Behold in emerald fire
The spotted lizard crawl
upon the Sun-kissed wall. [110]

Images such as these have softness and grace and are infused with sound and colour.

*Urvasie* opens with the exquisite image of the day:

Watching that birth of day, as if a line
of some great poem out of dimness grew,
slowly unfolding into perfect speech. [111]

And then -

The golden virgin, Usha....

sUnveiled, soft smiling, like a bride, rose cheeked,

Her bosom full of flowers, the morning wind.

Stirring her hair and all about her gold.[112]

The poet has pictured the outer tumult of love and the inexpressible joy of the lovers during their first supreme moments in countless images that colour the texture of *Urvasie.* How exquisitely significant is each excited image of love

.....a sea of mighty joy

Rushing and swallowing up the golden sand,[113]

or

..She o'erborne,

Panting, with inarticulate murmur lay,

like a slim tree half seen through driving Rail, [114]

or

So clung they as two Ship wrecked in a surge. [115]

It is such living and apt images that deserve the well-merited praise of K.D. Sethna, "So finely realised are Sri Aurobindo's word-pictures that they are as if on a canvas before us, or rather in three dimensional Nature"

Spiritual experiences have been rendered vivid, concrete and intimate by the imagery employed by him and we do not at all feel strain and labour when we are drawn by the charm of something beautiful. Sri Aurobindo has been able to make 'sense of road to reach the intangible' Images in *Savitri* illumine the inner meaning and reveal 'homelands of beauty shut to human eyes' here is an image in the very opening canto of the epic:

The darkness failed and slipped like a falling cloak

From the reclining body of a god. [116]

Sri Aurobindo has himself remarked in one of the letters about *Savitri* "Rapid transitions from one image to another are a constant feature in *Savitri* as in most mystic poetry."

Another unified kinesthetic image of joy travelling the roads of a solitary heart-

A jingling silver laugh of anklet bells

Travelled the roads of a solitary heart. [117]

Spring the season of joy and festivity when there is freshness and bloom everywhere and flowers splash their colour against the brown earth, is described with sensous richness-

The spring, an ardent lover, leaped through leaves,

And caught the earth bride in his eager clasp,

His advent was a fire of irised hues

His arms were a circle of the arrival of joy. [118]

It is significant to note that the image of the sea springs up time and again in Sri Aurobindo's poetry. It plays a vital role and it is particularly there when he refers to the poetic phenomenon. Then is in the *Songs of Myrtilla* the image of the 'blue sea dancing like a girl' and there is the metaphorical image-

Her mind, a sea of white sincerity,

Passionate in flow, had not one turbid wave. [119]

One may go on citing illustrations from his poems in order to prove that Sri Aurobindo has a unique mastery of imagery with the help of double vision, the corollaries and sensous images and vivid projections he builds a picture that not only delight and informs but carries many layers of meaning.

The lyrics such as *Songs of Myrtilla* and *Night by the Sea* in their sensous imagery, remind one of early Keats:

Or dewy bell, the maid undrest

with creamy childhood in her breast, [120]

or

many a girls lips ruby red

with their vernal honey fed..

Ruddy lips of many a boy

Blithe discovered hills of joy

Ruby guided through a kiss

To the sweet highways of bliss. [121]

Such passages are mingled sometimes with a keen sense of sadness :

Are we more than summer flowers ?
Shall a longer date be ours,
Rose and spring time youth and we
By the everlasting sea ?[122]

The poems *The Island grave, The lover's complaint* and *Love in sorrow marked by poignancy* of grief are moving poetic utterances. We have no testimony to know whether the poems are the personal emotions and feelings or are but as spontaneous outbursts of powerful feelings of human heart, his early lyrics are superb.

*Love in Sorrow* filled with the sense of misery and despondency smells of the poignancy of lyric note distinctly Shelleyan :

For there was non who loved me, no, not one
Alas, what was there that a man should love
For I was misery's last and frailest son
And even my mother bade me homeless rove
And I had wronged my youth and noble powers
By weak attempts, small failures, wasted hours. [123]

The Sonnet To *the cuckoo* is typical, thoroughly English, reminding one of Wordsworth's address to the bird. The poet discerns in the cuckoo the art of renewing 'fresh childhood in the obscured human heart':

The spent and weary streams refresh their youth
And that creative rain and barren grove,
Regain their face of flowers; in thee the ruth
of Nature rewakening her dead children moves. [124]

Another poem *O coil, coil* marked by the passionate intensity of lovers pain, is vibrant with-

The soft asoca's bloom, the laden wind,
And green felicity of leaves, the hush,
the sense of Nature living in the woods.[125]

He hails the bird as 'honied envoy of the spring' and 'tireless voice of spring'. The poems of this period are the sprouts of not only the creative emotions of joy and meloncholy, but also of imagination stirred by inspiring episodes like the Irish fight for freedom. Three poems *Charles Stewart Parnell, Lines on Ireland* and *His Jacet* were inspired by his sympathy of the misfortunes of Ireland. Even in his teens, the young poet was deeply interested in politics, particularly in Irish Politics, for it bore closeness to conditions prevailing in India -

.....Bleeding, chastised, bound,

Naked to imputation, poor, denied,

while alien masters held her house of pride. [126]

There are number of memorial poems in which he pays tributes to Goethe, Bankim chandra Chatterjee, Madhusudhan Dutt and his grandfather Raj Narayan Bose and these are perhaps the best pieces in the first anthology of Sri Aurobindo. With classical scholarship he calls Goethe:

A perfect face amid barbarian faces,

A perfect voice of sweet and serious rhyme,

Traveller with calm, inimitable paces,

Critic with judgement absolute to all time.[127]

In the poem *Bankim Chandra Chatterjee* and *Madhusudan Dutt*, he paid tributes to the literary glory of these two great writers of Bengal. He addresses Bankim Chandra as 'Master of delicious words' and 'The Sweetest voice that ever spoke in prose'. And Madhusudan Dutt:

Poet who first with skill inspire did teach

Greatness to our divine Bengali Speech [128]

The later three sonnets (more poems) are significant as they mark a departure from the poets early romantic poetry and provides a foretaste of the future poems. The poet himself was not satisfied with these early writing as is evident from his estimate of them in the last poem *Envoi*

Pale poems, weak and few, who vainly use

Your wings towards the unattainable spheres,
offspring of the divine Hellenic Muse,
Poor maimed children born of six disastrous years ! [129]

His Songs of *Myrtilla* embodies the out-pourings of a potentially rich and majestic hearts on a variety of themes. With a freshness and finish, 'spontaneity and inspired fluency, an abundant felicity of phrase and fancy, sweet sounds and apt images. To qoute K.D. Sethna, "who can deny either music or imaginative subtlety to Sri Aurobindo when in his *Songs to Myrtilla*, written largely in his late teens under the influence of a close contact with the Greek Muse he gives us piece after finely wrought piece of natural magic"?[130]

In Songs of *Myrtilla* we find Sri Aurobindo in the early workshop, reminiscent of Spenser, the Elizabethans and the Romantics whether we find him moved to joy or touched to melancholy by the hues and harmonies of life, there is a quality in him which proves that here is the first utterance of an exceptionally gifted mind.

The Baroda period reveals considerable literary activity marked by a variety of inspiration After a concentrated study of the great literature of India, he started writing poems on Indian subjects and surroundings. He revealed some of the beauties of Bengali and Sanskrit literature. From Sanskrit he made translations of 3 remarkable works : Kalidasa's *Meghduta* and *Vikramorvasie* and *Niti Shataka* of Bhartri hari. He translated or rather transmuted into English many lyrical verses of Chandidas and Vidyapati and many other Vaisnava poets of Bengali. Iyengar observes, "indeed, some of these so called translations are so good and so feast the ear and chasten the mind that they may more appropriately be described rather as transfigurations in terms of colour, sound and in wrought imagery ."[131]

We have in the poem *Urvasie*, abundance of sensous passages, exaltation of love and passion of beauty, effective use of epic similies and impressive sweep and flow of blank Verse. As Iyengar obserbs "Urvasie is a work of a youngman ; it has youths boldness, idealism, intution or romantic Imagery and feeling for the sheer beauty of language."[132]

# RERERENCES

1. V. Rai, *William Shakespeare* (Varanasi : Bhartiya Vidya Prakashan, 1966), P. 257.
2. F.E. Halliday. *The Poetry of Shakespeare's Plays,* P. 54.
3. Ibid., P. 34
4. I for Evans, *The Language of Shakespeare's Plays*, P. 2
5. F.E. Halliday, *The Poetry of Shakespeare's* Play, P. 42
6. Ibid., P. 47
7. Granville-Barker, *preface to Shakespeare,* P. 205.
8. Rylands, *Shakespeare the Poet,* P. 113
9. Ifor Evans, *The Language of Shakespeare's Plays,* P. 35
10. F.E. Halliday. *The Poetry of Shakespeare's Play,* P. 145.
11. V. Rai, *William Shakespeare* (Varanasi : Bharatiya Vidya Prakashan , 1966, P. 272)
12. Ibid., P. 274.
13. Ibid. , P. 268.
14. Ibid., P. 270.
15. Ibid. , P. 271.
16. Ibid., P. 255.
17. F.E. Halliday. The Poetry of Shakespeare's Plays. , P. 29
18. A.K. Sinha, The Dramatic Art of Sri Aurobindo (New - Delhi : S. Chand & Company Ltd. 1997), P. 165.
19. W. Knight : The Wheel of Fire (London, 1964), P.P. 14-15
20. A.K.Sinha, The Dramatic Art of Sri Aurobindo ( (New - Delhi : S. Chand & Company Ltd. 1997), P. 168.)
21. Sri Aurobindo : Rodogune (Pondicherry, 1958),

Act IV, Sc. i. P.100

22. Ibid., Act I, Sc iii, P. 29
23. Ibid. ; Act V. Sc. iv, P. 145
24. Ibid., Act V, Sc. iv, P. 148
25. Ibid., Act. IV, Sc. ii, P. 107
26. Sri Aurobindo : *Perseus the Deliverer* (Pondicherry, 1955), Act I, Sc. iii, P. 31
27. Ibid.
28. Ibid.
29. Ibid.
30. Ibid.
31. Ibid.
32. Ibid.
33. Sri Aurobindo : *Eric* (Pondicherry, 1960), Act I, Sc. i, P.4
34. Ibid., Act I, Sc. ii, P.9
35. Ibid., Act I, Sc. iv, P.29
36. Ibid., Act I, Sc. iv, P.33
37. Ibid., Act II, Sc. i, P. 35
38. Ibid., Act III, Sc. i, P. 70
39. Ibid., Act III, Sc. i, P. 63
40. Sri Aurobindo : *The Viziers of Bassora* (Pondicherry, 1959), Act I, Sc. ii, P. 8
41. Ibid., Act. II, Sc. iii, P. 69
42. Ibid. , Act. IV, Sc. vi, P. 191
43. *Sri Aurobindo : Vasavadutta* (Pondicherry, 1955), Act I, Sc. i, P. 8
44. Ibid., Act. I, Sc. i, P. 9
45. Ibid. , Act. I, Sc. ii, P. 17
46. Ibid., Act. V, Sc. vi, P. 147
47. Ibid., Act. V, Sc. i, P. 116

48. Sri Aurobindo : *Prince of Edur* (Pondicherry, 1961), Act II, Sc. vi, P. 76
49. Sri Aurobindo : Eric (Pondicherry, 1960), Act I, Sc. iv, P. 33
50. Sri Aurobindo : *Vasavadutta* (Pondicherry 1957), Act II, Sc ii, P. 46
51. Sri Aurobindo : *Perseus the Deliverer* (Pondicherry, 1955), Act, V, Sc. i, P. 117
52. Sri Aurobindo : *Rodogune* (Pondicherry, 1958), Act, IV, Sc. iv, P. 112
53. Ibid., Act II, Sc. i, P. 37
54. Sri Aurobindo : *The Viziers of Bassora* (Pondicherry, 1959), Act I, Sc. i, P.7
55. Sri Aurobindo : *Rodogune* (Pondicherry, 1958), Act V, Sc. iv, P.143
56. Sri Aurobindo : *Prince of Edur* (Pondicherry, 1961), Act I, Sc. ii,P. 11
57. Sri Aurobindo : *The Viziers of Bassora* (Pondicherry, 1958), Act IV, Sc. i, P. 127
58. Sri Aurobindo : *Prince of Edur* (Pondicherry, 1961), Act II, Sc. vi, P. 78
59. Sri Aurobindo : *Vasavadutta* (Pondicherry, 1957), Act II, Sc. i, P. 26
60. Sri Aurobindo : *Eric* (Pondicherry, 1960), Act V, Sc. i, P. 91
61. Sri Aurobindo : *Vasavadutta* (Pondicherry, 1957), Act II, Sc. i, P. 26
62. Sri Aurobindo : *Prince of Edur* (Pondicherry, 1961), Act I, Sc. v, P. 41
63. Sri Aurobindo : *Perseus the Deliverer* (Pondicherry, 1955), Act I, Sc. ii, P. 14

64. Sri Aurobindo : *Prince of Edur* (Pondicherry, 1961), Act I, Sc. V. P. 38
65. Sri Aurobindo : *Perseus the Deliverer* (Pondicherry, 1955), Act I, Sc. iii, P. 31
66. Sri Aurobindo : *Rodogune* (Pondicherry, 1958), Act II, Sc. ii, P. 46
67. Ibid., Act I, Sc. i, P. 4
68. Sri Aurobindo : *Vasavadutta* (Pondicherry, 1957), Act II, Sc. i. P. 34
69. Sri Aurobindo : *Prince of Edur* (Pondicherry, 1961), Act III, Sc. i, P. 83
70. Sri Aurobindo : *Rodogune* (Pondicherry, 1958), Act I, Sc. i, P. 7
71. Ibid., Act II, Sc. i. P. 44
72. Sri Aurobindo : *Eric* (Pondicherry, 1960), Act IV, Sc. i, P. 78
73. Sri Aurobindo : *The Viziers of Bassora* (Pondicherry, 1958). Act VI, Sc. v, P. 185
74. Sri Aurobindo : *Prince of Edur* (Pondicherry, 1961), Act I, Sc. iii, P. 19
75. Sri Aurobindo : *Rodogune* (Pondicherry, 1958), Act I, Sc. P. 10
76. Sri Aurobindo : *Vasavadutta* (Pondicherry, 1958), Act I, Sc. i, P. 10
77. Sri Aurobindo : Rodogune (Pondicherry, 1958), Act IV, Sc. V. P. 122
78. Ibid. , Act III, Sc. ii, P. 91
79. Ibid., Act V. Sc. iv, P, 143
80. Sri Aurobindo : *Vasavadutta* (Pondicherry, 1957), Act III, Sc. iii, P. 70
81. Ibid., Act IV, Sc. ii, P. 102
82. Sri Aurobindo : *Prince of Edur* (Pondicherry, 1961), Act III, Sc. i, P. 80
83. Ibid., Act III, Sc.i. P. 84

84. Ibid., Act. II. Sc. v, P. 70
85. Sri Aurobindo : *Perseus the Deliverer* (Pondicherry, 1955), Act I, Sc. iii, P.25
86. Ibid., Act III, Sc. ii, P. 68
87. Ibid., Act V, Sc. ii, P. 125
88. Sri Aurobindo : *Rodogune* (Pondicherry, 1958), Act II, Sc. i, P. 38
89. A.K. Sinha : *The Dramatic Art of Sri Aurobindo* (New - Delhi : S. Chand & Company Ltd., 1979), P. 176
90. Ibid.
91. Ibid.
92. Ibid.
93. Ibid.
94. Ibid.
95. Ibid.
96. Ibid.
97. Ibid.
98. Ibid.
99. Ibid
100. Ibid.
101. Sri Aurobindo : *Rodogune* (Pondicherry, 1958), Act II, Sc. i, P. 38.
102. Ibid., Act I, Sc. i, P.P. 12-13
103. Sri Aurobindo : *Eric* (Pondichery, 1960), Act III, Sc. i, P. 66
104. Sri Aurobindo : *Vasavadutta* (Pondicherry, 1957), Act IV, Sc. ii, P. 105
105. Sri Aurobindo : Rodogune (Pondicherry, 1958), Act IV, Sc. ii, P. 109
106. Ibid., Act III, Sc. iii, P. 96
107. Ibid.
108. Sri Aurobindo : *Collected Poems and Plays* (Sri Aurobindo Ashram, Pondicherry, 1942), Vol. I, P. 1.

109. Ibid., P. 2
110. Ibid., P. 3
111. Ibid., P. 39
112. Ibid., P. 40
113. Ibid., P. 58
114. Ibid.
115. Ibid., P. 59
116. Prem Tyagi , *Sri Aurobindo : His Poetry and Poetic Theory* (Saharanpur : Ashir Prakashan, 1988), P. 139.
117. Ibid., P. 140
118. Ibid.
119. Ibid., P. 141
120. Ibid., P. 36
121. Ibid., P.127
122. Ibid., P. 36
123 Ibid., P. 36-37
124. Ibid., P. 37
125. Ibid.
126. Ibid.
127. Ibid., P. 38
128. Ibid.
129. Ibid.
130. Ibid.
131. Ibid., P. 40.
132. Ibid., P. 42.

☐

# CHAPTER-VI

# Conclusion

To conclude, we can mention that within the scope of our studies, we have focused on the influences and parrallelisms to be found in the drama's and sonnets of the great English dramatist and poet, Shakespeare and our Indian writer, poet and philosopher, Sri Aurobindo. To read both their drama's and sonnets seperately and individually is a great experience of its own kind. But to compare them and to read them side by side, is a voyage of rich discovery One is struck by the amazing number of influences and parralelisms, that are to be found between two such different writers of different countries, different times and different circumstances. There are outstanding influences and marked parralelisms between the Drama's and sonnets of these two creative artists. Critics like M.K. Naik are absolutely right when they hear "Persistent and loud Shakespearean echoes in character, incident and even dialogue," in Sri Aurobindo's plays.

Considering the plays of both the dramatist, first we see a lot of difference in the quantity or the number of plays that are written by Shakespeare and Sri Aurobindo. The number of plays penned by Shakespeare are almost 37, whereas, Aurobindo has written only five complete plays and rest are only fragmentary. Even in this small collection of plays, the influences and the parralelism can be perceived in the Elizabethan pattern of writing that was chosen by Sri Aurobindo conciously. He divided his plays into five-acts, just like Shakespearean plays.

Then again in keeping with the Shakespearean tradition, he chose to write romances, except one tragedy *'Rodogune'*. Whereas Shakespeare has written not only romances, comedies, tragedies but tragi-comedies as well. The noted difference in their tragedies was that the crudeness and the excessive blood-shed of Shakespeare's tragedies was missing in Sri Aurobindo's tragedy. Here Sri Aurobindo's finer sensibilities cannot be overlooked. One more difference to be noted is in the title that he chose for his tragedy. He deviates from the Shakespearean tradition of naming the tragedies after its hero. For example-*Hamlet, King Lear, Macbeth* and *Othello* etc. Sri Aurubindo gave it the name of the heroine, *Rodogune*, but if we consider it from the protagonist point of view, then the change is only in the gender. Though the similarity or parralelism is to be found in the tragic suffering and pain that has a profound effect on the elevation of that character in the esteem of the reader.

Sri Aurobindo's romances reveal a lot of influence and parralelism of Shakespearean romances. They are sunny, bright and optimistic in their out-look and atmosphere. And the setting of every play is almost a different country and clime in the case of Sri Aurobindo, as generally it was for Shakespeare. The art of characterization, the field in which Shakespeare excels, the same kind of excellent handling can be seen in Sri Aurobindo's plays. They seem to have the same deep insight in to all their charactes. The language of the plays of Shakepseare, which is a combination of prose and poetry has been very much retained by Sri Aurobindo as well. They both seem to have been such experts in the deft handling of both these mediums, that one never stops marveling at this beautiful mix. They both use prose for common or ordinary kind of characters and poetry for the noble and exalted characters. The use of blank-verse by both these artists is also out-standing. Especially in the case of Sri Aurobindo, since no other Indian writer of that time even tried this medium. Sri Aurobindo admits that writing in blank-verse was quite a difficult and unique experience.

As Shakespeare was supposed to hold a mirror up to the nature, similar is the case with Sri Aurobindo's dramatic art. One more pronounced similarity between these two writers is that they both believe in 'artistic economizing' as Sri Aurobindo terms it. By this he meant that he also never invented his own story or plot but bodily lifted it from some known source. But, after giving it his own personal touch and treatment, he made it completely his own and absolutely outstanding and individual, just like the great master Shakespeare. Another marked influence and parralelism between Shakespeare and Sri Aurobindo can be seen in the endings of their romances.

They were always ending on the happy-note. And the single tragedy '*Rodogune*' written by Sri Aurobindo again shows the influence of Shakespearean tragedy with the tragic death of Rodogune, the main character and the heroine of the tragedy.

In the sonnets of Sri Aurobindo, we can also trace the influence of Shakespeare. The first trace can be detected in the structure of Sri Aurobindo's sonnets Shakespeare in his 154 sonnets uses Elizabethan or Shakespearean structure, which is quite different from its original Italian or Petrarchan structure. Sri Aurobindo seems to have used both the styles frequently. But his sonnets written in Shakespearean style out-number the Petrarchan sonnets. Out of the total of 77 sonnets penned by Sri Aurobindo, almost 54 have been written in the Shakespearean style. To name some - 'The Divine Hearing', 'The Indwelling Universe', 'The Witness spirit' 'Liberation', 'The Golden - light' and many more.

Coming to the subject matter and the themes of their sonnets, here again we find that Sri Aurobindo decides to be different from Shakespeare. Whereas Shakespeare's sonnets focus on 'love' as a basic theme, though he does talk of 'time' and its damaging and destructive properties, but again in reference to 'love' only. Where as Sri Aurobindo seems to be occupied by the spiritual feelings, the longing for the eternal and theme of the 'Nirvana'. In Shakespeare's sonnets there seems to be different kind of controversies about the two people that he writes about. First his friend whose identity seems to be unknown even after much speculation and his mysterious 'dark-lady', whose identity has eluded practically all the critics. But we do not find any such controversies in Sri Aurobindo's sonnets. They deal very specifically, with the spiritual themes, with his strong belief in the existence of soul and an after-life. In some of them we do find his humour surfacing, when he talks in a funny and comic attitude towards science. He even sounds very practical when he talks of the destructive effect of science. He sounds almost like a seer, as we can today see for ourselves too, the destruction caused by all the latest scientific inventions, like the nuclear bombs.

The comparitive study of both these greatwriters excelling in the field of drama and poetry has been the most rewarding experience so far.

□

# Select Bibliography

## 1. Primary Sources

**A. Shakespeare**

William Shakespeare: *The Complete works, ed.* A. Harbage (London, 1969)

**B. Sri Aurobindo**

Aurobindo Sri : *Collected Plays and Short Stories,* Part One Birth centenary literary vol 6. Aurobindo Ashram, 1971, Pondicherry, 1971.

---------------, *Collected Plays and Short Stories Part Two.* Birth centenary litrary vol, 7. Pondicherry : Sri Aurobindo Ashram, 1971

---------------, Collected Poems : *Birth Centenary Library Vol. 5 Pondicherry :* Sri Aurobindo Ashram, 1971.

---------------, *The Future Poetry and Letters.* Sri Aurobindo Ashram, Pondicherry, 1972.

Iyengar, K.R.S. *Sri Aurobindo : A Biography and a History* 4th ed. rev. Sri Aurobindo Internation Centre of Education, Pondicherry, 1985

Purani, A.B. *Evening Talks with Sri Aurobindo.* 3rd ed. rev. (complete in one vol.) Sri Aurobindo Society, Pondicherry, 1982.

*The Life Divine, Book one and Book two,* Part one, Birth centenary litrary vol. 18. Pondicherry: Sri Aurobindo Ashram, 1970.

*The Life Divine Book Two, Part two,* Birth centenary litrary Vol. 19. Pondicherry: Sri Aurobindo Ashram, 1970

*The Life of Sri Aurobindo.* 4th ed. rev.: Sri Auorbindo Ashram, Pondicherry, 1978

## 2. Secondary Sources

### A. Shakespeare

Barbar, C.L. *Shakespeare's Festive Comedy* : Princeton, 1959.

BOAS, F.S. *Shakespeare And His Predecessors* : Calcutta, 1963.

Bradbrook, M.C. "Authority, Truth and Justice in *Measure for Measure." Review of English Studies,* 17 (1941).

Brown, J.R. *Shakespeare and His Comedies* : London, 1957.

Campbell, O.J. *Shakespeare's Satire* : New York, 1943.

Chambers, R.W. Man's *Unconguerable Mind* : London, 1939.

Charlton, H.B. *Shakespearian Comedy* : London, 1938.

Clemen, W.H. *The Development of Shakespeare's Imagery* : London, W.H. 1959.

Coghill, N. "The Basis of Shakespearian Comedy." *Essays and Studies of the English Association,* 1950

Colie, Rosalie L. *Shakespeare's Living Art:* London, 1974

Dubree, B.Ed., *Shakespeare: The writer and His Work London,* 1964.

Dusinberre, Juliet. *Shakespeare And the Nature of Women*, London, 1975.

Duthie, G.I. *Shakespeare:* London, 1951.

Edwards, Philip. *Shakespeare And the Confines of Art.* London, 1968.

*Encyclopaedia Britannica, Vol. 2, 5, 6, 8, 16, 18, 21.* Chicago :

Encylopaedia Britannica Inc., 1967.

Evans, Bertrand. *Shakespeare's Comedies* : London, 1960.

Frye, N. "The Argument of Comedy." *English Institute Essays,* (1948)

Ghosh, P.C. *Shakespeare's Mingled Drama:* Calcutta, 1966.

Gardon, G. *Shakespearian Comedy and Other Studies* : Oxord, 1944.

Granville - Barker, H. *Prefaces to Shakespeare : London,* 1927-47.

Halliday, F.A. *A. Shakespeare Companion :* London, 1964.

Hazlitt, William. *The Round Table characters of Shakespeare's* Plays. D.V. Dent & sons, Ltd., London, 1936.

Iyengar, K.R. Srinivasa. Shakespeare *His world and His Art.* Sterling Publishers Private limited, New Delhi, 1964.

Kinght, G.W. *The wheel of Fire:* London, 1961.

Leavis, F.R. *The Common Pursuit* : London, 1952.

Leech, C. The 'Meaning' of Measure for Measure." *Shakespeare Survey*, 3 (1950)

Ludowyk, E.F.C. *Understanding Shakespeare.* London, 1964.

Merchant, W.M. *Shakespeare and the Artist :* London, 1959.

Nicoll, *A. British Drama,* 4h ed. rev. London: George G. Harrap & co. Ltd., 1958.

Perrott, T.M. *Shakespearean Comedy* New York, 1949.

Pettet, E.C. *Shakespeare and the Romance Tradition :* London, 1949.

Rai, V. *William Shakespeare.* Bhartiya Vidya Prakashan, Varanasi, 1966.

Rossiter, A.P. *Angel With Horns:* London, 1961. Sen Gupta, S.C. *Shakespearian Comedy*". Oxford university Press, Delhi, 1985.

Sharma T.R. *Essays on Shakespeare.* Shalabh Book House, Meerut, 1986.

Sharma, Ram Bilas, *Essays on Shakespearean Tragedy*. Shiva Lal Agarwala & company Educational Publishers, Agra, 1965.

Tilak, Dr. Raghukul. *Shakespearean Tragedy.* Prakash Book Depot, Bareilly, 1988.

Tillyard, E.M.W. *Shakespeare's Early Comedies:* London, 1966.

Traversi, D. "Troilus and Cressida." *Scrutiny*, 8 (1938).

Varma, R.S. *Papers on Shakespeare.* S. Chand & Co. (Pvt.) Ltd., New-Delhi, 1973.

Vyvyan, John. *Shakespeare and Platonic Beauty* : London, 1961.

Wilson, J.D. *Shakespeare's Happy Comedies:* London, 1962.

Foakes, R.A. *Shakespeare: The Dark Comedies to the Lasts Plays:* London, 1971.

**B. Sri Aurobindo**

Abrams, M.H. *A Glossary of Literary terms.* 3rd. ed. Madras : The Macmillan Company of India Ltd., 1979.

Acharya, K.D. *Guide to Sri Aurobindo's Philosophy :* Divya Jivan Sahitya Prakashan, Pondicherry, 1968.

Das, Manoj. *Sri Aurobindo-Makers of Indian Literature.* Sahitya Akademi, Delhi, 1972.

*Glossary of Terms in Sri Aurobindo's Writings.* Pondicherry : Sri Aurobindo Ashram, 1978.

Gokak, Vinayak Krishna. *Sri Aurobindo seer and Poet.* Abhinav publications, New Delhi, 1973.

Ghose, Sisir Kumar. *The Poetry of Sri Aurobindo :* A Short Survey, Chatuskona Pvt. Ltd., Calcutta, 1969.

Heehs, Peter. *Sri Aurobindo - A Brief Biography.* Oxford university Press, New- Delhi, 1989.

Jaiswal, S.S. *Sri Aurobindo's Plays - A Thematic study.* classical Publishing company, New - Delhi, 1993.

Mishra, L.N. *Sri Aurobindo's Dramatic Theory and Practice.* B.R. Publishing Corporation, Delhi, 1996.

Naik, M.K. *A History of Indian English Literature.* New - Delhi : Sahitya Akademi, 1982.

------------, *Perspectives on Indian Prose in English.* New Delhi : Abhinav Publication, 1982.

Narayan, Dr. Jagdish. *The Absolute in Sri Aurobindo and Alfed North Whitehead.* Anupam Publications, Patna, 1983.

Prasad, S.K. *The Literary criticism of Sri Aurobindo.* Bharti Bhawan, Patna, 1974.

Purani, *A.B. Sri Aurobindo's Life Divine.* Sri Aurobindo Ashram, Pondicherry, 1966.

Reddy, V.M. *Sri Aurobindo's Philosophy of Evolution. Hyderabad* : Institute of Human study, 1966.

Roarke, Jesse. *Sri Aurobindo.* Pondicherry : Sri Aurobindo Ashram Press, 1973.

Sarma, S. Krishna. *Seed of Grandeur- Commentary on Sri Aurobindo's poems.* Kamla Publications, Vijaywada, 1972.

Seetaraman, M.V. *studies in Sri Aurobindo's Dramatic Poems.* The Univeristy, Annamalainagar, 1964.

Sethna, K.D. *Sri Aurobindo; The Poet.* Sri Aurobindo International Centre of Education, Pondicherry, 1970.

Setha, K.D. *The Poetic genius of Sri Aurobindo.* Sri Aurobindo Ashram, Pondicherry, 1974.

Shanmukham, N. Jaya. *Sri Aurobindo and the Indian tradition.* Crown publications, New - Delhi, 1989.

Sinha, A.K. *The Dramatic Art of Sri Aurobindo.* S.Chand & Co. Ltd., New Delhi, 1979.

*The MLA Style Sheet.* 2nd ed. Hyderabad : American Studies Research Centre, 1970.

Tyagi, Prem. *Sri Aurobindo - His Poetry and Poetic Theory.* Ashir Prakashan, Saharanpur, 1988.

**A. Articles in Journals and Periodicals**

Bhatta, S. Krishna, "Plays of Sri Aurobindo : A survey". *Indian Literature*, vol. XVII. Nos. 1 & 2 (1974), New- Delhi.

Ghosh, P.K. "The Relevance of Sri Aurobindo Today." *Souvenir Volume.* Sri Aurobindo Samiti, (1975), Calcutta.

Ghosh, Sisirkumar. "A Survey of Aurobindonian Poetry." *Sri Aurobindo Circle.* No. 23 (1966), Pondicherry.

------------, "Sri Aurobindo : The Poet of Being." *Sri Aurobindo circle,* No. 36. (1980), Pondicherry.

------------, "The Literary Genius of Sri Aurobindo." Sri Aurobindo circle. No. 21 (1965), Pondicherry.

Iyenger, K.R.S. "Sri Aurobindo as a poet." *Sri Aurobindo circle.* No. 25 (1969), Pondicherry.

------------, "Sri Aurobindo's Impact on Indian Writing in English." *Sri Aurobindo Circle.* No. 30 (1974), Pondicherry.

------------, "The Evolutionary Dialectic in Sri Aurobindo's Dramas." *Indian Philosophical Annual.* vol. 8 (1972), Madras.

Maitra, Sisir Kumar. "Sri Aurobindo and Goethe." *Sri Aurobindo Mandir Annual.* No. 11 (Aug. 15, 1952), Calcutta.

NandKumar, Prema. "Eric : An Approximation." *Sri Aurobindo circle* No. 33 (1977), Pondicherry

------------, "Rodogune; A Study." *Sri Aurobindo circle.* No. 22 (1966), Pondicherry.

------------, "Sri Aurobindo's Dramatic Aesthesis." *The Banasthali Patrika.* No. 17-18 combined (July 1971 and Jan. 1972), Banasthali.

------------, "Sri Aurobindo's Interpretation of Indian Culture." *Sri Aurobindo circle.* No. 35 (1979), Pondicherry.

------------, "Sri Aurobindo's Unfinished Plays." *Sri Aurobido circle.* No. 19 (1963), Pondicherry.

------------, "The Capitivity Theme in Sri Aurobindo's Plays." *The Banasthali Patrika.* No. 12 (Jan. 1969), Banasthali.

------------, "The Heroic Theme in Sri Aurobindo." *Sri Aurobindo circle* No. 27. (1971), Pondicherry.

------------, "The Viziers of Bassora : A study." *Sri Aurobindo circle,* No. 23 (1967), Pondicherry.

------------, "Vasavadutta : A Study." *Sri Aurobindo circle.* No. 21 (1965), Pondicherry.

Lalita, K.S. "Sri Aurobindo's 'Perseus the Deliverer' : An approach." *Mother India.* Vol. 22. No. 7 (Aug. 15, 1970), No. 8 (Sept. 1970), & nos. 10-11 (Dec. 5, 1970), Pondicherry.

Vishwanathan, K. "Sri Aurobindo on Shakespeare." *The Banasthali Patrika.* Nos. 17-18 combined (Jly 1971 and Jan. 1972), Banasthali.

□□□